To Philemon,
God bless
you

Lakendra

10-4-08

In His Time

Lakendra Lewis

authorHOUSE®

AuthorHouse™
1663 Liberty Drive, Suite 200
Bloomington, IN 47403
www.authorhouse.com
Phone: 1-800-839-8640

First published by AuthorHouse 11/20/2007

ISBN: 978-1-4343-2500-6 (sc)

Printed in the United States of America
Bloomington, Indiana

This book is printed on acid-free paper.

For Taylor

Then the Lord answered me and said:
Write the vision
And make it plain on tablets,
That he may run who reads it…

~Habakkuk 2:2

SONG LYRICS CREDITS

Girl You Know It's True
(William Pettaway Jr./ Sean Spencer/ Kevin Lyles/
Rodney Hollaman/ Ky Adeyemo)

That's the Way Love Is
(Norman Whitfield/Barrett Strong)

Try Me
(James Brown)

Awesome God
(Rich Mullins)

It's My Turn
(Michael Masser/C.B. Sager)

Ain't No Way
(C.A. Franklin)

Walkin' the Backstreets and Crying
(Sandy Jones Jr.)

The Happy Song
(O. Redding/S. Cropper)

Que Sera Sera (Whatever Will Be Will Be)
(Jay Livingston/Ray Evans)

Introduction

I love watching talent shows. *Star Search* and the *Gong Show* used to be among my favorites. But I never watched *American Idol*.

Something about the show just never clicked with me and so I passed on having much to do with it. But since I wasn't a monk nor did I live under a rock, I couldn't get away from all of the hoopla surrounding the show; it was virtually everywhere I turned. And by its fifth season, I was enticed into sitting down to watch the auditions because frankly, the promos for them looked really funny.

When January of 2006 arrived and *American Idol* aired for its fifth season, I was pleasantly surprised at how much I enjoyed watching the show's auditions. Not only was it hilarious at times (do some of these people really believe they can sing or are they just that desperate to get on television???) but it showed that amid all of the kooks thrown in for the sake of ratings, were some folks who could actually sing.

One of them was Taylor Hicks.

Taylor was, initially to me, the embodiment of both of the categories *American Idol* auditioners seemed to fall into: he seemed a little odd but he had an advantage in that he could sing. I didn't see his segment at the beginning where he explained his premature gray hair. I like to channel surf during the commercials. But when I did tune back in I saw this guy—who looked to me to be about 42—saying he was going to sing Sam Cooke. And when Taylor opened his mouth to do "A Change is Gonna Come," well... to steal a tired quote from *Jerry Maguire*, he had me at 'hello.'

Given that I thought Taylor was about 42-years-old, his song choices made sense. But when I later found out he was only 28 at the time of his audition, I was doubly impressed. Having recently entered my 30s, I felt a kinship with the man. I'd grown up listening to the likes of Marvin Gaye, James Brown, Sam Cooke and Ray Charles. And now, here was one of my peers who not only appreciated those musical greats, but obviously had more than a mere passing familiarity with their work. It was refreshing to see someone like that on a show like *American Idol*.

I have to admit (much to my shame) that it didn't appear to me in the beginning Taylor had a snowball's chance of winning. Not because he wasn't talented but because he didn't fit the image of the type of Pop star the music industry is peddling these days. He was real. And for all his eccentric dancing and slight quirkiness, he did indeed have soul. I didn't want to see him get booted too soon. So, the show I had only intended to watch for a few minutes suddenly became a permanent fixture on my television set Tuesday and Wednesday nights. I *had* to find out if Simon's prediction that Taylor would never make it beyond the first round would come true.

But Taylor got the last laugh. He won.

It was around the time of his impending victory in early May of 2006 that I got the idea for a short story about an ordinary girl who falls in love with a reality TV star. The initial premise was a parody, my ode to mockumentaries like *The Rutles* and *This is Spinal Tap*. But as the story evolved, the idea developed until it was no longer merely a parody, but also a story of faith, love and the country's obsession with reality shows and celebrity.

I decided to base my fictional reality TV star on Taylor because I liked his style. And though Taylor was not the only performer on *American Idol* I liked, he did end up becoming the one performer I routed for continuously. Along the way, he stopped being that 'crazy, gray-haired guy' and became someone for whom I have a great deal of admiration and respect.

Ultimately, he is the one who got my vote.

It is said that imitation is the sincerest form of flattery. I hope so, because that is the spirit in which my story was written.

Hope you enjoy the ride.

~L.L. (December 2006)

Prologue

I met my future husband through the wonder that is reality television.

I was the spectator, he was the novelty act brought to me courtesy of Campbell's Chunky Soup and Mazda.

I wasn't much impressed with his looks at first, but he had a couple of things going for him that I liked: one of them being personality, the other talent.

Well, maybe three things. He also had drive.

The first time I saw him was purely by accident. I was at home eating Doritos and drinking a Diet Coke, completely bored and desperately channel surfing for something to watch, when I came across this show where singers were auditioning to be a part of some talent contest. The show was called *America's Next Big Star*, and it was the hottest thing on television. So hot, in fact, that it had single-handedly lifted the fledgling RAM network out of the hands of impending bankruptcy.

Before then, RAM had basically been a small fish swimming among the great network sharks of CBS, NBC and ABC without much success. It was considered the laughingstock of the primetime lot, known for cranking out program stinkers like *When Seniors Attack*, which showcased an excruciating half-hour of videos where elderly people became hugely irate about the little things in life, like opening a can of tuna fish, or the bigger things, like having a boy scout (played by some child actor) offer to walk an old lady across the street only to end up snatching the poor woman's purse. It was like a bad take-off of *Candid Camera*, but done at the expense of gullible senior citizens who would inevitably end up stomping and cursing into the camera—sometimes threatening to sue—all to the canned sounds of a laugh track.

Now RAM was having the last laugh. With the inclusion of *America's Next Big Star* in its seasonal lineup, it had joined the reality TV bandwagon and suddenly become a network contender. I'd read somewhere RAM picked up *America's Next Big Star* three years earlier as a mid-season replacement, a last-ditch effort to bring in younger viewers. The strategy worked. The show quickly became a huge hit not only with the 18-23 demographic but with just about everyone in the country. In fact, most of the planet had gone hog wild over it, but not me.

Normally, I would have loved a show like *America's Next Big Star* because I'd always enjoyed singing contests. I'd even participated in a few when I was younger, although I'd never won. But there was something about ANBS, as it would come to be known for short, which bothered me. There was an irritable quality about it that I didn't remember having seen in similar shows like *Star Search*. Maybe it was that the whole premise reeked of Hollywood phoniness to me…how television had merged with the music industry to crank out these plastic, cutesy cookie-cutter types who seemed to have more of a gift for looking good and getting into trouble than actually having talent. That and the fact that Clive Fowler, one of the show's three judges, had to be the rudest, most mean-spirited person I'd ever seen on or off television.

Already a well-known TV personality in his native England, Clive had earned the nickname "Fowl" Fowler because of his grumpy disposition and scathing commentary on just about any given subject. He was an executive producer of *America's Next Big Star* who had originally been brought in only as a guest judge for the first few episodes. But his bitter personality and caustic wit must have gone over well with the network execs. He was soon made a permanent member of the judges panel, which also included Reggie Thompson, a former session musician who'd played with everyone from Paul Simon to Engelbert Humperdinck, and Shasta Orenté, an ex-supermodel who'd enjoyed a successful albeit brief recording career.

Watching ANBS was, for me, like watching someone undergo a root canal. Reggie and Shasta were okay. Their criticisms were tactful and constructive for the most part. But Clive ripped into the singers mercilessly. He berated them with a venomous zeal that stripped away any shred of dignity, all of which perhaps made for exciting television, but in my opinion, it left real people who seemed to be doing their very best humiliated and spiritually deflated.

"That was beyond God-awful," Clive would snarl at contestants in his clipped, upper crust British tone. "A dying cat could maintain better pitch."

What's more, it was obvious Clive took great pleasure in making others feel small. It seemed to me the only time he cracked the remotest hint of a smile was when he'd reduced some poor singer to tears. The whole thing got to me and after a few minutes, I'd find myself wanting to cry before quickly grabbing the remote to change the channel.

Of course, nothing spells ratings like being publicly humiliated on live, national television. I think people were tuning in to hear Clive's cruel remarks just as much as they were to see who would finally walk away America's Next Big Star. Clive, for his part, had become America's newest imported media darling, the man everyone loved to hate.

"You know what I think?" he smugly remarked during an interview I once happened upon. "I think you Americans really love me but you're afraid to admit it. A lot of you have the exact same opinions I express on the show, only you don't have the guts to come out and say them."

He shrugged.

"I say what I think. If someone gets their feelings hurt over it, to me, it's a clear indication they're not cut out for this business. It's tough love. I'm doing these kids a favor. Better they realize now they have no talent than to invest 10 or 20 years of their lives in something that's never going to happen."

I remember thinking that what Clive Fowler needed was someone to show *him* some tough love, preferably in a dark alley late at night. So, when I was flipping through channels and came across Clive's smug mug, my gut reaction was to keep flipping. And I would have if the camera hadn't suddenly cut away from him and onto a young man with black, curly hair and a nice bone structure who had just walked into the room. He stood calmly before all three judges.

Even though I didn't watch ANBS, I was familiar enough with it to know that people had to audition before they could be on the show. I had never watched the auditions and slowly put down my remote to see what would happen. There was an awkward silence as the young man, who looked to be in his early 20s, simply stood in front of the judges' panel, looking at them. The judges looked back.

After what was edited to look like another five minutes of silence (the sound of crickets chirping was added for comic effect) and the camera ping-ponging back and forth between the bewildered expressions of the judges and the young man's blank expression, Clive spoke.

"Well, are you gonna just stand there or do you intend to actually do something?" he snapped.

"Yeah," was all the young man managed.

More silence.

"Wellll???" Clive coaxed, doing a get-on-with-it gesture.

The young man still continued to simply stare oddly at the judges. He very loudly cleared his throat.

"Right, that's it," Clive said. "Get out."

That got the young man moving. He took a clumsy step forward and put his hands out in front of him. "No, wait," he pleaded. "I was just about to do my thing."

"Do your thing?" Clive mocked. "You've been standing there for the past two bloody minutes and you haven't done anything but waste our time. Get out."

"No, no, I was trying to set a mood, that's all," the young man explained.

"Set a mood?" Clive looked at his fellow judges in astonishment. "Set a mood? You do realize this is a singing competition?"

"Honey, are you nervous?" Shasta asked the young man.

"No. Well, yes, a little–"

"Take your time, man, take your time," Reggie chimed in.

"No, he can't take anymore time," Clive objected. "We've got 200 more people to see and the day's half-shot already..."

Just then, the young man screamed at the top of his lungs, a piercing, undulating cry that made the hairs on the nape of my neck stand up. Clive dropped his pen. Both Shasta and Reggie also looked startled, their backs suddenly ramrod straight in their chairs.

"What the–?" Clive mumbled.

"*Girrrlllll!*" the young man screamed. He paused and closed his eyes dramatically, as if he needed to catch his breath. Reggie opened his mouth to say something, but the young man cut him off with another loud, off key shriek.

"*Girrrlllll!*" he screamed again.

Everyone sat frozen, their eyes wide with alarm.

"*Girl you know it's trooooo! Ooh, ooh, ooooohhh, I love yewwwww!*"

Reggie sat back in his chair with a groan and put his head in his hands.

The young man repeated the chorus again, half singing, half screaming at the top of his lungs, his voice cracking and wavering.

"Oh, dear God," Clive said.

Had I been a judge, just singing anything Milli Vanilli would have been grounds for immediate disqualification. But singing Milli Vanilla off key was even worse. Yet, the young man didn't stop there. To add insult to injury, he took three tennis balls out of his pockets and tried to juggle them as he attempted to rap the rest of the song. Unfortunately, his hand-eye coordination was even worse than his singing.

"I'm in love with you, girl, cause you're on my mind…" he shouted as he haphazardly threw all three balls in the air. *"…You're the one I think about most every time…"*

That was all he got out before he dropped one of the tennis balls and the other two also came bouncing down. The young man had to duck to avoid being hit by them. One of the balls rolled right next to Clive's foot. Clive bent down, picked it up and held it, eyeing the young man as if he intended to throw the ball directly at his head. Instead, Clive jauntily tossed the ball in the air, let it land back in his palm and called, "Next!"

"Wow," Shasta said flatly.

"So, am I in?" the young man asked expectantly.

The judges looked at each other. Reggie was the spokesman.

"No way, Gee," he said.

"No, really?" the young man said. He seemed genuinely surprised. "I mean, I-I know my juggling was a little off, I get dizzy in tight spaces but…" He trailed off. Then, in a refreshed, hopeful tone: "You sure?"

Both Clive and Shasta were adamantly shaking their heads.

"Positive, Gee," Reggie said.

"Can I have my ball back?" the young man asked as he walked towards the exit, holding the remaining two tennis balls.

"No," Clive said simply. "It's payment for having to listen to that utter crap you just subjected us to."

The young man seemed nonplused.

"Okay, keep it as a souvenir," he said and saluted before walking out.

"Good luck with the juggling!" Shasta yelled after him.

Clive looked at Reggie and Shasta and shook his head in disgust. "Un-bloody-believeable."

The next three or four people weren't any better. Not that I'm the best singer in the world, but I do know a good voice when I hear it and from what

I'd seen so far, some of these people were obviously auditioning simply for the sake of being seen on television.

"Whoever told you you could sing should be shot," Clive remarked to one girl with a purple mohawk and a nose ring. She had just finished singing a very nasally rendition of "When Doves Cry."

I hated to admit it, but watching folks make complete idiots of themselves in front of millions of people gave me a bit of a voyeuristic thrill. It was amusing entertainment that afforded its viewers a small boost of superiority.

I was beginning to see why the show was so popular.

It was at that point that a gray-haired guy wearing a Hawaiian flowered shirt and khaki pants walked in and stood before the judges.

My first thought was that ANBS must have upped its audition cut-off age. Last I'd heard, you couldn't be older than 25 to try out for the show. But this guy looked like he had to be at least 40.

Russell Hargrove, the show's cute and single 20-something host and commentator, hadn't said so but I believe it must have been towards the end of the audition day because Clive was looking even more grumpy and disgruntled than usual. He eyed the gray-haired guy noncommittally.

"What's your name?" he inquired.

The gray-haired guy coughed briefly into his cupped palm and spoke softly but firmly. "Tyler….Tyler Nicks."

There was just the slightest hint of a Southern accent when he spoke.

"Alright, Tyler," Clive sighed, crossing his arms in front of his chest. "What are you gonna sing for us?"

"I thought I'd do some Marvin Gaye, "That's the Way Love Is."

"Great, let's hear it," Clive replied flatly.

I remember sitting up a little straighter on the couch. Marvin Gaye? I loved him!

The gray-haired guy closed his eyes and began to sing. What came out of him was a voice that was smooth and soulful, a tad deeper and throatier than his speaking voice but melodic just the same. Nothing like what I expected.

"After many tears fall from your eyes…" he began, slowing the song down a little and pausing for effect. *"A thousand times you ask yourself why…"*

He sang with a gospel-type emphasis on the word "why" that made my eyes widen and gave me goose bumps. All the while, he kept his eyes closed, as if he was in another world.

"The one guy you love has departed," he continued. *"You're left alone and broken-hearted! Oh, love just comes and goes…"*

He didn't try to go up into falsetto on "goes" like Marvin but it sounded just as good. He was making the song his own.

"…how long it's gonna last nobody knows…"

By the time he got to the chorus, I was enthralled. His voice was somewhere in between Blues and Gospel.

The camera shot to the looks on the judges' faces. Reggie was bobbing his head appreciatively to the sound of Tyler's voice. Shasta's mouth was hanging open. Clive simply sat stoic, chewing thoughtfully on the tip of his pen.

"That's the way love is, baby!" Tyler continued, now completely engrossed in the song and rocking from side to side as he sang. *"I saaiiiid… THAT'S the waaay….love is baaaabaaay! That's how it is, ooooh, that's how it isssss!"*

He held the last note out until his voice faded and the sound penetrated the stunned silence in the room. Tyler opened his eyes as if from a dream, let out a small, anxious breath and clasped his hands together, waiting for a verdict. I didn't know about the judges but I'd already made up my mind. The gray-haired guy was definitely in! After what seemed an eternity, Reggie finally broke the silence.

"Wow," he said. "That was, that was pretty hot, Gee."

"Thank you," Tyler said quietly, a tiny smile crossing his lips.

"I have to admit, I didn't expect something like that to come out of you, but that was…..wow."

"I agree," Shasta said, nodding enthusiastically. "It was very good, good vocal control."

Tyler again quietly expressed his thanks. Only Clive remained outwardly unimpressed.

"Well, I heard all I need to hear," Shasta announced. She looked at Clive and Reggie. "I say he's in."

"Me too," Reggie agreed. "In."

Tyler smiled and looked expectantly at Clive. All three judges had to reach a unanimous decision in order for a contestant to be put through to the next round.

"Clive, man, whaddya say?" Reggie asked. "In or out?"

Clive continued to study Tyler with the interest of a scientist who's stumbled upon a new specimen.

"I dunno," he said slowly, still chewing on his pen. "Granted, that was pretty good, but I don't know if it's good enough."

Shasta and Reggie looked at each other with oh-boy-here-we-go-again expressions on their faces. Shasta rolled her eyes while Reggie let out an exasperated sigh.

"What do you mean 'not good enough?'" Shasta frowned, gesturing in Tyler's direction. "This guy's good. He's the best we've heard today–"

"You want him to sing something else?" Reggie asked. The camera cut to Tyler, who seemed more than ready to do an encore if necessary.

Clive thought about it for a moment. Then: "No, I don't think I need to hear him again."

Now it was Reggie's turn to frown. "Well, if you don't need to hear him again, what's the hold up?"

Clive let out a longsuffering sigh. "Well, to be quite frank, I don't know that this bloke's got the star quality America's looking for."

The gray-haired guy chuckled ruefully and shook his head as if to say, "I can't believe this."

Shasta and Reggie were hurtling objections on top of each other.

"What? Are you serious?"

"Man, this is about singing. America's looking for a singer, Gee."

"Yes, but it's not just about the singing, is it?" Clive reasoned, pointing at Tyler. "I mean, look at him. He looks like somebody's dad, like he could be the father of one of those kids out there." Then to Tyler: "You aren't, are you?"

"Clive!" Shasta chided, giving him a reproachful but harmless smack on the forearm.

"Well, are you?" Clive pressed, ignoring Shasta.

In an endearing gesture, Tyler put his head down for a second then raised it again good-naturedly. "No."

"Why'd you come to this audition?"

Tyler shrugged, as if the answer to that question should be obvious. "Cuz I want my voice to be heard," he said simply.

"Uh-huh." Clive cupped his hand under his chin. "You think you have a voice?"

"Yeah, I do," Tyler firmly answered.

"How old are you?"

"29."

Clive raised his eyebrows. "Get on, you're 29?"

The gray-haired guy nodded. "Yessir."

For the first time since Tyler walked in, Clive smiled. "You just barely made it, then, didn't you?"

I didn't know what Clive meant by that comment at the time, but I later found out 29 was the new ANBS cut-off age.

"I guess so," Tyler said.

"And you've already got gray hair," Clive mused. "Is it real?"

"Yeah, it's real."

Clive turned to the others. "See, this is my point," he said. "He's almost 30-years-old, he's got gray hair, he's got an okay voice but really, he looks like he should be singing round at Joe's Pub or at a piano bar somewhere, but not on any wide scale level."

Reggie was shaking his head vehemently. "I completely disagree. I think this guy could be big."

Clive studied Tyler again. "I don't know, I don't see it."

"Just try me out," said Tyler. "Let the people decide."

"Yeah, Clive," Shasta added. "Let the public decide what they want."

"If," Clive raised his pen as if in a toast. "*If* I say yes and we let him through, the American public will *not* vote for him."

I almost jumped off the couch when he said that. Never in my life had I wanted so badly to pummel someone.

"Well, let's find out," Shasta insisted. "We won't know if we don't put him through, right?"

Clive chewed thoughtfully on his pen some more, then put it down and swiveled his chair around to Shasta and Reggie.

"This is against my better judgment," he said hesitantly. "But....alright, you want him in, he's in!"

"Yesss!" the gray-haired guy clapped his hands. There were shouts of approval from Shasta and Reggie.

"I'm sure I'll live to regret this," Clive stated over all the hubbub as Tyler walked to the exit with a pink card in his hand.

Reggie called out to Tyler, "Yo, we'll see you in Hollywood, Gee!"

"Alright," Tyler said, waving as he left the room.

I don't remember any of the other auditioners after that. What I do remember is making a conscious decision to watch the show next week.

I was curious to see just how far that gray-haired guy would go.

Chapter 1: Revelation

ost people look forward to Fridays; Sharla Davis loved Thursdays.

It was her favorite night in the week for several reasons.

Sharla had been working for the last two years as a news assistant at the *Agape Gazette*, the only major newspaper in her hometown of Agape, Texas, population 300,000.

Her schedule required her to come in in the afternoon and work late into the night Sunday through Thursday and some weekends, depending on what was happening. But a plum spot had recently opened up for a general assignments reporter, and Sharla's hard work and writing skills had gotten her the position.

The promotion meant not only a raise in pay but also 9 to 5-ish, Monday through Friday hours, which allowed Sharla time to do some things she hadn't been able to before, like joining her church choir which practiced on Tuesday evenings, or being able on Thursdays to watch *ER*, one of her favorite shows. But the best thing Sharla liked about Thursdays was watching *America's Next Big Star*.

As with *ER*, ANBS had become one of Sharla's primetime passions ever since she'd happened upon the show's auditions back in September. The show aired two nights a week. Wednesday was competition night, when each contestant was given the opportunity to showcase their vocal skills, usually singing to music based on a particular theme. Thursday was results night, when all of the votes that had been generated by the viewing public for each singer's performance the night before would be tabulated, and the contestant with the least amount of votes was sent home.

One of the singers in particular, a quirky, gray-haired guy who went by the name of Tyler Nicks, had especially caught Sharla's attention. She'd happened upon his audition and become an immediate fan upon hearing his amazing, soulful voice. Sharla felt a kinship with Tyler because (1) they were around the same age (she was 32, he was 29); (2) they both seemed to have an unabashed love for music; and (3) with his age, premature gray hair and unorthodox performance style, which included dancing around onstage like a man who'd just stepped in a giant pile of fire ants, Tyler had gone into the competition an obvious underdog. As a reporter and as a person, Sharla tended to lean towards the underdog.

During the ANBS auditions, Clive Fowler had predicted—no, almost vowed—that Tyler would never win the American public's votes. But three months into the show, Tyler was still in the running for the title of *America's Next Big Star*, having sung his way into the coveted Top 30, which, over the passing weeks of elimination, was whittled down to the Top 15 and then the Top 10.

Now there were only seven hopefuls left: Eddie Mellenger, an amiable young man in his mid-20s whom Sharla felt also had a nice, bluesy voice; Chelsea Kitchens and Megan O'Reilly, both of whom were pretty, had decent voices and certainly could fit easily into today's female Pop star image; Maya Fox, an eclectic 19-year-old from New Jersey with spiky hair who favored Techno music, tons of black eyeliner and dressed Goth; Reese Bridges, who, with his dreamy, bedroom eyes, hunky good looks and smooth, non-threatening vocal style, was a favorite among the ladies; Geneva Tucker, a feisty little 17-year-old with a big, jazzy voice who saw herself as the next Ella Fitzgerald; and of course, Tyler, who, contrary to Clive's pronouncement, had amassed a formidable fan base known as the Soul Squad, whom he frequently gave shout-outs to during the telecasts.

Wednesday night's theme had been "Swing Music," with all of the remaining contestants having to sing a song from the Big Band/Swing era.

Given the musical aspirations of the group left—Maya a Goth, Techno singer; Chelsea a twangy Country girl; Tyler more Soul; Eddie more R&B, etc.—the show's theme made for an interesting night of television.

Out of the bunch, Sharla surmised the theme would most compliment Geneva with her Jazz vocal style and Reese, who was a natural crooner. But strange things can happen under pressure. While Geneva started out strong with her version of Duke Ellington's "It Don't Mean a Thing," she forgot the second verse, flubbing the words and mumbling her way through until the live stage band brought her back to the chorus.

Reese sang "Misty," which could have been a showstopper had he sang it in a lower key and refrained from trying to add too many vocal gymnastics. Surprisingly, Sharla felt the night's standouts were Maya, who did a conservative, heartfelt version of "Someone to Watch Over Me," and Tyler, who picked an up-tempo Frank Sinatra tune, "Witchcraft."

Sharla normally didn't call in to vote. She simply enjoyed watching the performances. But occasionally, if she felt a singer had done a particularly good job, she'd dial the toll-free 877 number that flashed across the screen for each contestant and cast her vote for whomever she'd felt had sung the best that evening. Now that the number of contestants was dwindling, the competition was getting tighter and the voting harder. Sharla was finding herself having to define her loyalties.

Last night, she'd voted for Tyler.

After a brief recap of each singer's performance and the judges' comments from the night before, Russell Hargrove, the show's host, got down to business. When the show opened, all seven contestants were sitting in an area to the left of the stage Reggie had affectionately dubbed the G-Zone. But when the camera cut back to Russell, Tyler was now standing next to him, waving and mouthing "Soul Squad" into the lens.

"Welcome back," Russell smiled into the camera, addressing the TV audience. "Standing next to me is Tyler Nicks…." Applause for Tyler from the audience and the G-Zone.

"…who I asked to come up during the recap. Tyler, do you know why I asked you up here?"

Tyler, who Sharla noticed was sporting a new, shorter haircut that framed his face and brought out his eyes, smiled at Russell and shook his head. "I have no idea."

"Well, I'll tell you," Russell said matter-of-factly. "It has something to do with last night's voting results."

Tyler didn't say anything, but his eyebrows went up in an 'uh-oh' expression and he lowered his head. Grim oohs and aahs could be heard in the television audience.

"As you know," Russell continued, gesturing first at the contestants in the G-Zone then back at Tyler, "Someone on this stage will be going home tonight."

Boos were now coming from the audience. The camera cut briefly to Shasta. She was holding her hand over her mouth and looking as if she was about to cry. Clive looked glib as usual. Sharla was vaguely aware her palms had become moist. Russell had never singled out a singer to stand next to him on results night. The only time that happened was when that singer was going home, and from the looks of it, Tyler was being given the boot. Sharla felt she could at least console herself with the thought that Tyler had gotten farther than Clive, or anyone for that matter, could have ever predicted. That alone was an awesome accomplishment.

Well, he had a good run, she thought sadly. *Maybe someone will offer him a record deal.*

On television, Russell had to raise his voice in order to be heard over the rising din.

"Would everyone in the G-Zone please stand up?"

Slowly, all the singers rose from their seats as the commotion in the audience subsided. Sharla looked around her apartment living room and realized her friend Lindsey White, who'd been an ANBS fan since Season Two, was not in the room with her. She'd gone to the kitchen to get a glass of sweet tea.

"Lindsey, get in here!" she called. "They're about to say who got voted out."

"Okay, okay," Lindsey called back, scuttling into the living room with two large glasses of iced tea. She sat one of the glasses on the coffee table in front of Sharla.

"Thanks," Sharla said, taking a sip.

Lindsey plopped down on the opposite end of the sofa. "What'd I miss?"

"Looks like Tyler's getting the ax," Sharla said glumly.

Lindsey leaned forward. "What? He was good last night."

"Apparently not good enough," Sharla shrugged. "Russell just called him out in front of everybody."

"Oh," Lindsey frowned.

On television, Russell was instructing the contestants in the G-Zone to form a single line facing him. He then asked them to divide themselves into two groups of three by having the two people in the center of the line take three steps away from each other. The people on either side of them followed suit. When that was done, Russell again addressed Tyler, who had been calmly standing by with a pensive but determined countenance.

"Tyler," said Russell, "Last night, you sang 'Witchcraft.' America voted…"

Tyler nodded but remained silent, his face serious.

"And out of all of the singers last night," Russell continued. "You…" he paused dramatically. "….received the highest number of votes."

A momentary frown lit across Tyler's face, as if he hadn't quite understood what he'd just heard. But the frown was quickly replaced by a huge grin that made Sharla want to smile. The crowd broke into spontaneous applause as Tyler visibly relaxed, letting out an audible sigh. Sharla and Lindsey also let out sighs of relief.

Thank God, he's still in it, Sharla thought.

Russell put a hand on Tyler's shoulder. "Tyler, you will not be going home tonight…" He then turned back to the other contestants. "….but one of your peers will."

"There are two groups," he continued, the camera panning the faces of first the group on the right, which consisted of Maya, Reese and Geneva, then the group on the left, made up of Eddie, Chelsea and Megan.

"One of these two groups had the lowest average of votes last night," Russell explained. "Tyler, I want you to go stand with the group you think got the higher average of votes."

"What?!" Lindsey exclaimed.

Sharla put a hand up to her mouth in shock. More oohs and ahhs and even a few boos from the audience. Tyler shook his head in disbelief and briefly turned his back to the camera.

"Think about it for a minute, Tyler," Russell instructed. Then, into the camera: "We'll be right back."

The ANBS theme music swelled as the screen went temporarily black before going to commercial.

"Well, that's just not right," Lindsey said, angrily leaning back on the couch. "They didn't have to put him on the spot like that."

Sharla agreed. Poor Tyler. What people wouldn't do for ratings.

"Which group do you think Tyler's gonna pick?" Lindsey asked.

On TV, a Wilfred Brimley-type gentleman was touting the benefits of Heartland Health Insurance.

Sharla shook her head. "I don't know. It's such a close race."

On the surface, she was thinking about what had just transpired and how unfair it was to put Tyler (or anyone) in a position where he would have to point a finger at his fellow competitors and basically say, "You don't cut it." That kind of action, depending on how it was executed, could turn the tide of goodwill Tyler had so far generated with the American public against him. Not to mention the tension it could potentially cause with the other singers.

Under the surface, Sharla couldn't stop thinking that there seemed to be something different about Tyler lately. Or to put it more succinctly, there was something different about her feelings towards him. She wasn't sure if it was his clothes or his new hairstyle or maybe the fact that he'd toned down his performances the last couple of weeks, or maybe all of the above, but she found herself thinking about him sometimes when the show wasn't even on. And tonight, in his button down shirt and faded blue jeans, he looked better than she'd ever seen him.

But that was to be expected, Sharla mentally reasoned. All of the singers looked better than they did when they first got on the show. It was all part of being groomed for their new image.

Still, that Tyler....

"Welcome back to *America's Next Big Star*," Russell interjected, breaking into Sharla's thoughts.

"I'm here with Tyler Nicks, who was asked just before the commercial break to go stand with the group he thinks will not be going home tonight. Tyler, if you would, please go stand with whichever group you think is safe."

With an air of determination, Tyler began walking towards Maya, Reese and Geneva, the group on the right. But instead of standing with them, he quickly but warmly hugged Maya and then Geneva before firmly shaking Reese's hand and giving him a friendly pat on the shoulder as he murmured "I'm sorry" under his breath. He then strode quietly over to the group on the left and positioned himself among them.

A few whistles and cheers from the audience.

Sharla was stunned. Russell also looked momentarily dumbfounded but quickly regained his composure.

"Tyler," he remarked, with just a twinge of wonder in his voice. "You have chosen the correct group."

The studio audience erupted into cheers and applause. Chelsea, whom Tyler was standing next to, screamed and began jumping up and down. She and Megan hugged each other, then the two of them went to hug Tyler, who smiled wanly and gave each girl a perfunctory pat on the back. Sharla could see in Tyler's face that he wasn't thrilled with what he'd been asked to do. Her heart went out to him. He'd handled it well. A heck of a lot better than she imagined anybody else would have, herself included.

"Well, that was a smart move," Lindsey replied. "Way to go, Tyler."

She got up and headed for the bathroom.

"Yes, it was," Sharla said to no one in particular. "Yes, it was...."

Something weird was happening but Sharla didn't know what. She was sitting frozen in front of the television, her eyes huge and distant, transfixed on Tyler as if she were seeing him for the first time. In a way, she was. Watching him then, Sharla saw for the first time not a quirky, gray-haired guy with a good voice who jumped around on stage, but a kindhearted, generous individual, who now that she thought about it, wasn't all that bad to look at. Especially since the ANBS stylists had cut his hair.

Sharla continued to consider...

Yeah, he really was kind of cute, what with him dressing more casual on result night. Jeans and sharp-colored button down shirts that made him look more his age and more....

"Sexy!" Sharla gasped, then realized she'd said it aloud.

Reflexively, she clamped her hand over her mouth and looked around to see if Lindsey had heard but she was in the bathroom.

Sharla turned back to the television. A commercial for some kind of feminine hygeine product was promising her and millions of other women that it would leave them feeling 'fresh all day.'

Sharla's mind drifted back to Tyler and this overwhelming attraction to him that had so suddenly overtaken her. She shook her head and closed her eyes. It was what he'd done that had gotten to her. How he'd so graciously walked up to the losing group and made it a point to hug each one of them and shake their hands. How the awkwardness of his position registered on his face as he made his way over to the winning side of the stage. Never had Sharla seen anyone involved in a competition of this nature do what Tyler had done. Most people would have pointed to the losers and walked, no almost ran, over to the safe side, saving their goodbyes until after the show, if they did it at all. But Tyler had taken the time in front of millions of people to show that even though this was a competition, he still cared about the feelings of his peers. It was an unselfish act that revealed to Sharla something of Tyler's heart, and in the process, touched hers.

But so what? So he'd shown what a nice guy he can be. Was that any reason for her to all of a sudden get all gooey over him?

"This is crazy," Sharla whispered to herself.

"What'd you say?" Lindsey asked, sitting back down.

"Oh. Nothing," Sharla said.

On TV, Russell was back, standing with the seven remaining contestants. Sharla's eyes immediately went to Tyler who was standing in the center of the group. She was having a great deal of trouble taking her gaze away from him. That's when the revelation was dropped into her spirit. The more she looked at him, the clearer it became.

The man she was staring at was her husband.

Chapter 2: Bad Love

T here was no great, white light.

The heavens didn't open before her.

The hand of God failed to appear and write a pronouncement on her apartment wall, but Sharla knew with certainty the reason she had become drawn to Tyler, possibly the reason she'd even begun watching the show, was so that God could present her with her future husband.

God had opened her eyes; she'd seen a glimpse of Tyler's spirit. A sweet, childlike spirit that moved something within her. It spoke to her because within her was a similar spirit that was also open and childlike. But much of her true self had been buried under hurt, pain, unforgiveness and relational setbacks. The most recent being the end of a tumultuous, three-year relationship with a 37-year-old financial advisor named Paul Grant.

Sharla met Paul while working as a temp in the brokerage firm he worked for. She was the receptionist and Paul had struck up a conversation with her. It all happened during a particularly low point in her life and her self-esteem, a period when she wasn't walking closely with God. She had, not surprisingly, just come out of a bad relationship. Paul was handsome and seemed decent enough. They soon began dating and though she kept her own apartment, Sharla spent most of her time at Paul's. It was nice for a while. He was nice. But over time, Sharla began to see little inconsistencies in Paul's behavior. He was prone to severe mood swings.

Paul was never physically abusive, but he had a mean streak in him that, as the relationship wore on, made him verbally abusive. What started out as cute, sarcastic quips evolved into frequent tongue lashings that undermined Sharla's self-confidence until the only thing she felt she was remotely good at was writing, which oddly enough, was the one talent for which Paul praised her.

Sharla discovered she had a knack for writing while attending Agape Junior College. An avid reader, Sharla had always done well in English. And though it wasn't her major in college, she found both English and American Literature fascinating. She fell instantly in love with the poetry of Keats and Browning, the prose of Poe, the fluidity of Thoreau, and the plays and sonnets of Shakespeare. While at AJC, Sharla dabbled in writing short stories and even worked on some articles for the *AJC Informer*, the college's weekly student newsletter.

Paul was a bookworm himself; it was one of the few things they had in common. Sharla showed Paul some of her old short stories she'd written in college and he seemed impressed. He told Sharla she should think about one day becoming a professional writer, maybe even try to pen a book. Sharla initially took the comments with a grain of salt but when Paul told her he had a friend who'd studied journalism, which was a great way to learn the art of writing and perhaps eventually find a niche in the business, Sharla secretly began to consider the matter more seriously. She had always been interested in journalism and she did love to write. Besides, she certainly didn't want to work as a temp the rest of her life. Later, when Sharla mentioned to Paul in passing that she was thinking about possibly furthering her writing career, he seemed to like the idea.

Until she got a job at the newspaper.

Once he saw that Sharla actually meant to turn her writing hobby into a profession, Paul became sullen and withdrawn, often taking his insecurities out on her, ridiculing her at every turn and always reminding her of how she never did anything right. His opinion of her as an author suddenly took a 180 degree turn. Writing a few mediocre short stories was one thing, but what made her think she could be a real writer when she'd only had two years of junior college? It took years to be a great writer; she didn't know the first thing about journalism, etc. All of which was probably true but Sharla thought she'd give it a shot anyway. She prayed to God to help her, to open a door, any kind of door. Soon after, a position for a full-time news assistant opened up at the *Agape Gazette*, no experience necessary.

Sharla applied and was hired. Two years later and through prayer and a lot of hard work, she was a full-fledged reporter. Of course, Paul had dropped out of her life long before then. Soon after she started at the paper, Paul began seeing one of Sharla's co-workers behind her back. A tall, thin gorgeous type who worked in the advertising department. It was around this time that Sharla decided to go back to church and make a reconnection with the Lord. That was where she met Lindsey. The two became fast friends, and Sharla confided in Lindsey her troubles with Paul.

It was Lindsey who'd told her about Paul and Sarah, the woman in the advertising department. She'd seen them out together, quite cozy and serious, at a local bistro one crowded lunch hour. Sharla didn't want to accept the truth. She never confronted Paul about it. Her self-esteem was almost non-existent. She was afraid Paul would blame her for the breakdown of the relationship. She tried to overlook the distance that had grown between the two of them, praying that maybe if she just ignored the problem and had faith, things would change.

They didn't.

She came home from work one night to find all of the belongings she kept at Paul's apartment packed up and stacked neatly in boxes on her front stoop. There was a handwritten note in an envelope sitting on top of the first box. The note had three words: "It's over. Paul."

Sharla had just enough self-preservation left not to grovel. When that ran out two days later, she called Paul hoping they could talk things out. The iciness in his voice was telling.

"The relationship's dead, Sharla," Paul said coldly. "Just accept it and move on."

"Fine," Sharla said, trying to sound as if her heart wasn't in her throat. "I'll just drop off my set of keys."

"Don't bother," Paul said. "I had the locks changed."

Three weeks later, Sharla learned Paul and Sarah were engaged. She came across the announcement, ironically, in the paper while she was at work helping one of the reporters do background research on a city council pipeline story. There was a photo of Paul, smiling and happy with his bride-to-be underneath the caption, **Grant-Cummings** in the Marriages/Engagements section. The picture looked like it had been taken outside on the patio of Paul's apartment. Without thinking, Sharla quickly tore the photo from its page, folded it so it fit in her pocket and went to the ladies room.

Once in the bathroom, Sharla checked each stall to make sure she was alone. She then unfolded the photo, smoothed out its edges on the sink and studied it more closely. The date at the top said it was printed last week. That meant people that knew her—people she worked with—had to have seen it, yet no one had said a word to her. Her parents took the paper (dad read it cover-to-cover) but had said nothing. Then again, why would they? They'd never liked Paul. They were glad when the relationship was over. They probably figured it was for the best, as Lindsey had said when Sharla told her Paul had ended things. Sharla imagined everyone else had kept silent out of pity. Poor Sharla, what a shame, she imagined them saying as they shook their heads, their tongues producing that annoying ticking sound people made whenever they heard about something that was particularly pathetic.

Sharla refolded the clipping so she could toss it in the trash but somehow, it ended up back in her pocket. Funny how Paul had so quickly changed his view on marriage. Every time Sharla had brought up the subject, he dismissed the idea, claiming marriage was a dead institution, a passé symbol of outdated traditionalism. What a load of bunk that turned out to be. He just hadn't wanted to marry *her*. That much was now painfully obvious.

A lump welled in Sharla's throat. All her denial came crashing down. She hadn't cried when she came home and saw her things piled up on her front doorstep, all her little knick knacks, love letters, pictures and mementos that represented the good times she and Paul had shared. She hadn't cried when she'd read Paul's painfully short note that didn't seem to do the three years of her life she'd devoted to him justice. He hadn't even had the decency to break up with her in person. But she cried in the *Agape Gazette* ladies room when she saw that engagement photo in all its grainy black-and-white glory. She managed to get through the rest of the day, then went home, put on Aretha Franklin and cried all weekend, until her face was swollen and puffy and all she could do was thank God that the advertising division was downstairs and she worked upstairs so she at least wouldn't have to run into that miserable slut.

Cummings. That was the tramp's last name.

That had been about two years and 50 extra pounds ago. Last she'd heard, Paul and Sarah had gotten married and moved to Miami. In the meantime, Sharla had vowed she would never allow herself to be party to an unhealthy relationship with any man ever again. Consequently, she hadn't been on one date with anyone in almost two years. It was simply too much trouble. She was overweight and depressed. The last thing on her mind was finding a man. She had her job, her family, a few good friends and her God. She'd talked herself into believing she didn't need anything else. But the real truth was, she'd given up on hoping someone would love her. Then, Tyler Nicks, this young man with the premature gray, simply by being himself, had pierced Sharla in a core of her soul that she hadn't known existed. And when she looked at him, she knew he held the missing piece to her heart.

Sharla blinked several times, trying to shake off the feeling that had been thrust upon her. Tyler was it. He was the one. It felt right. Sharla knew it was right. The Soul man had permeated her soul.

That's when she began to panic.

It couldn't be, she thought. This was all too sudden. It didn't make sense. A few weeks ago, this guy was just another talent show contestant! How could he now be the love of her life? Were her feelings real or was this some kind of odd post-30 crisis?

Little beads of sweat began to form on Sharla's upper lip as Russell prepared to announce the night's ousted contestant. All the while, Sharla's expression remained stunned, her eyes glossy as they fought with the camera to stay trained on Tyler, whose 6-foot-2-inch frame made him the tallest of the seven contestants.

After dismissing Tyler, Eddie, Chelsea and Megan back to the G-Zone, Russell focused his attention on the group left onstage.

"America, who is going home tonight?"

He gestured to the remaining three contestants. The television audience became deathly quiet. Only the sound of a sustained, eerie note on a synthesizer in the band broke the stillness.

The camera cut quickly to Tyler, Eddie, Chelsea and Megan sitting in the G-Zone. All of them looked tense as they directed their gazes towards their peers onstage.

Russell addressed each by name.

"Geneva…..Maya…..Reese…," he said. "Unfortunately for one of you, this is the end of the journey."

Geneva nodded her head. Maya stared straight ahead. Reese managed a weak smile and let out a nervous breath. They all held hands.

Russell lifted a card and looked at it. After another brief, dramatic pause, he spoke: "Maya, Reese, go sit down, you're safe."

A mixed roar of murmurs and shouts rose up from the crowd. Maya put a relieved hand to her chest; Reese's smile widened.

"Geneva, I'm sorry," Russell said, walking over to her. "You're going home."

Geneva closed her eyes and nodded, seeming to take the moment in stride, as if she'd been expecting it. She quickly hugged Maya and Reese before giving a small speech about what an exciting experience being on *America's Next Big Star* had been, and that it was not the end of her journey but only the beginning. Russell put an arm around Geneva and directed her towards a huge monitor that hung high above the center of the stage.

"Geneva," he said, "Let's take a look at that journey."

The giant screen became lit with images of Geneva's time on the show—beginning with the innocent, shy-looking little girl who walked into the auditions in her home state of Indiana and blew everyone away with her big voice and magnetic personality—to the gradual, visual and aural evolution that had brought her to where she currently stood next to Russell. Throughout the montage, Danny Sugar's runaway hit of the summer, "Your Luck Ran Out," played in the background. It was the standard farewell for every ousted contestant.

Sharla was sick of the song. They played it each week at the end of every results show, but she couldn't help singing along with the catchy chorus, which had become embedded in her head:

Your luck ran out,
You didn't quite win
You got dealt a bad hand
But you take it on the chin
Your number came up,
So you face it with a grin
You feel the tide rising
And you're goin' in!

Your luck ran out
But it's alright

You're walkin' thru the fire
You'll make it thru the night
Your luck ran out...
Your luck ran out!

After the video montage, Russell turned the stage over to Geneva one last time.

As she sang her exit song from the night before, she was joined onstage halfway through by the other contestants. When she finished, the first person to go up to her was Tyler. His eyes were filled with compassion as he grabbed Geneva and gave her a huge bear hug, comforting her as a big brother would his little sister.

Awww, what a sweetheart he is, Sharla thought.

"Wow, I thought for sure it was gonna be Reese tonight," Lindsey said.

The show's credits began to roll.

"What do you think about Geneva getting voted off?.......Sharla?"

Sharla heard but didn't answer. She couldn't take her eyes off Tyler. Her tongue felt glued to the roof of her mouth.

"Sharla?" Lindsey noticed her friend was staring at the TV with her mouth slightly open, as if she were in a trance. She got up and waved a hand in front of Sharla's face.

"Sharla? You okay?"

As the show ended and Sharla could no longer see Tyler before her, her paralysis broke, but the image of him hugging his peers and telling them how sorry he was had been emblazoned in her heart. Slowly, she came around and looked blinkingly at Lindsey.

"There you are!" Lindsey said. "I got worried for a second. You looked almost catatonic. Where'd you go?"

"Nowhere, I was right here."

"No, I mean in your head," Lindsey replied. "You were daydreaming about something. Or somebody." She smiled. "Judging from the look on your face, I'd say it was somebody."

Sharla averted her eyes so Lindsey couldn't see how right she was. After a long pause, she said, "I just thought it was sweet how Tyler hugged Geneva when she lost."

Lindsey's eyebrows went up. "Oh?"

"Yeah," Sharla cleared her throat self-consciously. "He seems like a nice guy."

"Yeah, that was nice." Lindsey was looking at Sharla suspiciously, as if she was trying to figure out something. Sharla didn't like it. It was making her nervous, and when she was nervous, she tended to ramble.

"I think the way he handled what happened tonight was pretty classy," she went on. Then almost as an afterthought: "I like his hair. It looks good shorter."

"Who's hair?"

"Tyler's," Sharla said absently, almost dreamily. "Didn't you notice he cut it? It looks nice. Makes him look.....younger....kind of you, you know, more attractive."

Lindsey sat back, a smile forming on her lips. "Are you talking about Tyler Nicks, the gray-haired guy?"

Sharla gave Lindsey a who-else-could-I-be-talking-about look. "Yeah."

Lindsey's smile grew bigger. "I thought you said you thought Tyler was kind of weird."

Sharla hesitated. "Well, I do. I did! I mean, it's just that since he's toned it down the last couple of weeks, I guess it's allowed me to see another side of him. A calmer side. Maybe he's not so crazy all the time as he appears to be."

"So....what?" Lindsey probed. "You think he's gonna win?"

Sharla frowned and circled the rim of her tea glass with the tip of her finger. "I dunno," she said. "Probably not but I hope he can at least make it into the Top Three."

"Well, I hate Geneva got cut," Lindsey sighed, mercifully removing her whimsical, suspicious stare. "I really liked her. I was sure it would be Reese. I didn't like that song at all he sang last night."

Sharla didn't hear. She was picturing herself standing in Geneva's place as Tyler came over to hug her.

"You know, Tyler's not all that bad looking once you really look at him," she said.

Lindsey's whimsical stare came back but Sharla didn't notice. "I hadn't really thought about it."

"Well, neither had I," Sharla answered quickly. Perhaps too quickly. "I just happened to notice tonight that he looked better than usual…."

Sharla trailed off, feeling she'd probably said too much. From the smile on Lindsey's face, she could see she had.

"Sharrrrlaaa," Lindsey cooed, leaning forward. "Do you like Tyler?"

Sharla thought for a moment.

"Sure," she answered innocently. "I think he's got a good, soulful voice and a lot of stage presence."

"That's not what I mean and you know it!" Lindsey emphasized the word "know" by dunking her fingers in her iced tea and playfully flecking some of the liquid in Sharla's direction.

"Quit playing dumb. You've got a thing for him, don't you?"

Sharla picked up her iced tea and let out a huge, frustrated sigh. She made sure to look anywhere but directly at Lindsey. "You know, I don't have to sit here and listen to this."

With that, she got up, grabbed both tea glasses and headed for the kitchen. Lindsey sprang up in hot pursuit.

"Why are you trying to avoid the question?" she teased.

"I don't know what you're talking about," Sharla replied, somehow managing to keep a straight face.

"It's so obvious!" Lindsey continued. "Oh, didn't Tyler look good tonight? And oh, isn't he cah-lassy? I should have known something was up the way you've been staring at the TV all lovesick. You were checking out Tyler–"

"Oh, please!" Sharla said weakly.

"Sharla," Lindsey reminded her. "You're not a very good liar. You can't lie to me and you shouldn't lie to yourself. You've got a crush on that guy, you've had one for weeks."

Weeks?! Sharla's mouth dropped. Had it been that noticeable? And if it had, why hadn't she really noticed before now? Up until tonight, the only thing she'd been aware she felt for Tyler was admiration for his talent.

"What? I have not had a crush on him for weeks!"

"Oh, yes, you have," Lindsey countered. "Every week since the Top 30, you've been saying, 'Oh, look, there's that gray-haired guy, Lindsey, you've GOT to hear him sing! If he doesn't make it to the next round, this show's fixed! For weeks, that's all I've heard about him from you. You get so excited when he comes on, Sharla, I've been watching."

"Well, that's because he's good!" Sharla objected. "I always thought that. But I like some of the others too. Eddie and Maya and—"

"Not the way you like him, Sharla," Lindsey said seriously. "Your eyes don't light up when they sing."

Sharla was quiet.

"Maybe you hadn't noticed it, but it's there," Lindsey said.

"That's ridiculous," Sharla waved, grabbing a rag to wipe off the countertop, more so she wouldn't have to look at Lindsey than in any real desire to tidy up.

Finally, she looked up. "I admit that tonight, yes, I did see something about him I'd never seen before, but Tyler's never meant anything more to me than any other contestant on that show."

"Maybe you just weren't ready to face it," Lindsey pointed out. "But it's been there, believe me."

"But he's not even my type!" Sharla confessed. "He's so…..out there!"

"Well," Lindsey suggested, "Maybe you're more out there than you'd like to think you are."

Sharla remained silent. As much as she hated to admit it, there was some truth to that statement.

"So," Lindsey asked, putting her elbows on the counter. "What did you see tonight that made you see Tyler differently?"

Sharla didn't know how to answer. How could she tell Lindsey what she'd seen in the Spirit? If she was having trouble believing Tyler Nicks was destined to be her husband, how could she expect anybody else to believe it? She'd be carted off to the loony bin. A snippet of "They're Coming to Take Me Away" played briefly in her head.

No, until she could get more from God on what she'd seen, Sharla was going to stay mum.

"I guess it was just the way he looked with the new hairdo and the trendier clothes," she explained instead. "And you saw how he handled what Russell put him through tonight. I liked that. It was very thoughtful. I like thoughtful guys. I guess it made me see there's more to him than all the dancing antics he does."

"You think he'll dye his hair to go with his new look?" Lindsey asked.

Sharla shuddered and wrinkled her nose. "I hope not," she said. "I like his hair the way it is. So what if he's prematurely gray? Being prematurely gray didn't hurt Steve Martin."

"I don't have a problem with it," Lindsey agreed. "But you know how it is when you get a little money and some fame. People change their look all the time."

Sharla crossed her arms over her chest. "Well, I hope Tyler doesn't. I mean, it's his hair and he can do whatever he wants with it but personally, I think at this stage, if he were to change his hair color, it'd be selling out, you know? Like he was agreeing to simply lie down and be molded into this bland rock star image that's so prevalent nowadays. His gray makes him stand out. I'm glad he doesn't look like every other singer out there."

"Well, I must admit, I do think Tyler has charisma," Lindsey said. "He may dance funny but he's got heart and I like that."

Sharla didn't say it aloud but she liked Tyler's heart too.

Chapter 3: Upside Down You're Turning Me

As the days passed, Sharla's feelings for Tyler only intensified.

The first two weeks after she realized how she felt about him were the worst. She would lay awake thinking about Tyler, about his beautiful, boyish smile and dark brown eyes.

He was the first thing on her mind when she awoke in the morning and the last thing she thought about before finally falling asleep at night. She lost interest in food and seemed to go through her days in a lovesick haze.

Before Sharla realized she was in love with Tyler, watching *America's Next Big Star* had been a casual, fairly entertaining way to pass the time on Wednesday and Thursday nights. Now, watching the show had become mandatory. For one hour, two nights a week, Tyler had the floor. Everyone who knew Sharla quickly learned not to call her while ANBS was on unless it was an absolute emergency.

Her routine hadn't changed. It was still get up, go to work, come home, go to church. But now, all of it was done in a fog. Sharla felt especially guilty when she was at church. She could hardly pay attention to the pastor's sermons for thinking about Tyler. And when she sang in the choir, it was all she could do to keep her mind focused on the songs and not have it wander back to Tyler and his sultry, gray mane. Almost everything Sharla did, she did with Tyler in mind. She'd even started exercising, an activity she loathed. But if God was in this and she did meet Tyler, Sharla didn't want him to see her looking so heavy. She'd been meaning to lose weight anyway but the thought of Tyler had given her an added incentive. It wasn't so bad once she got a routine down.

But even exercising did little to halt the emotional rollercoaster that was now riding her in every direction.

Sharla began to feel like Sybil. One minute, she was certain she loved Tyler, the next minute, she wasn't so sure. One minute, all of this was the hand of God, the next minute, she was sure she was under demonic attack. She would laugh, then cry, then do both at the same time. And through it all she couldn't shake the million dollar question ringing in her head: how could she suddenly be in love with someone she'd been looking at for months without—at least until recently—having felt even so much as the slightest tingle? Better yet, how could she be in love with someone she didn't really know?

Sometimes, Sharla lay awake in tears, wondering if she'd lost her mind. She'd been in relationships where she'd thought she was in love. She'd certainly thought she was in love with Paul. But never in her life had she felt about any man as she felt about Tyler. In her quest to get information on the man she'd fallen madly in love with, Sharla began scouring the Internet.

She found more than she bargained for.

Thanks to Google, Sharla was made aware that scores of women felt about Tyler just as she did. The information was downright frightening, not to mention disheartening. Tyler's growing popularity had turned him into a reluctant sex symbol. Almost overnight, he'd become like George Clooney or one of those other famous, good-looking men over which women like Sharla only dared fantasize. Tyler Nicks web sites were popping up all over Cyberspace.

"Why, God, why?" Sharla cried one night during a particularly bad bout. "Why does he have so many women after him?"

She ranted and threw up her hands in bed, tearing at the sheets like a child having a super tantrum.

"I could see if he wasn't famous, but God, he *ISSSSSSSSS!*" she wailed, plunging her head like a dive-bomber onto her pillow.

"Why couldn't You have me fall in love with some guy at church....or at least someone in the same state?!" she hiccuped, looking up at the ceiling of her bedroom with tears streaming down her cheeks.

Between huge, gasping sobs that would have been comical had her heart not been so full, she would pause, then cry, "Jesus, this is torture! You could have at least showed him to me before he got on the show. He's got women swooning over him left and right now. He's unreachable. He's so big and I'm so...so....uhhh, God, *whyyyy?????*"

In between bouts of despair, Sharla patiently combed through Tyler Nicks websites and forums, as well as the ANBS message boards in search of information.

Sharla learned Tyler's middle name was Joel. He was born February 25, 1977 in Taylorsville, Georgia. He'd been a musician most of his life, a passion that began at age 8 when he heard Marvin Gaye sing "Pride and Joy."

After high school, Tyler did a short stint at Georgia State University where he studied psychology, something Sharla found interesting. She too had studied Psych in college. Tyler was an accomplished musician who played several instruments, including the piano, guitar and saxophone. He'd been in numerous bands over the years, the most recent being The Tyler Nicks Experience, which traveled anywhere they could playing clubs, bars, honkytonks, weddings and birthday parties.

A few years prior to ANBS, Tyler had released an independent CD titled "Under the Influence," an out-of-print gem that briefly resurfaced in the form of downloadable MP3's. Thanks to Amazon and Tyler's growing popularity, the album had achieved a type of cult status among members of the Soul Squad.

Tyler was single, had never been married and had no children. His parents were both alive and had been married 37 years. His father was a successful chiropractor in Smyrna, Georgia, and his mother a retired nurse. He had two siblings: a younger brother, Andy, and an older sister named Janice, who was married and had two children.

Tyler had been living in Atlanta with two roommates—his pet cockatoos, Sam and Dave—when fate intervened.

A busted water pipe flooded his apartment and forced him to temporarily vacate. By sheer coincidence, some friends in Kansas City happened to call Tyler the day of the flood asking if he was available to play for their cousin's Bar Mitzvah that weekend. Since it was such short notice, his friends offered to pay his plane fare and provide him with a place to stay until his apartment dried out. After safely depositing Sam and Dave in the care of his parents, Tyler agreed and happened to be in Kansas City at the exact same time *America's Next Big Star* was holding area tryouts. At the urging of his siblings, Tyler decided to audition.

From the moment he made the Top 30, there was a lot of talk in several of the forums about Tyler mentioning that if he won ANBS, the first thing he was going to buy was a bed. Apparently, living on a traveling musician's wage hadn't afforded Tyler the cash to buy a decent bed, so the poor guy had been roughing it sleeping on an old air mattress. Some pictures of Tyler's vacant apartment were being circulated online and Sharla got to see for herself just what kind of condition the air mattress was in.

The apartment itself looked like the typical bachelor pad, albeit a bit sparse. It was pretty clear Tyler didn't spend much time there. The only evidence the place was inhabited were a few plants and some old saxophone reeds on a nightstand. The hardwood floors, which had been damaged in the flood, had reportedly been repaired, though Sharla thought she noticed a few random water stains.

The much-talked about air mattress was pretty tattered, so much so that the ends of it were frayed. But what amazed Sharla about that mattress is that towards the end of the show, some fan broke in and cut off a piece of the thing to have as a souvenir. That of course, ended the amazing life of Tyler's air mattress. The remains would later be scrunched up into a baggie and sold on E-Bay.

The ANBS message boards also contained some pretty interesting tidbits. The site had a separate web page for each of its Season Three finalists. On Tyler's page, Sharla found a snippet of the standard ANBS questionnaire all auditioners are asked to fill out. Some of Tyler's answers made her chuckle:

When did you first start to sing?
In the hospital delivery room.

What other talents do you have?
I play a pretty mean game of pool.

If you are eliminated from *America's Next Big Star*, what will you do?
Keep playing music.

What album would your friends be surprised you own?
Weird Al's Greatest Hits.

What artist/performer do you most admire?
James Brown.

What is your most embarrassing moment?
Throwing up in a restaurant's fish tank. At least the tank was empty at the time.

What has been the proudest moment in your life so far?
The birth of my niece and nephews.

If you couldn't sing, which talent would you most like to have?

To be a painter, an artist.

What would people be surprised to learn about you?
I can do a few magic tricks.

How has this experience changed your life?
Ask me again when this is over.

Do you have any lucky charms?
A buffalo head nickel.

What's been your toughest obstacle in life?
Overcoming life's obstacles.

If you win, who will you thank first?
God.

Another part of Tyler's page told her that in addition to James Brown, his favorite male vocalists were Marvin Gaye and James Taylor. His favorite female artists: Pat Benatar and Debby Harry.

Sharla liked Tyler's answers. Seems they even had some things in common outside of music. But inside, she still felt confused and overwhelmed. Being on television every week had made Tyler a celebrity. He was among the rich and famous now. Sharla imagined he was probably having the time of his life in California going out with all those tall, beautiful, bone thin Hollywood women who were no doubt throwing themselves at his feet. Why would he want a nobody like her?

Sharla would mentally work herself over thinking that none of what she felt made sense. There had to be something wrong with her. She had to be deluded. Then she would get calm and quiet, listening for that still, small voice within her that told her nothing was impossible for God. A person's fame was no barrier for Him, if she had faith but as big as a mustard seed. The peace of God would overwhelm her then, and she'd again be pumped with faith that God was somehow going to make this happen.

"Hurry, Lord," Sharla would sometimes say. "Give me confirmation that what I saw in my heart is true."

But the confirmation was already there. She felt it inside of her whenever Tyler came into view.

Chapter 4: Try Me

Ferris Park was uncharacteristically warm and sunny on the Saturday afternoon Sharla went down to the lake.

The park was only a few blocks from her apartment. In the center of it was a small lake Sharla sometimes went to whenever she needed to think or meditate. The air there always seemed fresher, and there was a family of ducks nearby she liked to watch waddle and squawk around the grounds.

Aside from the occasional jog around the park itself (she was trying to fit it in as part of her new exercise regime), Sharla hadn't been to the lakeside in some time. There hadn't really been anything pressing to think about lately.

Until Tyler.

Now, it seemed that in the blink of an eye—or maybe more appropriately, the touch of her remote control—Sharla had been given a lot to think about, matters for which she felt utterly unprepared.

She took a seat on a park bench and sighed. The water was a murky shade of gray due to the early January chill. The weather had been rainy and sleeting with temperatures in the low 30's since before Christmas. Snow wasn't usual in the area of Texas where Sharla lived, though every year, the forecast seemed to threaten it. Today was the first day the sun had come out in weeks. The temperature had risen into the late 60's, a perfect day to grab a jacket, take a reprieve from household chores and go for a walk.

Sharla tried to simply sit and concentrate on the scenery or on the sound of the birds chirping in the trees but her mind simply wouldn't let her. It always somehow drifted back to thoughts of that gray-haired guy on *America's Next Big Star*.

Who was Tyler Nicks? And what did Sharla really know about him except what ANBS and a few websites had told her? Had she really seen what she'd thought she'd seen? Surely, she'd been mistaken. The loopy, paranoid thought that maybe Lindsey had slipped something in her tea that night—pixie dust, perhaps—was beginning to look more and more like a logical explanation.

Hard as she tried, Sharla just couldn't shake what she'd seen, what she'd felt in her spirit. She thought at first that maybe what she was experiencing was some type of latent infatuation, a crush that would run its course and quickly run out of steam. That's the way her crushes had always worked in high school. But it had been weeks and still the thought of and the attraction to Tyler had not lessened. If anything, it had become stronger.

Sharla frowned deeply.

This was crazy! Even if there was a possibility of meeting Tyler, there was no guarantee he would be attracted to her. Or her to him, for that matter. Thinking you were in love with someone from afar was one thing, but what if that person wasn't who you thought they were up close? Couldn't it be entirely possible, Sharla thought, that she was only in love with the *idea* of Tyler, just like Scarlett O'Hara's obsession with Ashley Wilkes in *Gone with the Wind*? And anyway, Sharla reminded herself for the umpteenth time, Tyler was in another world now, one that included celebrities and hobnobbing in wealthy inner circles. What could a woman like her who was so…so ordinary, have to offer him now?

On the walk over, Sharla had been listening to James Brown on her CD walkman. The song "Try Me" came up just as her thoughts turned to the possibilities with Tyler, as if the Godfather of Soul himself would plead her case. The song's lyrics echoed Sharla's desires:

> *Try me, Try me!*
> *Darlin', tell me*
> *I need you*

Try me, Try me!
And your love will always be true
Oh, I need you (I need you)...

Sharla listened intently, the cool, January air caressing her face as James pleaded for the object of his affection to hold him, talk with him, walk with him. As the last strains of the tenor sax brought the song to a close, Sharla removed her headphones from her ears and let them drop around her neck. She closed her eyes and lowered her head.

"Father," she silently prayed. "I didn't want to believe what I saw the other night, but it's gotten a hold of me and I can't shake it. So now, God, I'm asking you again for a confirmation. I need You to show me or tell me in some way that what I believe I saw in my spirit was from You and not my imagination." She squeezed her eyes shut tighter. "Please, Jesus, I feel like I'm going crazy and I desperately need to hear from You."

Sharla said "amen" aloud and opened her eyes. The ducks, who had been lingering close by, had disappeared but Sharla could just hear them on the opposite side of the lake. On the hiking trail, she noticed a couple walking towards her arm in arm headed for the bench, there eyes locked lovingly on each other.

Sharla got up to leave; three was a crowd.

She replaced her headphones back over her ears and pushed "play." James' undeniable scream introduced "I Feel Good," one of Sharla's favorites.

Maybe the song was a good omen.

Sharla smiled a little and began the trek back to her apartment.

Chapter 5: Tell Me Something Good

The next morning, Sharla got to church a few minutes early so she could have some time alone with the Lord.

The choir was already gathering up on the platform but Sharla wouldn't be joining them today. She didn't think she should be up there right now, not when she wasn't able to fully concentrate.

Instead, she found her usual spot in the fourth row near the front—center aisle—and sat down, but something inside her felt she should go to the altar.

Sharla walked over to the side and knelt down. She prayed, again asking God to give her confirmation as to what she thought she'd seen in her spirit six weeks ago. Was she really destined to be with Tyler Nicks, a man who didn't even know who she was and who, as far as she was concerned, lived on the other side of the country?

"Please God," she silently entreated, "Let me know if I'm losing my mind!"

Sharla was on her knees like that for awhile, desperately pleading with God for help and on the verge of tears, unaware of the time or how long she'd been at the altar.

The first few notes of "Awesome God" from the praise band brought her out of her thoughts. Slowly, she began to arise, her legs feeling stiff and wobbly. By the time she was finally standing, the congregation had just finished the first verse of the song and was singing the chorus:

> *Our God is an awesome God,*
> *He reigns from heaven above*
> *With wisdom, power and love*

Our God is an awesome God!

Sharla quickly murmured "amen" and went to her seat.

Normally, the worship was the best part of the service for Sharla. She loved entering into God's presence through song, but it just wasn't happening right then. She sang and lifted her hands to the sky in praise, but her heart was not quite into the music. The more she tried to concentrate on worshipping God, the more her thoughts returned to Tyler. His face, his voice. No matter how she tried, she couldn't shake him. And in church, of all places! Sharla lowered her hands and wondered half-seriously if she was going to hell.

By the time Pastor Mike got around to giving his message, Sharla was mentally rebuking the devils that had dropped off that wild, dancing guy in her head and left him there.

I won't think about him, I won't *think about him!* She kept telling herself, which only made the situation worse. It was like telling someone not to think about a pink, polka-dotted elephant.

Had she later been asked what the pastor's sermon was about, Sharla wouldn't have been able to repeat a word. She had been too busy involuntarily thinking about what a sweet smile Tyler had and how she hadn't noticed before that he had dimples. But what she would have been able to say she did remember was the prophecy she received that night, the one that got her to thinking perhaps she wasn't so crazy after all.

It happened towards the end of the service, when the pastor asked all those who were in need of a breakthrough in their life to come forward for prayer. Sharla had enough presence of mind to hear that and immediately stepped forward. She was prepared to tell the pastor everything, to repent at his feet and throw herself at the altar if necessary. Anything to rid herself of this ache she had for a man she didn't even know!

When the pastor got to Sharla, instead of simply laying hands on her and saying a prayer, he stopped and looked at her. Sharla had closed her eyes when he came to her, but after a few seconds, she opened them to see Pastor Mike staring at her.

Oh God, She thought wildly. *He knows. He knows I didn't hear a word of what he said and he's going to call me out in front of everyone for thinking about a man other than Jesus in church!*

"God's got a word for you," Pastor Mike said, pointing directly at Sharla. He took a step towards her and laid a hand on her shoulder. The music grew softer and Sharla could see out of the corner of her eye that the entire congregation was looking at her.

"What you saw," Pastor Mike said slowly, as if searching for the words, "What you saw in your spirit was from Me, says the Lord."

Sharla's eyes became huge; her jaw dropped.

"Now, I don't know what that means," Pastor Mike said. He was looking Sharla squarely in the face. "I don't know what you saw in your spirit, but God is telling you not to doubt."

"Yes," Sharla nodded.

There was a brief pause as the pastor closed his eyes. He opened them again and continued, "Sister, God is going to show up in your life and it's going to be in a way that you'll have no doubt it was Him!"

The congregation burst into applause. Sharla released a great sigh of relief. Her shoulders sagged as she did so, as if she'd just had a huge burden lifted from her shoulders.

"Thank you, Jesus," she whispered.

"Get ready, things are gonna change for you," the pastor said softly. "*You're* going to be changed."

He touched Sharla's arm, and a jolt went through her body that sent her reeling back into the arms of one of the church helpers, who gently laid her down and covered her with a blanket.

For several minutes, Sharla lay slain in the Spirit, marinating in the presence of God's awesome power. When she was finally able to get up with the assistance of the same kindly church helper, she was still thinking about Tyler, but now, she had peace.

God was in this. She was going to be changed.

———————————————————————

After church, Sharla and Lindsey decided to have lunch.

They each took their own cars and met at Frenchy's, a little mom and pop establishment that served the best enchiladas in Agape.

"So, why weren't you in choir today?" Lindsey asked after they'd been seated. "We could have used you. Most of the altos are out sick."

"I know," Sharla sighed, settling into the booth. "But I wasn't feeling too hot myself."

A waitress came and took drink orders.

"Is everything okay?" Lindsey asked when she'd left.

"Yeah," Sharla shrugged, a bit hesitant. "Just post-holiday stuff."

"Oh, tell me about it," Lindsey agreed and launched into the saga of her cousin Jeffrey and his wife and three rotten, ill-mannered kids who'd come down for Christmas to a family gathering at her parent's house in Kilgore. Now, here it was mid-January and they still hadn't left. Lindsey's mom was calling her practically every night complaining she was at her wit's end.

"They won't leave!" Lindsey said in a dignified, high-pitched voice that almost perfectly mimicked her mother's. "I mean, doesn't this man have a job? They don't do anything but lay around all day and those little monsters of his are eating us out of house and home."

"So, I said, 'Well, mom, just tell Jeff either he's gonna have to pack up and get out or start paying rent'," Lindsey continued. "You're not running a hotel. This guy has always, always been a user, Sharla, even when we were little. I told mom that before she and dad invited him. The only time he ever shows up is when he wants something. But you know how they are, they just want to help everybody and Jeff knows that so he takes advantage…."

The waitress returned with drinks and took food orders. Lindsey ordered the enchiladas, Sharla a loaded baked potato and a garden salad. When the waitress had gone, Lindsey continued.

"He probably got fired again and doesn't want to tell my parents—"

"Who probably got fired?" Sharla asked. She was only half listening, the prophecy Pastor Mike had spoken over her that morning still fresh in her thoughts.

"Jeff, my cousin." Lindsey said.

"Oh," Sharla nodded. "Yeah, that is tough."

"Hmmph! Tough for anybody that tries to help the guy," Lindsey replied bitterly. "I mean, I know we're supposed to be Christ-like and have compassion and all, but Jeff is nothing but a professional moocher. And now he's raising that demon seed of his to be the same way…"

Sharla looked out the window next to the booth at the fantastic view of the restaurant parking lot and it's dumpster. Listening to Lindsey talk reminded Sharla of a girl she'd known in school, Camy Willis. They'd met in band when Sharla was in the ninth grade. Sharla played French horn, Camy the clarinet.

Camy was a year older and a real out-going, free spirit. She loved music, especially classic Rock and Soul. Sharla had grown up in a very religious, conservative home. Both her parents were devout Catholics with musical tastes that leaned mainly towards light classical and traditional Gospel hymns. So it was a mind-opening experience for Sharla to have her ears suddenly invaded with the sounds of groups like Led Zepplin, Jimi Hendrix, The Who, Eric Clapton and The Beatles.

Sharla fell in love with the music instantly.

Always an avid reader, she immersed herself in rock star biographies and the history of Rock, Pop and Soul music. At night before going to bed, she would put on headphones and tune her little Walkman to the oldies or the classic rock station while she slept.

Sharla developed a special affinity to Soul music, how the lyrics and the rhythms seemed to, many times, convey what she was feeling. Listening to it gave her a safe outlet to express herself. Whenever she felt depressed or alone, she would take out her secret stash of R&B tapes and let Aretha Franklin, Marvin Gaye, Otis Redding or Ray Charles sing out the blues for her.

The music also gave her the courage to do things. Like entering a few talent contests in high school, where Sharla discovered she had a decent singing voice. She never won (the closest she got was second place) but just having been involved in the contests gave her an opportunity to break out of her natural shyness.

Sharla smiled. She hadn't thought about Camy, about any of that stuff, in years. After they graduated, Sharla lost touch with Camy. Last she'd heard, Camy had gotten married to a lawyer and was living somewhere overseas, perhaps in Ireland, Sharla recalled. But it was easier to find people now with the advent of the Internet. Sharla thought maybe she'd try looking her old friend up sometime. After all, in an odd way, Camy was indirectly responsible for Sharla's interest in Tyler.

The man God says I'm going to marry, Sharla thought warmly, her mind replaying what Pastor Mike had told her.

"So, then," Lindsey said, looking directly at Sharla, " These aliens in a spaceship came down and kidnapped me, and took me to their home planet where they pledged me in marriage to their king."

"Uh-huh," Sharla said, still gazing out the window. "We're getting married at 3:00 today on the planet Fahlahful," Lindsey continued.

"Mmm." Sharla continued to stare out the window and pick at her food, which she was barely aware had been brought to the table several minutes ago.

Lindsey sat back in the booth. "The groom is only three inches tall…"

No response from Sharla.

"..and I'm already pregnant with our first child. It's a boy…I think. Can't be sure with aliens."

Sharla slowly turned around and looked at Lindsey with a blank expression. "What?"

"Nothing," Lindsey sighed. "Just talking to myself….apparently."

Sharla smiled faintly. "Oh…I'm sorry. I, um, I was just thinking."

"I could see that," Lindsey said. "Wanna talk about it?"

Sharla shrugged and leaned back in the booth. "I don't really know if I can."

"What is it?" Lindsey leaned forward, concerned. "Are you sick?"

"No, no, I'm not sick," Sharla said.

"Then what? You look like you need to get whatever it is out."

Sharla tried to take a bite of her potato and ended up letting the food on her fork fall limply back to her plate.

"I haven't been sleeping very well," she admitted.

Lindsey nodded slowly. "Is it work? Are you stressed out?"

"Well, work is always stressful," Sharla sighed. "But no more than usual. No, it's not that…" She trailed off. Sharla tried to look at Lindsey and couldn't. Lindsey didn't say anything, only waited patiently for Sharla to speak as she thoughtfully chewed her enchiladas.

Sharla was debating whether she should say anything about Tyler. Not because she didn't trust Lindsey but because the whole thing was so crazy. Despite the new confirmation, she was afraid her best friend would confirm Sharla's worst fear that she was losing her mind. But then, she pictured Tyler. A huge smile stretched across Sharla's face, which was turning a bright shade of crimson.

Lindsey stopped eating and set her fork in her plate. "Okay, what's going on?" Her eyebrows went up. "Are you in love?"

Sharla didn't speak, only sat back in the booth and smiled wider.

"I should have known," Lindsey said. "No wonder you've been acting so weird. So, who is it? Do I know him?"

Sharla thought a moment. "Well, sort of. You know *of* him."

"Oh, come on, please don't make me play 20 Questions," Lindsey pleaded. "Who is it?"

Sharla leaned forward and lowered her voice. "Okay but before I tell you, keep an open mind."

"Okay," Lindsey said slowly, a tinge of suspicion in her voice. Then: "He's not a drug dealer, is he?"

"No!"

"Did he just get out of jail?"

"What?! Oh, for goodness sake—"

"Did he used to be a she?"

"Lindsey," Sharla gasped. "God, no! What kind of a person do you think I am?!"

"Well, you said to keep an open mind," Lindsey reasoned.

"Not that open," Sharla quipped. "You remember about a month ago when we were watching *America's Next Big Star* at my apartment and you asked me why I was acting so strange?"

Lindsey thought a moment. "No, I don't think so."

"You know, when it was down to the top seven and Russell asked Tyler to choose a side?"

Lindsey thought again, a puzzled expression on her face, followed by dawning recognition. "Oh, yeah!" she said finally. "When Geneva got voted out."

"Right."

"Yeah, I remember. What about it?"

"You said I was acting strange and you asked me why. Remember?" Lindsey took a sip of her iced tea. "Well, you've always been a little strange…"

Sharla rolled her eyes and smiled.

"…but you were acting kind of out of it that night, come to think of it." Lindsey continued slowly, talking like a detective who is speaking aloud for the benefit of those present of how she came to solve a mystery.

"And I said I thought you had a crush on Tyler but you denied it, even though you'd been going on about him for weeks. So, I was right. You did have a thing for Tyler!"

Sharla nodded. "Right."

Lindsey looked pensive, almost as if she were afraid to ask the next question because she already knew the answer. "And how does that tie in with you being in love?"

Sharla took a deep breath. She couldn't believe what she was about to say. "I saw my husband that night."

Lindsey's eyes widened. "Where?"

"On the show."

"What show?" Lindsey asked, perplexed. *"America's Next Big Star*?"

Sharla nodded and said 'yes' in a voice that was barely audible.

Lindsey looked at Sharla as if she was seeing her for the first time. She let out an amused laugh.

"You're kidding, right? You're not serious?"

"Yes," Sharla said. "I'm very serious."

Lindsey stared at Sharla, her eyes searching her friend's face for the punch line to this odd joke. But Sharla's face showed no sign she was joking. Finally, Lindsey spoke, not sure just what to say next.

"Who's your husband?" she finally asked.

"Brace yourself," Sharla warned. "Tyler."

Lindsey nearly choked on her drink. "Tyler Nicks?!" she coughed.

"Yeah," Sharla nodded.

"Are you sure?" Lindsey gasped.

"Yeah, I'm positive."

Lindsey was dumfounded. "Well…how?"

"I don't know!" Sharla shrugged helplessly. "That's what's so crazy about all this. I-I don't understand what happened. I mean, up until about six weeks ago, I didn't even think Tyler was all that cute. Now, I look at him and I see….I see…"

"Your husband," Lindsey finished, her voice dripping with skepticism. Sharla decided to pretend she hadn't noticed.

"Yes," she said. "I know it sounds odd—"

"You got that right," Lindsey interjected.

"—But I know what I saw."

"Just exactly what did you see?" Lindsey asked, folding her arms.

"It's not so much what I saw, I guess," Sharla explained. "But more what I felt in my spirit. And Lin, I know how crazy this seems but I looked at Tyler that night and I just knew in my heart that he and I were meant to be together. He's my husband, I can't explain it any better than that."

"Uh-huh." Lindsey took another sip of her tea but remained silent. Sharla could see Lindsey was struggling with this. She couldn't blame her. She'd been struggling with it herself.

"You know how couples talk about how they saw their future spouse and just knew that was the person they would marry?"

Lindsey nodded.

"Well, that's how it was with Tyler. I looked at him and I just knew."

"But Sharla, you've been looking at Tyler for months now."

"I know," Sharla admitted. "Maybe sometimes it doesn't take right away, I don't know. All I know is that something's come over me and I believe it's Holy Spirit-driven. There's no other explanation for this sudden feeling I have about this guy. I have never felt this way about any man, not even Paul. It has to be God, Lindsey! Believe me, I have wrestled with this thing for weeks, thinking I was losing my mind. But I've been praying for confirmation from God and this morning…"

Sharla's voice went up and she became more animated. "….this morning, I got my confirmation. I'm not going crazy after all, Lin, it is God!"

Lindsey leaned forward again. "What happened this morning?"

"Don't you remember when Pastor Mike spoke a word over me?"

"Oh, yeah, but I couldn't really hear everything he said."

"He spoke a word over me," Sharla repeated. "He told me that what I saw in my spirit was God and to have faith!"

Lindsey's features softened a bit at hearing this. "Had you told him about any of this?"

"No! That's just it," Sharla went on. "He had no idea what I'd seen. I hadn't told anybody. I wanted to be sure first that it was God and not just me having some major mental breakdown. That's why I didn't tell you when you brought up Tyler that night."

Then Lindsey stated the obvious. "But Tyler doesn't even know who you are."

Sharla shrugged, then smiled and took a bite of her potato. "Yeah, well, God can change that."

"True," Lindsey agreed. "I just want you to be cautious, Sharla. You don't really know anything about Tyler."

"I know. And believe me, I know how ridiculous this sounds. But it has to be God. Why would I all of a sudden have this intense feeling about someone I don't know and didn't even really have an interest in until recently if it's not God?"

Lindsey thought a moment. "Is there anything about Tyler that reminds you of Paul?"

Sharla sighed. "I thought about that and honestly, no, he doesn't remind me of Paul at all, thank God. It's not that. I've thought about this from every angle there is. I've asked God to search my heart and there's no underlying reason for this. It's just like us being believers, Lin. We know-that we know-that we know-that Jesus is Lord, right? Well, it's the same with Tyler. I just know."

For a while, the pair ate in silence. The waitress came and brought the check and refilled drinks, which gave both women a moment to collect their thoughts. After the waitress had gone, Lindsey spoke.

"You know, I hate to say this, but you kind of sound like some of those stalkers you hear about on TV, Sharla. The ones that claim they were 'meant to be' with Jennifer Aniston or Whitney Houston or Madonna or whoever?"

She leaned over and took Sharla's hand. "You know I say that as a friend, right?"

Sharla chuckled. "Yeah, I know. And I do know how wacko it sounds. But it's not like that. I'm not making plans to camp outside Tyler's house or send letters threatening him to marry me or else. This either happens completely through God or not at all."

"So, you're really in love with Tyler?"

"Well," Sharla answered, "I think so. I certainly am attracted to him. He's all I've thought about for weeks. I can't sleep, I can barely eat. I can't concentrate. If he's not in the front of my mind, he's in the back of it. Does that sound like love?"

"Eh, maybe." Lindsey waved off. "Could just be lust."

"No," Sharla said. "There is definitely a physical attraction but it goes deeper than that. I mean, let's be honest. You know me. If I was gonna go for just the physical, I would have gone for Reese. No, this is beyond lust."

Lindsey nodded then looked at her watch. "Well, I'm gonna have to be going. I promised my elderly neighbor I'd stop in and check on her. Then I've got to call mom and see if she took my advice and put her foot down about Jeff."

"Okay," Sharla said, leaving a tip for the waitress.

"Just keep praying about this, Sharla," Lindsey said as they walked out of the restaurant. "I'm not saying it couldn't happen. If it's really from God, anything is possible. But just be careful, okay?"

Sharla hugged her friend. "Of course." Then: "Do you think I'm crazy?"

"Honestly, no." Lindsey said. "Now, if you weren't concerned that you *might* be crazy, I would be worried…"

Sharla laughed.

"..but since you are concerned and you seem pretty sold that this is God's choice for you, then no, I don't think you're crazy. I have to admit, though, this is a little hard to swallow…"

"I know," Sharla agreed. "It was for me too in the beginning. But I thought about how sometimes, God tells us things that don't make any sense in the natural. Telling Noah to build a huge boat when it had never rained, that didn't make sense. Or asking Abraham to leave his home and go to some unknown land, I'm sure that didn't make sense either. I don't fully understand what I saw or why I feel the way I feel, but…" Sharla shrugged. "…I'm gonna trust God. If it's not Him, it won't happen, right?"

Lindsey agreed. "Well, just keep praying and see what happens. And keep me posted."

"I will."

Sharla got in her car and let out a sigh. It felt good to finally tell someone what had been on her heart for so long. But she couldn't help wondering, confirmation aside, if perhaps she hadn't spoken too soon.

Chapter 6: Thunk

Going into a Tyler Nicks Internet forum could be quite an adventure.

Not only was it a good way to keep up with Tyler's comings and goings, but people sometimes posted some pretty interesting stuff.

Sharla found there were various types of Tyler web sites. Some focused solely on him as a musician, others on his new reality TV celebrity status. Some combined all aspects of him as a person and as a musician; some were clearly for entertainment purposes—like the web page dedicated to his pet cockatoos, Sam and Dave—while others fixated on his sex appeal.

The latter sites were particularly amusing to Sharla. One of them, Tyler's Place, was a favorite hot spot among diehard female Tyler fans or "Nicks Chicks," as they called themselves.

Sharla didn't consider herself a Nicks Chick and frankly, wasn't crazy about the term. She didn't want to be lumped in such a general category with thousands of other women, all of whom were oogling the same man. She wanted to stand out to Tyler, to somehow be viewed by him as different. Branding herself a Nicks Chick made her feel insignificant, just another face in the crowd. But the forum itself held some interesting discussions, although the talk often tended to get a bit racy and in a few cases, bordered on pornographic.

Sharla normally skipped past the more raunchy posts, usually opting to read the funnier ones. She'd even learned a new word that had recently become part of the Nicks Chick vernacular: "thunk," which was a complimentary term women used to describe how Tyler made them want to swoon or pass out. Another phrase, "the apple," was being used as a reference to Tyler's derriére. Sharla couldn't figure out why Tyler's backside was being compared to a piece of fruit but it made for some interesting chatter:

··That Tyler Nicks has got the cutest apple! *thunk*

·They say an apple a day keeps the doctor away.

·With an apple like Tyler's, who needs a doctor?

·He is to die for. Yum…

·I must admit that ever since I discovered Tyler, I have become a proud, card-carrying member of Tylerholics Anonymous. In fact, I'm overdue for a meeting now. Gotta run!

·Holy cow, it's hot in here! (pants) Is it just me or does that man get more good-looking with every new pic??? *thunk*

·Well, he may have a nice tush but I think the rest of him is pretty thunkworthy too.

· "Thunkworthy." I like that. Can I borrow it?

Farther down, Sharla read more food-related subject matter:

·Okay, here's something to think about. If Tyler was a dessert, what kind of dessert would he be?

·That's easy. An apple pie, of course. Light, flaky and sweet.

·I like donuts so I'd liken Tyler to a box of one dozen assorted Krispy Kremes. Sometimes he's filled with inner yumminess, other times he's smooth like chocolate or tangy like a lemon tart. But whether he's glazed or powdered, he's always delicious, sweet, and highly addictive!

·LOL, Great analogy!

Another funny topic caught Sharla's eye—**Tyler or George Clooney**:

·Definitely Tyler. George Clooney has shifty eyes. I don't trust men with shifty eyes.

·Tyler, no question. He's much more down to earth than Clooney.

·I agree. Clooney's this huge movie star type. But Tyler has that-hot guy-next-door quality about him. Definitely more approachable.

·Tyler is da bomb!

·Who's George Clooney?

·On a scale of 1 to 10 on the 'ol Thunk-o-Meter, I'd say George gets a 7 and Tyler is a perfect 10.

·I think Tyler and George are both handsome in their own way. But since this is a Tyler forum and I could be stoned for saying otherwise, I'll go with Tyler.

0

·Good choice. (Drops stones). Ha, ha. Kidding…

Sharla was torn. She'd never seen such lust for one man in one place and didn't know what to think. While she was physically attracted to Tyler and did agree that he took a nice picture, she could never be as bold to say some of the things these women did. She was too afraid Tyler might see it and she'd be embarrassed. What would he think? What *did* he think of comments like these?

As she scrolled through the messages, Sharla found a very interesting one from someone who obviously didn't share in the Nicks Chick ardency:

Tylerlover1: I've been lurking in this forum for some time and have never felt the desire to post a comment. Normally, I am not an outspoken person but the continuous, sexual degradation of Tyler Nicks, who, in my humble opinion, is a fine, upstanding human being, must be addressed. I am appalled at the behavior of some of the people on this board who claim to possess intelligence. I suppose I will be hated and ostracized for what I am about to say but since this was still a free country last I checked and you all have had your say, I'd like to have mine. No one in this thread seems to appreciate Tyler for his talent. You have reduced him to nothing more in your minds than a piece of grade-A sausage to be salivated and fought over like a pack of rabid dogs in heat. Your comments sadden me. Tyler Nicks is a person. The man deserves to be talked about with respect, not as if he were a mere sex object or some Chip & Dales stripper. You all ought to be ashamed of yourselves. There, I've said it. Somebody had to. I will now go back into lurkdom and leave you to your depravity.

Sharla's mouth dropped. She couldn't wait to see what people had to say about this. The next comment answered her question.

Grand_dame: So we're nothing more than a pack of rabid dogs in heat, eh? Well, Tylerlover, let me tell you something. Yes, it is a free country and you do have a right to your opinion but who are you to come in here and suggest that we/I don't appreciate Tyler for his talent? Just because we laugh and joke around about how attractive he is doesn't mean we don't respect him. We're just venting about how he makes us feel and if that bothers you, than you don't have to come in this thread. Which leads me to another question. If you're so holier-than-thou about sexual commentary, what the heck are you doing in this thread in the first place?! Shame on us? No. Shame on *you*!

Ladysoul: you are certainly entitled to your opinion and I respect that. Believe it or not, I respect Tyler too.

Tysbabe: Comparing Tyler to grade-A sausage? Now THAT is an insult. He is 100% USDA approved Porterhouse STEAK all the way, honey!.

---

nickychicky: Okay, I admit it I'm guilty. Looking at Tyler reduces me to a quivering piece of moronic mush. So sue me. I don't see how any warm-blooded female can stand next to him and still be able to speak in coherent sentences.

---

lady_marmalade_65: You're right, Tylerlover1, it is a free country, which means you're free to get out of this forum.

Quilty: I had the opportunity to meet Tyler during a taping of ANBS and I was able to speak to him in coherent sentences. Yes he is beautiful in person but he's also very relaxed and easy to talk to, which makes a person feel comfortable. I took my three grandchildren with me to the studio and Tyler was kind enough to autograph Soul Squad bandannas for each of them.If anyone would like to see the photos, e-mail me.

Barb: Tylerlover, please excuse my lack of intellect (I'm just a dumb fan who recently graduated from Brown University with a BA in Aerospace Engineering) but your post leads me to believe you think you're better than most here because you appreciate the music, while us other gals, blithering idiots that you feel we are, are too low-brow to see beyond Tyler's good looks. Since it is a free country as you pointed out, and you're free to refer to me as a rabid dog in heat, I am therefore free to call you an arrogant, snotty, uptight prude who desperately needs someone to surgically remove that stick from up her backside. As a music lover, Tyler moves me. I did vote for him, after all. But as a woman, I am not ashamed to admit that he also moves me in other ways. Thank you for letting me revel in my so-called depravity. Sounds to me like you could use a good dose of the stuff yourself. It might make you a nicer person.

Blue-by-u: Why can't Tyler be both handsome and talented? Why must it be one or the other? Speaking only for myself, I do think I may get a little out of hand sometimes with my comments, but it's all in fun and it certainly doesn't mean I lack intelligence. I love every aspect of Tyler, which happens to include his looks. Can he sing? Yes. Is he talented? No question. But the guy is also friggin' HOT, and all those music snobs out there who pretend not to notice that he is need to get over it.

shrek: Good looks doesn't mean less talent and an abundance of talent doesn't have to mean an artist can't have sex appeal. It certainly didn't hurt Elvis Presley, Prince or Bruce Springsteen...I could go on and on. Honestly, I doubt that the ramblings of a few lovestruck fans will hurt the chances of Tyler's music being taken seriously. Handsome or not, the music stands on its own. That's my two cents.

Tysbabe: Tyler as a Chip & Dale...mmm....must....go...take...cold... shower....

---

scuba77: Tylerlover, I admire your moxy and I agree with everything you said. Tyler should be respected for his talent not his looks. ANBS is not a beauty pageant it's a talent show. Tyler has so many fans because of his talent and his mass appeal to people of all ages. To me, his looks are irrelevant. I am in love with his voice.

Sharla chuckled. She was in love with Tyler's looks and his voice. So, in what category did that put her? Luckily, she didn't care enough about the matter to label herself. When it came to Tyler, Sharla simply loved who he was. Or at least, what she'd seen and heard of who he was. She had a hunch that upon meeting him, her perception would not be dispelled. It seemed with Tyler, what you saw was pretty much what you got, and that was good.

Sharla didn't want anything less than all that Tyler was.

Chapter 7: Homecoming

The week Sharla was given her revelation was the last week *America's Next Big Star* was aired live until after the New Year.

In a season first, the show had given each of the remaining contestants two weeks off to go home for Christmas break. The change was due largely in part to a public outcry that started when a few ousted ANBS alumni from the first two seasons complained to the press that the show's break-neck schedule hadn't afforded them any time with their families during the holidays.

Sharla read in one Tyler forum that the producers were not happy about having to sacrifice the ratings momentum the show had built up so far this season, but had reluctantly given in for fear the public would boycott the show altogether. It was decided ANBS would run Season 3 highlights for the two weeks the contestants were on break.

Of course, Sharla quickly learned that with ANBS, there was no such thing as a real break. When everyone came back live in early January, it was learned each finalist had been given songs to work on and perfect during their time off. The cameras also had not stopped documenting their movements.

Although she was happy the contestants were given small reprieves, the break from the show personally hadn't done anything but make Sharla long for Tyler. The two weeks she wasn't able to see him perform were the same two weeks in which she went through a lovesick stupor. Not even spending Christmas with her parents and brother and his family took her mind away from him for long. But, as promised, ANBS came back live the first full week into the New Year and over the next three weeks of elimination, Sharla fervently prayed Tyler would not get voted off the show.

So far, God had been listening. Now it was down to Tyler, Maya and Eddie.

The night of the results for the Final Three, Sharla was at home in bed with a slight fever and a sore throat. She'd called in sick from work but it was more than simply having a small head cold. Sharla was sick for another reason.

Tonight, Tyler could face elimination.

The previous night's competition had been tough. Both Maya and Eddie had given some great performances, but Sharla was pretty sure no matter how good those two were, Tyler would be in the finale.

Still….it didn't pay to become cocky.

Her head feeling as if it might explode at any moment, Sharla put on some Van Morrison, fixed herself a cup of hot tea with lemon and honey, fell asleep and slept through the entire show. When she awoke, it was 9:30. Sharla jumped out of bed as if she'd been stung and ran into the living-room.

"Please God, please tell me I set the VCR," she mumbled frantically as she turned on the TV.

Turns out she was in luck. There was a tape in the VCR. Sharla breathed a deep sigh of relief and pushed "rewind."

While she waited for the tape to cue, Sharla noticed there were several messages on her answering machine. She must have really been exhausted not to have heard her phone ring. It was probably Lindsey and another friend, Roxanne, calling to discuss the show's results. She'd call them tomorrow after she'd had a chance to view the tape.

Sharla had read online that the final three contestants were allowed to travel back to their hometowns for a day and that footage from their trips would be aired during the show. As she fast-forwarded past the opening credits and a brief recap of the showdown the night before, Sharla found out the rumors were true.

The first person profiled was Eddie, who went back to his hometown of Bartlesville, Oklahoma, where he sang the National Anthem at a local football game. Next was Maya, who returned to her native New Jersey for a visit with family and friends. After their clips, both contestants sang a song they'd performed the night before.

Tyler had been saved for last.

A knot formed in Sharla's stomach as she watched Russell banter briefly with Tyler about his visit back home, which Tyler said included "plenty of biscuits and barbecue."

Russell chuckled. "Well, let's take a look at what happened when Tyler went home to Atlanta."

The segment began with Tyler getting into a limousine as Ray Charles crooned "Georgia On My Mind" in the background. Sharla smiled to herself.

Of course, what else would they play? She thought.

While Ray sang, Tyler talked to the camera, explaining that he was on his way to a television studio to be interviewed by the local network affiliate. There was a short clip of the studio interview in which Tyler said he appreciated all the fans' support. Sharla felt like melting into the sofa as she watched him speak. She sighed deeply and thought briefly about what a lovely profile he had.

After an edited montage of Tyler doing a mock sports report and clowning with the news desk anchors, he was back in the limo on his way to a radio station, where he was greeted outside by a large group of enthusiast fans, some of whom had been there since 2:30 in the morning. Many of them were waving banners and had come armed with signs that read "Tyler is Our Georgia Peach."

One of the fans had what looked like a ferret. The ferret was wearing a tiny Soul Squad shirt. Tyler was shown holding the animal and petting it affectionately. Watching him hold the ferret made Sharla long to trade places with it. Her heart skipped and her skin tingled as she watched Tyler put his arm around a fan and muss a child's hair. She didn't think it possible, but she was falling more and more in love with Tyler just watching him. She marveled at his gentleness and warmth. When he smiled, it made her weak. Clad in a cream-colored button down shirt, blue jeans and a navy blazer, Tyler looked handsome and relaxed. Sharla couldn't take her eyes off of him.

As Ray still sweetly called "Georgia," Tyler's limo was seen speeding down the fairway flanked from the front and behind by a police escort. With all the security, Sharla wondered if Tyler didn't have the President in the car with him. The camera panned to a banner baring Tyler's likeness. It read: "ATLANTA...WHERE AMERICA'S NEXT BIG STARS COME FROM."

At the foot of the banner stood the mayor of Georgia, who, amid thunderous cheers and applause, presented Tyler with a key to the city. As the mayor placed the key around Tyler's neck, Sharla felt an overwhelming desire to give Tyler her own kind of key: the key to her heart. She wanted to put it on a ribbon and place it around his neck. Tyler, for his part, seemed both awed and thrilled at the huge reception he'd drawn. As he waved to the crowd and blew kisses, Sharla wished she could have been there to catch a few of them.

Next, Tyler was shown riding through the streets of downtown Atlanta sitting on the backseat of a open-top convertible, waving to the vast crowds as a parade in his honor followed closely behind with trumpets sounding and brass cymbals clanging. His salt and pepper bangs hung loosely on his forehead the way he seemed to like them, free of the hair gel the ANBS stylists had lately grown so fond of using on him. It was a silly idea, but Sharla thought Tyler looked as if he'd been born to ride in the back of a convertible with ticker tape falling all around him.

Observing him glide with charismatic ease from television studio to radio station to the streets of Atlanta, Sharla was, as always, struck by Tyler's graciousness. He had a humble way in which he responded to all of the well-meaning chaos that encircled him. Sharla loved how no matter what was going on around him, Tyler would break from narrating to the camera to thank a fan or a group of bystanders on the street. He'd taken so naturally to all that was going on yet he seemed to take none of it for granted. His demeanor was so easy-going and warm. Watching Tyler lead, Sharla felt she could follow him anywhere.

Just at that moment, Tyler made a 'follow me' gesture and got back in the limo. The next scene showed him being met by the governor of Atlanta and the governor's wife, who blushed and giggled like a schoolgirl when Tyler politely shook her hand. After a brief speech, the governor declared the day Tyler Nicks Day. In appreciation, Tyler signed autographs and presented both the governor and his wife with bright-colored Soul Squad bandannas. Then the camera cut to Tyler back in the limo, informing the good folks of America that he was now headed to the town of his birth, Taylorsville, for a performance at the local shopping mall. Judging from the crowd that met Tyler there, it seemed as if the whole of Atlanta had followed him.

Tyler remarked that Taylorsville was a small town with a population of about 300 residents. But the army of fans who showed up to greet Tyler was as far as the eye (or the camera) could see. There had to be at least nine or ten thousand people there, Sharla guessed, and that was a conservative estimate.

Sharla was dumbfounded. She knew Tyler was popular, but if those crowds were any indication of his appeal, Sharla had a gut feeling Tyler was destined to become a huge star. Throngs of people of all ages, from small babies to 80-year-old grandmothers, were packed onto every level of the three-story mall cheering and screaming hysterically. Sharla couldn't remember the last time any public figure, a musician no less, had this kind of effect on people. The reaction to him was unbelievable. There hadn't been anything like it to her recollection since the Beatles, or perhaps, in more recent years, Michael Jackson.

Thousands upon thousands of voices sent up a collective shout as Tyler, accompanied by a small entourage that included the mayor of Taylorsville, made his way down the mall's escalator to a makeshift stage where Tyler was set to play with his band.

Sharla was enthralled. She was so happy to see Tyler back in his natural element as a live performer, playing guitar, singing and gleefully boogying about the place. Able to take a breather from what was, at its basest level, the world's biggest karaoke competition.

The scene made Sharla want to leap off the couch and dance around the room. There was no doubt about it now—with or without *America's Next Big Star,* Tyler was going to have a very promising future.

Then, as quickly as it had begun, the segment was over. It had only lasted about three-and-a-half minutes at the most, but Sharla planned to keep it forever.

As the big ANBS screen went black, the stage lights revealed Tyler standing next to Russell. Just as with Eddie and Maya, Russell asked Tyler to sing a song from the previous night's competition. Tyler chose to sing a slower number, "Your Song" by Elton John. Sharla was ecstatic. She loved "Your Song" and was pleased Tyler had chosen it. Now he was singing it again and with each swelling note, Sharla couldn't help feeling he was singing it just for her. In fact, she thought he sounded even better than the night before.

Then Tyler did something that nearly made Sharla cry. Before he was even at the song's chorus, Tyler gestured for Eddie and Maya to come center stage with him, which they did, and the three of them sang the chorus all huddled around Tyler's microphone. Gosh, but that man was just so sweet! Even with his neck possibly on tonight's chopping block, he was still nothing less than gracious. Sharla shook her head in amazement. She loved it when he did beautiful things like that.

When the song was done, the audience erupted into ear-shattering applause and Sharla somehow knew Tyler was going to be in the Final Two.

She relaxed a little (but only a little) and took in small, stilted breaths as Russell prepared to announce who would be moving on to next week's finale. The urge to fast-forward past all of the suspense was strong, but Sharla fought it, placing the VCR's remote control under a couch pillow so she wouldn't be tempted to use it. She had come this far with Tyler and thoroughly intended to see him through every nail-biting moment, no matter how difficult.

"The voting results last night were extremely close," Russell told the audience. "In fact, never in the history of *America's Next Big Star* have we had such a close race."

He turned to the contestants, who were all nervously holding hands.

"Maya, Eddie, Tyler, you've all done a fantastic job. But one of you is going home."

He then turned to the big screen. "Let's see who it is."

All eyes went to the screen. Slowly, a name materialized in large black letters:

EDDIE MELLENGER

There was an audible gasp from the audience, then the camera cut to reactions from Maya and Tyler's families before showing Eddie's father and sister, both of whom looked disappointed but composed. Both Maya and Tyler hugged Eddie as Eddie walked over to where Russell stood.

Russell gestured toward Maya and Tyler. "America, your Final Two."

Although she was sad to see Eddie go, Sharla felt a wave of excitement wash over her and let out an involuntary yelp. Tyler had made it! She'd known he would.

Eddie was singing his goodbye tune as the credits rolled and Sharla finally fished the remote out from under the pillows to turn off the tape. She wanted to rewind back to Tyler's homecoming segment. Those crowds back in Atlanta had helped get Tyler into the finale. Now it was time to pray he would become *America's Next Big Star.*

After she'd watched Tyler's homecoming a few more times, Sharla was still feeling a little drowsy, possibly from the medication she was on, so she decided to crawl back under the covers. As she drifted back to sleep, she sent up a prayer of thanks to God for letting Tyler make it into the Final Two.

Sharla's last coherent thought was a fleeting awareness that her throat no longer bothered her. She smiled and thought warmly of Tyler.

He always had a way of making her feel better.

Chapter 8: Forum.com

T he following week was chaos for ANBS fans.

The show's web board stayed busy with talk about the finale and the Final Two. In just about every Tyler forum, the Soul Squad was on hyper- alert.

It was crunch time. The finale was only a day away, just in time for February Sweeps. But tonight, Tyler and Maya would be battling it out one last time for America's votes.

As had become her daily ritual, Sharla logged on to tylerfanzine.com to see what the buzz was on the night's showdown. Under "New Posts," she saw a topic titled **Maya Fans Threaten Tyler**. She clicked on it. The starting message was from somebody called "topsyturvytexan" who wrote:

Hey, everyone,

I don't mean to scare you but I found this message posted on the ANBS boards. It was posted by an obvious Maya fan. I think it has since been deleted but I thought you all should look at it. Not everyone loves Tyler and we have GOT to continue to make sure he wins this thing. Let's make him America's Next Big Star, ya'll. WOOOO!!! GO SOUL SQUAD!!!!

FROM ANBS MESSAGE BOARD

A warning to all the soul squatters out there: Tyler Nicks is going down! Tonight's the night we send that grey-haired Confederate packing. Maya Fox is America's Next Big Star, everyone knows that. Stop deluding yourselves. WE WILL OUTVOTE YOU. Funk is dead. Soul is dead. Techno RULES! Long live the music of Maya! Peace.

Sharla scrolled down to read some of the replies:

Tonight's the night we send that grey-haired Confederate packing.

Soulgirl: "Confederate???" OMG, are they serious?! Does whoever wrote this know the Civil War is over?

---

nathanmod: Guess they didn't get the memo.

---

db73: Maya has a lot of fans on the East Coast. I guess the 'yanks' are trying to start an ANBS civil war with our southern boy. I'm with Ghandi. I prefer non-violence. But if it's a fight those people want, it's a fight they'll get.

Tyfan4life: Amen! Bring it on! Tyler's gonna open a can of whoop-butt on that girl tonight. Those Maya freaks and Clive are going to eat their words. Soul Squad, we gotta burn up the phone lines now fa sho!!

Tyler Nicks is going down!

HelloKitty: What? Oh NO they didn't! Nobody messes with my Tyler! They better not make me have to come through this computer. I will it tear it UP! You better believe!

Margaret: Folks, this so-called threat was posted by idiotic, misguided people. They are lashing out in pathetic desperation because they know the country loves Tyler and he's got Maya fans running scared. Don't give this a second thought. Just stay focused and vote, vote, vote!

---

nathanmod: Kitty, how could someone with such a cute screen name be so angry? Please, vent your wrath by voting up a storm tonight. You don't want to be watching the finale from a jail cell.

Ladysoul: It's a good thing I'm a Christian. Otherwise, I'd be tempted to go over to that ANBS site and cuss those hateful people out. God Bless you, Tyler! Love in Philly, Liz.

tylerswoman: I wouldn't be surprised if this message was posted by the ANBS producers.

I_wud_die_4_Tyler: No, no, Tyler CANNOT crash and burn! I'm going to vote tonight until my fingers bleed. I LOVE YOU, Ty! ~Connie

SallyG: Question-Who's Ghandi? Is he on the show?

Voodoopriestess64: I've been praying and chanting all afternoon and I am very powerful, people. So don't be surprised if Maya comes down with a severe case of laryngitis. Or food poisoning. I haven't decided which.

I'm going to vote tonight until my fingers bleed.

Funkadelic: Well, I'm gonna dial till my fingers fall OFF and you can take that to the bank!

nathanmod: Take what to the bank, man? Your fingers???? Dude, that's sick. :P

Rochelle: Voodoo, thanks for your obvious enthusiasm. I'm sure Tyler would appreciate it. But I believe he wants to win this competition on his own merits, not through witchcraft.

Margaret: I agree, Rochelle. I don't think Tyler would want to see anyone hurt so he can win. Sally, if you want to know who Ghandi is, rent the movie with Ben Kingsley, hon. It's very informative. *HuGs!*

I believe he wants to win this competition on his own merits, not through witchcraft.

groover: Not that I'm trying to start trouble, but why not fight fire with fire? Everyone knows Maya's family has hired a well-known psychic to do her astrological chart every day and advise her on what songs to sing. And there's talk that her aunt has personally paid $75,000 to have a Brazilian witch doctor flown in to burn incense and chant incantations over Maya while she stands waist deep in a tub of Peruvian pig's blood before the final show. If she can have all of that, why can't Tyler use voodoo? Just my two cents.

Ladysoul: No offense, topsy and voodoo, you're entitled to your beliefs. But if GOD has ordained Tyler to win America's Next Big Star, then he *will* win, no matter how many witch doctors, psychics or Clives come out of the woodwork to try and stop him. That's *my* two cents.

---

cutiepie_32: Amen and AMEN, Lady! Father, I thank you for Tyler and his tremendous talent. Lord, we his fans believe you have called him to be America's Next Big Star. We pray that you will keep him refreshed, calm and grounded as he walks out on that stage tonight, and that NOTHING, be it voodoo spells or howling at the moon, will deter him from giving each performance his all. In the mighty name of Jesus, we pray. Amen.

Sharla quit reading and put her right hand up to her forehead.

The posts had given her a headache. Still, she had to chuckle in spite of herself. Voodoo spells, witch doctors, Peruvian pigs blood???

"What is wrong with people?" She asked herself aloud. "It's just a competition for goodness' sake!"

But it was an important competition. Just about anyone who'd become hooked on ANBS because of Tyler would never admit it (they knew they'd be locked up if they did) but the fate of the country, no, the entire planet, now rested upon the performances of Tyler Nicks and Maya Fox, two people who up until five months ago, no one had heard of. Now they were pitted against each other in the mother of all musical duels. Who would win? The gray-haired Soulman with the honey-smooth voice or the Goth chick with the long, black fingernails and piercing green eyes?

Sharla opened the medicine cabinet in the bathroom and popped the top off a bottle of Excedrin. She dropped two aspirin into her palm, popped them into her mouth and downed them with some water.

Tyler had to win, she thought. In the name of all that was decent and holy, he had to win. How could America live with itself if he didn't?

"God, please be in this," Sharla muttered, and went back to her computer to stare at the latest photo of Tyler she'd saved to her desktop. Tyler stared back at her with his good-natured smile and dark baby brown eyes.

Sharla wondered briefly if he had any idea how beautiful he was.

He'll win, she thought. *I know he will.*

"Good luck, Tyler," Sharla said to her desktop and raised a hand to briefly rest it on the monitor near Tyler's cheek.

"I'll be praying for you."

Chapter 9: The Finale

The day of the finale, Sharla almost had a car accident.

She was doing 50 in a 35- mile-per-hour zone, trying to rush home from work to prepare for the ANBS finale party—thinking of a million things at once (all of them having to do with Tyler)—when she looked up just in time to realize she was about to run head-on into the back of a pickup truck stopped at a red light.

Sharla yelped and jammed her foot on the brake. The tires of her Honda Accord squealed and the car weaved slightly out of control as she bared her hands down on the steering wheel, bracing herself for impact. The Honda came to a screeching halt, its front bumper stopping only inches from the tailgate of the pickup truck.

With her heart pounding almost out of her chest and her breath coming out through her teeth in short, syncopated pants, Sharla closed her eyes and tried to calm herself. Thank God no one had been behind her. She could smell burning rubber.

At least her underwear still felt dry, that was good.

The light turned green. Sharla gingerly put her foot on the accelerator. No more speeding. She wanted to be sure she got to see the finale in one piece.

When she got home, she heard a message from Lindsey reminding her not to forget the six-layer dip.

Sharla had three close girlfriends: a co-worker, Roxanne Solis, who worked in the *Agape Gazette* accounting department and was an ANBS fanatic; Diane Simms, whom Sharla had known in school but recently reconnected with through church; and Lindsey, who was the only one in the group who lived in an actual house. It was decided a finale party would be thrown at Lin's since she had more space.

Sharla quickly changed into what had become her ANBS attire—a pair of worn, comfortable blue jeans and a faded Led Zepplin T-shirt— and grabbed the chilled container of six-layer dip she'd made the night before from her refrigerator.

Before she left, she checked a couple of the Tyler forums to see if there had been any updates (a rumor was circulating Tyler was to sing a duet with B.B. King during the finale), but found nothing new. After offering up her 27th quick prayer of the day for Tyler's success tonight under her breath, Sharla checked her VCR one last time to make sure it was set to record the show, and headed for the door.

Roxanne and Diane were already at Lindsey's when she arrived. Everyone was busy milling around, getting things ready for the party. Of course, Lindsey and Sharla were Tyler fans, both pulling for him to win. But Roxanne and Diane's loyalties were divided.

While Roxanne really liked Tyler and thought he had a good voice, she felt Maya possessed a stronger, more marketable personality and would come out the victor. Diane was a Maya fan all the way. Somehow, everyone had agreed to disagree. But it sometimes quietly grated on Sharla how Diane would make snide remarks about Tyler's dancing. In retaliation, Sharla teased Diane that she and Clive would make a great couple. Lindsey had promised Sharla she would not divulge the vision God had given her, and Sharla trusted that she hadn't. But all the girls knew Sharla had a crush on Tyler—it had become obvious over the course of the season—and Sharla felt Diane sometimes made fun of him just to irritate her.

"Alright, the dip is here!" Lindsey exclaimed as Sharla entered the kitchen. "The party can bee-gin!"

"Hey, is that the only reason you invited me?" Sharla frowned good-naturedly, putting her hand on her hip.

"No, that's not the only reason!" Lindsey said, giving Sharla a hug. "We also like your sweet potato pie."

"Ha-ha," Sharla said, setting the dip on the kitchen table. As she did so, her eyes spotted what looked to be a bottle of champagne sitting in an ice chest.

Roxanne noticed Sharla eyeing the bottle. "That is to be opened upon the announcement of the winner," she said.

Sharla picked up the bottle. "You brought this?" she asked, turning to Roxanne.

"Yeah, I picked it up at the store on my way over here."

"It's non-alcoholic," Lindsey said.

Sharla's eyes widened. "Non-alcoholic champagne?" She'd never heard of that before.

"Yeah, it's the latest thing. They've got non-alcoholic beer now too," Roxanne reported.

"Wow, go figure," Sharla shrugged. "What will they think of next?"

"Maybe non-addictive crack," Diane quipped, getting out some napkins.

As they set up, the girls talked about the finale and the guest celebrities, rumored and confirmed, scheduled to make appearances. Since its debut two years ago, *America's Next Big Star* had become the new springboard from which already established pop stars, simply by appearing on the show, could rejuvenate their careers and introduce themselves to a whole new generation of music lovers. Roxanne, the resident ANBS expert, remarked that tonight's finale was to be the most star-studded one to date, though she'd found out from a supposed "insider" on the ANBS boards that B.B. King, much to Sharla's chagrin, would not be performing.

Inevitably, the talk turned to voting. Lindsey admitted she'd voted for Tyler a few times last night, and everyone knew who Sharla and Diane had pegged to win. But Roxanne, who liked both Tyler and Maya, refused to say to whom she'd given her vote.

"There are three things I do not discuss in mixed company," she replied half-seriously. "Religion, politics, and who I voted for on America's Next Big Star."

"Oh, come on, Roxanne, that's ridiculous," Diane coaxed. "You're among friends. It's just a TV show."

"I know, but to be honest," Roxanne slowly confessed. "I'm kind of superstitious. I feel like if I tell who I voted for, they won't win."

"Roxy, it's a vote not a wish," Lindsey smiled, heading for the living room.

Roxanne crossed her arms over her chest and shook her head from side to side adamantly. "I don't care, it's just how I am. It's like a tradition for me. I'm not telling and that's all there is to it."

There was a finality to her voice that told the others there was no use trying to press the subject. In the living room, Lindsey was announcing it was almost show time.

"We got about....two minutes," she said, looking at her watch.

Sharla felt a warm flush of excitement. She was sure Tyler would win, she'd been feeling it in her spirit for months. His performances the night before had been beyond stellar. She'd voted for him at least 100 times. Between divine favor and the Soul Squad, how could he lose?

By the time each of the women got something to drink and took their seats in front of the set, it was on, the moment the country had been anticipating for five long months.

The camera panned in on an empty stage. Slowly, lights came up and music swelled as Maya's voice was heard just offstage. A few seconds later, she was walking onstage with microphone in hand, wearing a smart, black pantsuit. Her makeup was tasteful and conservative, devoid of the gobs of black eyeliner that had become synonymous with her Goth image. Only her jet black hair, which was done up in a spiky style with pinkish glitter shining in it and a tiny silver stud in her nose, showed that despite her moderate new garb, Maya was still a Punk at heart.

Sharla and the others were stunned. Who knew that underneath all that black gunk was such a pretty girl?

Diane jumped up from the couch. "What's she done to herself?!" she yelled at the television.

"Looks like she washed her face," Sharla smirked; she couldn't resist.

"Oh, this is what the Mayans were all riled up about!" Roxanne gasped, pointing at the TV. "I read on the boards Maya was gonna do something her fans felt was a cop out, but I didn't expect this."

"You're darn right it's a cop out," Diane huffed, running a hand through her hair in exasperation. "She looks like…like Britney Spears broke into a glitter factory!"

"No," Sharla said. "Isn't Britney blonde this week?"

"She looks beautiful," Lindsey interjected. "She should have 'copped out' a long time ago."

"She still has that dark and broody thing going," Sharla added. "Just with a little more class."

"I bet her aunt talked her into doing this," Roxanne said, speaking in a confident tone that made it sound as if she knew Maya and her aunt personally. "Maya's aunt is like her manager," Roxanne explained. "There's been a lot of talk on the boards that the producers secretly want Maya to win, so her family's been grooming her and trying to get her to change her image so she'd get more mainstream votes."

Sharla chuckled. She hadn't heard that one. Come to think of it, Maya's performances last night had seemed a little less edgy and her eyeliner a tad less heavy. Was Tyler that much of a threat?

Then, almost as a fearful afterthought, Sharla said aloud: "But it's not up to the producers, right?"

Roxanne shrugged. "Depends on who you talk to."

Sharla frowned. If Tyler didn't win, she'd have her answer. Nothing personal against Maya, but she hoped her aunt's strategy was too little too late.

On television, Maya was belting out the opening lyrics to "It's My Turn" by Diana Ross as the audience cheered and applauded. Then, from nowhere it seemed, came Tyler, looking stunning in a tailored, black suit and matching black dress shirt. As he crossed the stage to Maya, he sang:

> *Because it's my turn*
> *With no apologies.*
> *I've given up the truth*
> *To those I've tried to please*
> *But now it's my turn…*

Sharla was holding a glass of iced tea. When Tyler came out, she almost dropped it.

"Holy moly!" Lindsey leaned forward. "Is that Tyler?! He is lookin' GOOD!"

Diane rolled her eyes and muttered "Give me a break" under her breath.

Roxanne was sitting next to Sharla and gave her a playful elbow in the side. "There's your boyfriend, Sharla," she teased. "He cleans up pretty good, don't he?"

Sharla swallowed. She could barely speak.

The thunk was happening.

Oh, God, she thought. *I'm going to pass out!*

The room began to spin. Sharla could hardly catch her breath. She grabbed on to the back of the sofa she was seated on and tried to get her bearings, but the back of the sofa looked blurry and off-kilter. She put a hand to her chest, then to her forehead. It was slightly warm.

"Sharla, are you blushing?" Diane leaned over to see her better. "You look kinda feverish. Ya'll, doesn't she look feverish?"

Sharla jerked away reflexively. "I-I'm fine," she stammered. "I'm just….
it's kind of warm in here…"

Ooh, that suit!

"Hey," Diane announced. "Somebody call the fire department 'cuz it
looks like Tyler's got Sharla hot under the collar!"

"No….I'm fine," Sharla lied. When she looked at Diane, she could swear
there were two of her.

"Yeah, I can see that," both Dianes smiled.

"Diane, leave the poor girl alone," Roxanne said. To Sharla's ears, it
sounded like she was speaking from inside a tunnel. "She's just happy to see
her man."

"I'm just…surprised at how good he looks," Sharla replied weakly.

Dear Lord, he's gorgeous!

"He has come a long way since the auditions," Lindsey agreed. "Sharla, I
think you may have to share Tyler with me."

Never! Sharla thought, but was too felled to speak.

"I thought you only liked blonde-haired guys," Diane frowned.

"Silver hair, blonde hair, same thing almost," Lindsey waved off.

"Guys, I can't hear what they're singing!" Roxanne complained.

Once Sharla's double vision cleared up a few moments later, she thought
she might be able to continue watching the finale without fainting. Once she
regained cognitive speech a few minutes after that, she was positive she could
settle into the show and just how good Tyler looked in it.

Later, Sharla found out she was not alone in her reaction to Tyler's
entrance. Many people—all of them women— commented on it the next
day in the online forums. Pictures of him in his black suit surfaced all over
the Internet. There was even a headline story about a woman in Wisconsin
who suffered third degree burns to her face and hands while watching the
show. She apparently came out of her kitchen holding a hot TV dinner and,
awed by how handsome Tyler looked during his entrance, tripped over her

own two feet and fell headfirst into the TV dinner. The woman filed a multi-million dollar lawsuit against Swanson foods, makers of the hot TV dinner, as well as the creators of *America's Next Big Star* for not putting up an advance disclaimer warning people there would be "hot guys" on the show. Sharla later heard a rumor Tyler found out about the incident and sent the woman get-well wishes and a Soul Squad T-shirt. Her lawsuit was eventually dismissed.

The finale continued without incident as the typical end-of-season entertainment program. Performers voted out earlier in the season were brought back for another chance to go down memory lane, clips from past performances, a video montage of some of the auditions.

Sharla watched it all with the others, commenting on the clothes (she'd counted eight wardrobe changes for Tyler alone) and the celebrity-filled crowd, but in the back of her mind, she just wasn't that interested in seeing the ANBS clan sing group songs or duet with other celebs. She simply wanted to know one thing: had Tyler won? For almost two hours, she sat in anticipation, her heart throwing in a few extra beats every time Tyler appeared.

After what seemed like an eternity, the moment finally came. One last commercial break and then there were three people standing on the ANBS stage: Russell, Maya and Tyler.

Maya and Tyler had again changed outfits. Maya was now wearing a sleek, powder blue off-the-shoulder evening dress with matching high heels, while Tyler sported a dazzling white suit and white dress shirt. A tiny red carnation was stylishly pinned on his right lapel.

Sharla thought he looked like an angel.

"Ladies and gentlemen," Russell announced. "The moment you've been waiting for has arrived."

He held up a small gray envelope. "America, last night you voted and boy, did you vote. More than 65 million of you jammed the phone lines to crown either Maya Fox…" Russell gestured toward Maya. "…or Tyler Nicks…." He nodded in Tyler's direction. "…America's Next Big Star. Maya, Tyler, are you ready to hear the results?"

Both Maya and Tyler nodded and instinctively drew closer together. The two of them smiled nervously at each other and locked arms.

The audience fell quiet as Russell opened the envelope. "And America's Next Big Star is…."

Russell paused for what seemed an eternity. Maya and Tyler both watched him with muted looks of anticipation. Sharla, Lindsey, Roxanne and Diane all held a collective breath. Sharla placed her hands anxiously over her mouth, her eyes already brimming with tears.

"…..TYLER NICKS!!!!"

Before Russell had gotten out the second syllable of Tyler's first name, Sharla was on her feet screaming, laughing and crying, all at the same time. Lindsey and Roxanne also let out smaller victorious cheers. Diane simply leaned back on the couch, shaking her head.

Tyler, for his part, was—at least outwardly—extraordinarily calm. Upon hearing his name, he broke into a huge smile and immediately hugged Maya. She held him a long time and eventually whispered something in his ear before he finally let go of her and faced the audience.

Meanwhile, the camera had cut to some place in Atlanta where hoards of Tyler fans holding signs and banners were going wild with excitement over the news. Back in the auditorium, the audience also was on its feet applauding and cheering. The camera panned in for a reaction from Tyler's family, all of whom were ecstatic.

"Tyler, do you have anything to say?" Russell asked, handing Tyler his microphone.

Tyler took it and yelled out two words: SOOOUL SQUAAAAD!!!!!! SOOOUL SQUAAAAD!!!!!"

Sharla stopped screaming and simply started crying. The audience erupted into even more cheers as Tyler walked to the center of the stage to sing what would be his first single, "Did I Do Alright."

As Tyler sang his song and basked in his new title of *America's Next Big Star*, Sharla stood in the middle of her best friend's living room, staring at the television, her emotions spent, her girlfriends forgotten. The millions of viewers at home and the people in the television auditorium all disappeared and it became just Sharla and Tyler for the moment.

I knew it, Tyler, I knew you'd win, Sharla mentally chanted over and over again as she watched the man she'd come greatly to admire, and to love. Never had she felt personally so proud of anyone. Watching Tyler come out from under to capture the title of *America's Next Big Star*, Sharla couldn't have felt more joy than had it been herself that had done it. In a way, it was. Tyler was up there representing people like her. The underdogs who had hidden dreams they'd perhaps given up on and put away. Now, simply by standing on that stage and singing with his all, Tyler Nicks had become living proof the Everyman's dream could be made a reality. Perhaps the music industry wasn't dead after all. Perhaps her dreams weren't dead after all.

On television, a choir was flanking both sides of the stage, ready to join Tyler for the song's chorus:

> *I just want to be the one*
> *When the race is finally won*
> *To cross the finish line*
> *With every promise kept in sight*
> *But before I go down that road*
> *There's something that I need to know*
> *Did I do alright!*

Sharla was beaming. Tyler had done more than alright. He had given her hope. She only wished she could be there in person to share in his victory.

A loud popping noise brought Sharla back into an awareness of her surroundings. She turned around to see everyone in the kitchen. The girls were holding out plastic cups as Lindsey poured out non-alcoholic champagne for a toast. Even Diane had put aside her anti-Tyler attitude and was laughing and joining in the celebration.

Sharla looked back at the television in time to see the credits roll. Everyone had come onstage now to hug Tyler and congratulate him as ticker tape fell around them.

Sharla had to hand it to Tyler. He was acting so poised through it all. How had he gotten through that song without passing out? Without *freaking* out? Sharla surmised he was probably in shock. Surely, it hadn't all quite sunken in yet. She wanted so very much to be there for him when it finally did. What a pity that wasn't possible.

Sharla turned her head back towards the kitchen in time to catch Roxanne looking at her. Embarrassed, Sharla began swiping at her tears with the back of her hand. Roxanne simply smiled, walked over to Sharla, handed her a plastic cup of champagne and whispered, "I voted for Tyler."

Sharla looked at Roxanne, surprised. Roxanne put a finger to her lips in a hush gesture and winked.

The two women shared a smile and went to join their friends.

Chapter 10: I've Just Gotta Get a Message to You

A fter the finale and consequently, *America's Next Big Star* ended, Sharla started going through withdrawal.

She missedseeing Tyler.

For almost six months, two nights a week, he'd come into her living room, making her feel for those few brief moments that he was with her, even if it wasn't in the flesh.

Sharla still saw him periodically on television via the numerous talk shows and entertainment news programs he'd been appearing on following his win, but it wasn't the same. The consistency she'd grown used to was gone.

Her Wednesday and Thursday nights were now wide open and she was restless. In the meantime, Tyler's career was off to a great start. His first single, "Did I Do Alright," had reached No. 1 on the Billboard Top 100 and gone gold within days of its release. It's B-side, a cover of "How Sweet it Is to Be Loved by You," sung more in the style of James Taylor but with Tyler's own definitive vocal flavor, was also doing well on the charts where it had settled at No. 17.

Entertainment Daily was reporting that according to the Nielsen television ratings system, the Season Three finale of *America's Next Big Star*, which was watched by about 40 million people, was ranked as the highest-rated show in its time slot, not to mention it was also the most widely-viewed show in ANBS history. And the more than 65 million votes that Tyler, who never once during the show was in the Bottom Three, received on finale night was more votes than the President had gotten during the last election.

The Soul Squad had done their job. But now that Tyler had achieved his dream of superstardom, there didn't seem to Sharla to be anything more left to do for him. She felt almost like a proud mama bird who'd done all she could for her baby chick, and now that he'd left the nest and was flying on his own, she'd lost her sense of purpose.

Ever-appreciative of his fans and sensing their collective anxiety, Tyler had assured them in interviews and through personal online messages that ANBS was only the beginning. There would be plenty more on the horizon for him and the Soul Squad once he finished the ANBS All-Stars tour and set to work on his first major album with the new label he was now signed to, SATURN Records.

Sharla planned to sit tight and wait for the new album. She was extremely happy for Tyler and kept him in her prayers, but neither the vision she'd had regarding him nor the fact that he was no longer in front of her on a weekly basis cooled her feelings towards him. He still consumed her every thought. Seeing him on television all the time helped to dull some of the ache, but once the show was over, Sharla realized she was going to have to find another outlet for her emotions. She toyed with the idea of sending Tyler a heartfelt letter but then thought better of it. The man was wanted by thousands, no probably millions of women, and she was just one of many. How could she tell him how she felt without sounding like every other Nicks Chick on the Internet? So, to vent her frustration, Sharla did the only thing she knew how to do—she wrote.

Whenever she had a moment, she would take out a notebook and freewrite. Usually, it began with Tyler's name and simple word association. Other times, she reverted back to junior high and put her name and his inside a big heart, or she'd simply write his name over and over again until the sound of it ringing in her head stopped.

When that didn't prove to be enough, Sharla bought a journal, filling it with her deepest thoughts and emotions. In it, she wrote letters to Tyler which she never intended to send, for even if she had, she was sure Tyler would never see them. Surely his fan base had become too wide for him to bother with such trivial things as drippy fan letters. Besides, Sharla was certain that what she had to say would be too simple and cliché for Tyler to take any real notice even if he had the time.

That was when Sharla decided to vent her frustration by making up a short story. She decided it would be a spoof. A satire on the country's obsession with *America's Next Big Star* and its latest hopeful, Tyler Nicks. As with the journal, Sharla wrote the story purely for herself, no one else would ever see it. It was just an outlet, a way to get out the heartache of not being able to tell the only man she'd ever felt connected to how she felt about him.

Sharla decided to base the story loosely on what she was going through. She invented Dora Harris, a spinster-type who sees Trevor Reams, Tyler's alter-ego, a 28-year-old, prematurely gray blues singer from Tennessee, on a reality TV talent show and instantly falls in love with him. After she had her basic premise, the words seemed to flow from her keyboard. It was as if the muses would not let her up until she'd written her entire sad tale in a form that was palatable, at least to her. Writing out her story was beyond therapeutic. It enabled her to turn her tears into laughter, to poke fun at the situation and still possess some dignity. The more Sharla thought, the more she wrote.

About a month or so into the writing, Sharla realized she had more than a short story on her hands. She might have a novella.

Maybe I should publish this, she thought to herself. *Who knows? It might not be any good.*

But as Sharla read back what she wrote, she felt that it was good. Could be good, anyway. Certainly, it had its moments. As a test, she printed out the first few chapters and gave them to her girlfriends to read. All of them brought her favorable comments.

"I like it," Lindsey told her. "It's funny and it's sweet."

"What a cute idea!" Roxanne gushed. "Let me know when you finish. I'd like to read the rest of it."

Surprisingly, Diane, who would never be one of Tyler's biggest fans, offered the most sage advice.

"It's good," she said simply. "I think you should try having it published."

"Really?" Sharla asked.

Diane shrugged. "Sure. It's said that everyone has a book in them. This could be yours, Sharla. I mean, it's not *War and Peace* and it probably won't end world hunger, but it has a lot of feeling in it, a lot of soul. Trevor Reams is an interesting character. I imagine if Tyler read it, he'd like it."

That was all Sharla needed to hear. If Tyler liked it, that would mean everything, especially since her feelings for him refused to cease even as her story grew. Sharla found that no matter how much she wrote or how funny it was, she was still in love with Tyler. And no pretend Tyler could change that.

Nightly, she prayed for God to take the feelings from her. They were too much. It hurt too deeply. The man had too many fans. He was too big now. He'd never notice her. He wouldn't want *her*. There had to be a mix-up. But every time Sharla prayed, she got the same reassurance in her spirit– that it was true and that Tyler would want her.

That somehow, God was going to make it happen.

———————————————————————————————

In the meantime, Sharla's parents (namely her mother) had begun to grow concerned about their daughter. What had started as a harmless interest in some reality TV person had now, in their eyes, become a full-blown obsession. The mere fact that Sharla was writing a book on this man was proof she had gone off the deep end, her mother told her.

"It is not a book about him, it's a spoof partially *based* on him, Mom, there's a difference," Sharla explained one morning in April as she sat at the kitchen table of her parents' house while both of them perused her manuscript.

"I don't care what you call it," Ida Davis told her daughter. "Honey, you're obsessed. For months now, all I've heard from you is Taylor this and Taylor that—"

"It's *Tyler*, Mom," Sharla corrected.

Ida rolled her eyes. "Taylor, Tyler," she said. "Whatever his name is, he's got a hold on you and you have got to let go!"

"Well, maybe with this book, I can do that," Sharla reasoned.

Richard Davis, Sharla's father, had been thumbing through the manuscript as his wife and daughter debated. He now removed his reading glasses and gingerly put the thick stack of papers aside.

"What do you intend to do with this?" he asked Sharla, gesturing towards the manuscript.

Sharla sat primly with her hands in her lap, as if she were a little girl being interrogated. "I think I'm gonna shop it around, see if I can get it published."

Her father, a retired plant manager with Reynolds Metal Co., smiled. In his younger days, he'd done a little dabbling in writing himself, most of it poetry, none of it ever published. "You do know it's not easy to get a book published these days. Not if you intend to submit it to a publishing company."

"I know, Dad," Sharla said. "But I've prayed about it and I want to try."

Richard sighed and looked at his wife. "Alright. Just as long as you realize it won't be easy. But I'm proud of you, kid." He touched a corner of the manuscript. "Looks like you've got yourself a book."

Sharla beamed. If Dad approved of the book, that was a good sign. "Yeah, I can hardly believe it."

"Sharla," her mother asked. "Now that you've written this thing, do you think you can forget about Tyler and start to….to….you know, find yourself a real man?"

Sharla's smile quickly faded. She'd been silently wondering how long after she walked in the house it would be before her mother started in with her about settling down. She looked at her watch. It had taken exactly 15 minutes, a new record.

Sharla sighed inwardly and decided it would probably be rude not to take the bait. "What do you mean, Mom?"

Ida looked at her husband briefly then back at Sharla. "I mean this Tyler is not real! He's a fantasy, honey. You don't know him and he doesn't know you. It's time you got out and started dating again, don't you think?"

Sharla sighed. "Mom, we have talked about this and you know what I told you…"

"Right," Ida interrupted hotly. "That God told you you were going to marry this Tyler Hicks—"

"Nicks," Sharla corrected.

"Hicks, Nicks, whatever," Ida went on. "It doesn't make sense to me. Why would the Lord show you your husband but not give you any other instructions on how to get him? Personally, honey, I think you're using this so-called vision you had as an excuse not to get out and mingle."

Sharla felt a little stung. "No, Mom, it's not that. I just have faith. You say you believe in God. Where's your faith?"

For the moment, Ida didn't have a comeback.

"I guess God will let me know more in time. For right now, I'm just waiting."

"More like wasting," Ida muttered.

Sharla rolled her eyes. Every visit lately seemed to end with this tired conversation.

"Ida, let the girl alone," Richard said, getting up to pour himself another cup of coffee. "She'll start dating again when she's ready."

"And when is that?" Ida asked over her shoulder. Richard didn't respond but instead took a sip of his coffee and headed for the living room and the morning paper.

"Sharla, I just don't want you to let the best years of your life pass you by," her mother said. "You're such a sweet girl not to have a special man in your life. And let's be honest. You'll be 33 in October." She reached over and took her daughter's hand. "The clock is ticking."

Sharla hated it when her mother talked to her like this, as if Sharla had no idea she was getting older and that she didn't have a man in her life. Why did everything have to center around having a man? But Sharla didn't feel like arguing and she didn't think her mother would understand if she did.

"Mom, I'm just not ready," is all she could muster. "What happened with Paul was very…very hard. Not to mention humiliating."

"Yes, but Sharla," Ida said sympathetically. "How long do you intend to stick your head in the sand and lick your wounds? What happened with Paul was a long time ago."

"Two years isn't that long," Sharla protested.

"Okay, two years. Isn't two years enough? How much longer are you going to use what happened as an excuse not to move on with your life? He certainly moved on with his!"

Sharla crossed her arms in front of her chest. Mom could be so blunt sometimes. "Thanks for the reminder."

Ida softened her voice. "I didn't say that to rub it in, but Sharla, you've got to stop feeling sorry for yourself. You're not the only woman whose ever had her heart broken. You have to forgive and move on. Your father and I just want to see you happy with someone before we die." Then, as an afterthought: "And it would be nice too if you gave us some grandchildren before we died."

That did it; it was time to go.

"You already have a grandchild," Sharla said, getting up from the table. Derek, her younger brother who lived in Austin, was married with an 18-month-old son.

"Yes, but I'd like to see *you* with children," Ida countered.

"I have to go," Sharla said, grabbing her manuscript and kissing her mother on the cheek. "I need to mail off some copies of my book before I go to work."

"Good luck, kid," her father said as she planted a kiss on his forehead on the way out. "Let us know what happens."

"I will, Dad," Sharla said, walking to the door. Her mother was close on her heels.

"Sharla," she called as her daughter stepped onto the walkway outside. "You know what I say I say out of love."

Sharla nodded. "I know, Mom."

"Good," Ida leaned in the doorway. "Then leave that Tyler alone and get yourself somebody tangible."

Sharla shook her head in that stubborn way that was so much like her father. "Mom, I know it sounds crazy and it makes no sense but I know what I saw in my spirit, and I was given a confirmation."

"Well," Ida said half-heartedly, "I guess we'll just have to wait and see, then." Sharla could tell the fact that she'd gotten a confirmation meant nothing to her mother. Her parents were diehard Catholics who went to confession every Saturday whether they had anything to confess or not. They had very little understanding when it came to the kind of 'church' Sharla attended.

Sharla took her mother's hands in her own. "I have faith," she said firmly. "So, don't worry. God has someone for me."

With that, Sharla hugged her mother and turned around to leave.

As she watched her daughter walk to her car and get inside, Ida Davis couldn't help wondering if perhaps her next door neighbor, Agnes Gillespie, who didn't watch television and didn't even own a set, hadn't been right when she'd said that TV was nothing but pure evil, the seemingly innocent vehicle by which our children were being driven straight to hell?

Chapter 11: The Set-Up

———————————————————————————————————————

"**H**ave you been talking to my mother?"

Sharla posed the question to Lindsey as they browsed through the racks of a clothing store in the mall. Lindsey, in her not-so-subtle manner, had just suggested Sharla take a stab at going out with someone again.

"No," Lindsey frowned, admiring a pair of slacks. "Why?"

"Because that's been her anthem lately," Sharla said. "She's been on me constantly to start dating again and it's driving me nuts."

"Well," Lindsey started cautiously. "She may have a point. You haven't been out with anyone in a while."

"Yeah, and you know why," Sharla answered.

"Not all men are like Paul, you know," Lindsey chided.

"It's not just that," Sharla shrugged. "I'm waiting on God."

Lindsey put a hand up to her mouth and cleared her throat. "Yeah, what's happening with that, since you brought it up?"

Sharla put a pair of jeans up to her waist, trying to imagine how good they'd look on her if she were 15 pounds lighter. "Well, Tyler is on tour with the ANBS All-Stars right now, and when he's done he'll start recording his album."

"Yeah," Lindsey replied, "I heard about that. But what I meant was what's happening with you and him?"

Sharla put the jeans back on the hanger. "Umm, nothing right now. Like I said, he's on tour."

"Are you going to see the tour?"

"Nope. I think I'm gonna wait till he tours on his own."

"Have you tried to contact him?"

Sharla stopped sifting through clothes and looked at Lindsey. "You're full of questions today."

"I'm just trying to take an interest in your love life, that's all," Lindsey smiled.

"Well, there's no update, sorry. I did think about writing Tyler but I figured he probably wouldn't get it anyway, he's so busy. So, I've decided just to leave the situation to God." Then, so that Lindsey wouldn't have time to reply, she quickly added: "What about your love life? How'd your date with that guy you met on ChristianMatch.com go?"

"Please," Lindsey grimaced, putting a hand to her stomach. "I just ate."

"Hey, here's some news," Sharla chuckled. "I have so far collected five rejection letters from various publishing companies regarding *Chasing Trevor*.

"Chasing Trevor?" Lindsey looked confused.

"My book," Sharla explained. "It's called *Chasing Trevor*."

Recognition lit across Lindsey's face. "Oh, yeah! Well, don't give up, it's a good story."

"I'm not," Sharla assured her.

"Look, I know you probably don't want to hear this," Lindsey said, "But I really do think you should try going on a date with someone."

Sharla sighed in exasperation. Why couldn't everyone leave her alone about dating? She was content, really! Why did people automatically assume a single woman must be miserable and unfulfilled if she didn't have a man?

"You're right," Sharla said, crossing over to a set of sweaters. "I don't want to hear it."

"I don't mean just anyone," Lindsey said. "I mean a certain someone."

Sharla put down an attractive blue sweater and stared at her friend. "What certain someone?"

"Someone from church," Lindsey remarked slyly.

Sharla's eyes widened. "Oh, no! No way, Lin. I don't know what you did but you're gonna have to undo it!"

"I haven't done anything!" Lindsey said innocently.

"Then why have you got that look?"

"What look?"

"That look that says you did something?"

Lindsey opened her mouth but thought better of it. She paused and then said, "Before you shoot him down, let me just tell you a little about him—"

"You *have* been talking to my mother," Sharla muttered, reaching into her purse for her cell phone. She was going to call that lady and tell her to butt out!

"No, I haven't, I swear," Lindsey said. Sharla studied her face for a moment and decided she was telling the truth. Sharla put away the phone.

"I just think this is a nice guy, he seems interesting and I thought you two might hit it off."

"Lin, I know you're just trying to be a friend, but really," Sharla sighed. "I'm not interested."

"Well, I may have given him your number," Lindsey said quickly and made a beeline for some blouses hanging up near the register.

Sharla stopped short as Lindsey began sifting through the rack of blouses, pretending not to notice Sharla's reaction, which was absolute shock.

"You may have what?" she almost shouted.

"*Sssh*, keep your voice down, we are in a store," Lindsey said nonchalantly, her eyes never leaving the blouses. She took one off the rack by its hanger and held it up to her to test its fit. "I know you don't like being fixed up but I think you'll like this guy. He's very nice aaand he's a Christian."

Sharla walked over to Lindsey with as much control as she could muster. She felt as if she was seconds from going ballistic. "Oh, he's a Christian, huh? Well, that just makes it all better, thanks!"

"There's no need for sarcasm," Lindsey said, holding up another blouse to her chest as she looked in the store's full-length mirror. "What do you think?" she said, turning to Sharla. "You think this is a good color on me?"

"Forget the blouse!" Sharla hissed. "I wanna know why you gave some guy my phone number without telling me?!"

Lindsey sighed and turned back to the mirror, shaking her head in a she-just-doesn't-get-it gesture. "Because if I had asked you, you would have said no."

"You're darn right I would've!"

Deciding the blue blouse looked better, Lindsey draped it over her arm and put the other color back on the rack. "See? You see how you act? That's why I didn't tell you. Plus, you know this guy. He's in the choir."

"In the choir?" Sharla frowned, frantically trying to picture all the men in the choir, none of which she'd ever thought were very promising. "But all the men in our choir are married." Then, as an afterthought: "Or in the middle of a divorce."

"Not true, not true at all," Lindsey corrected. "There's a few single ones. You've always got your nose so buried in the music it's a wonder you ever see anything that goes on. This guy is new. He's only been going to the church for about a month now."

Sharla gave Lindsey a puzzled look that said she still couldn't place this man in her mind.

"I wanna try these on," Lindsey said, heading for the dressing rooms. Sharla followed.

"You know the shy guy, dark hair, real quiet, sits in the tenor section?" Lindsey continued, entering a dressing booth. Sharla waited outside.

"Shy guy, quiet…tenor…" Sharla muttered. She couldn't think of anyone in the tenor section that fit that description. Then a light went on. Come to think of it, there was a new guy in the choir. His name was Dan or Dale or something with a D. He was a decent-enough-looking guy. Quiet like Lindsey said. Pretty good voice, from what she could tell. At least he could sing on key. Sharla vaguely remembered some of the women talking about him not long after he showed up but she hadn't really thought much about him herself.

"You mean that guy that sits in the back? The one some of the women have been going on about 'cuz he's single?"

"That's the one," Lindsey remarked through the dressing room door. "His name's Denny. He's really sweet once you get to talk to him."

Denny! That was it!

"And how is it that you just happened to end up talking to him?"

"Because I'm a friendly person, I talk to everybody," Lindsey said. Then, more to herself: "Shoot. I don't think this is gonna fit. I knew I shouldn't have eaten that last piece of cheesecake."

"You mean you're a nosy person," Sharla quipped.

"That too." Sharla could hear Lindsey smiling. "Anyway, it turns out he's new in town and doesn't know a soul, poor thing."

"And you volunteered me to show him around."

"No," Lindsey said, trying to sound hurt. "He brought you up first, if you must know."

Sharla eyebrows went up. "Really?"

"Yeah. He asked who you were and I told him."

Sharla's nose was almost buried in the dressing room door. "He asked who I was? What did he say?"

"He said, 'Who is that?'" Lindsey replied flatly.

"You know what I mean!" Sharla snapped. "What did he want to know?"

Lindsey opened the dressing room door and came out with blouses in hand. "I thought you weren't interested."

"That was before you said he asked about me first," Sharla said, following Lindsey out on the department store floor.

"He just asked what your name was and I told him. He said he'd noticed that you have a very pretty singing voice."

A big smile appeared on Sharla's face. "He did? Well, that was sweet. What else did he say?"

"That was it," Lindsey shrugged, placing the clothes she was going to buy on the cash register counter. A young salesgirl began ringing up the purchase. "But I thought it was enough to suggest that he give you a call some time. I could see he liked you and Lord knows you could use a date!"

The salesgirl let out a little giggle and tried to keep her focus on folding up the blouses.

"You wanna say that a little louder, Lin?" Sharla asked. "I don't think the people over in Sportswear heard you."

"All I'm saying," Lindsey said, handing the salesgirl her credit card, "Is that it would do you good to go on a date. It'd get your mind off…"

She trailed off, looking at the salesgirl. "….other things."

Recognition lit on Sharla's face. Lindsey was talking about Tyler. "Oh, you mean…"

"Yeah. That's what I mean."

Sharla shrugged. Maybe Lin was right. God hadn't said she couldn't date anyone while she was waiting for Tyler. And everyone seemed to be after her to start dating again. Maybe it was time. Maybe it might be fun.

"But we know next to nothing about this guy," Sharla said as she and Lindsey walked out of the store. "We don't know where he comes from, what he does. He could be a serial killer and you're giving him my phone number!"

"He's from Chicago, he's 34, single, and he works at the university as an assistant librarian."

Sharla looked at her friend with a new respect. "Wow, you're good," she said. "You should have been a reporter."

Lindsey chuckled. "Thanks." She loaded her shopping bag into the back seat of her Saturn. "Anyway, I'm a pretty good judge when it comes to people and I have a feeling Denny's a good guy," she said, getting in behind the wheel. "Besides, he might not call. He didn't say he would for sure."

Sharla got in on the passenger side. "You didn't give him my home number, did you?"

"No," Lindsey said, backing out of the parking space. "I gave him your cell, which by the way, happens to be listed in the church directory."

Sharla blew out a sigh of relief. "Well, that's good."

"So, when did you manage to get all of this information out of him?"

"Last night, after choir rehearsal."

"Oh." Sharla tried to remember why she didn't see Lindsey and Denny talking, then remembered that she bolted from rehearsal as soon as the choir was dismissed. She wanted to get home to watch a special encore presentation of *America's Next Big Star* that featured highlights from Season Three. She'd recorded it while at rehearsal and couldn't wait to fast-forward to Tyler's scenes.

"Well," she sighed. "He probably won't call anyway."

"You're right," Lindsey agreed. "He probably won't."

Sharla shot Lindsey an I-can't-believe-you-just-said-that look.

"I was kidding!" Lindsey laughed, playfully slapping Sharla's arm. "Of course he'll call. He seemed very interested."

"If he's so great, how come you're not going out with him?"

"Oh, he's not my type," Lindsey said, shaking her head. "He's sweet, but you know me. I like 'em blonde."

Lindsey braked at a red light. "But you two," she continued. "I think you'll get along. He's into music....just like Tyler."

Sharla let out an amused grunt. "Yeah, but he's not Tyler."

"Just give him a chance," Lindsey reasoned. "You never know."

Chapter 12: Breaking Up is Hard to Do

enny didn't call. Instead, he struck up a conversation with Sharla at the next Tuesday night choir rehearsal. Afterwards, (and with some slight hesitation on Sharla's part) they ended up going for coffee at the Pancake House, an all-night diner next to the church.

Lindsey was right—Sharla found that she and Denny did share a love for music. As a new Christian (he'd only been saved for about eight months), Denny confided in Sharla that he found it refreshing to be able to talk to another Christian about secular music without feeling judged. Sharla sympathized. She remembered the disapproving glares she sometimes used to get in the company of believers if she happened to mention a non-Christian song or band.

She could understand how some secular music could be looked upon as dangerous or evil, she told Denny. But she loved all forms of music. She could find spiritual in the secular and secular in the spiritual. It was all about one's outlook, in her opinion. Music, be it Christian or otherwise, spoke to her, and if there was ever a song she was listening to that offended her ears or left her feeling convicted to turn it off, she did. But she felt to only listen to one type of music out of a sense of religious duty rather than a genuine leading of the spirit was limiting. Denny agreed. The pair ended up talking for well over an hour just about music, although Sharla also learned that even though they weren't born the same year, she and Denny's birthdays were just days apart. He was born October 7; she, October 9.

When they finally left the diner nearly two hours later, Sharla had agreed to have dinner with Denny that Saturday. She still had some trepidation. Outside of his love for music, Denny didn't look anything like Tyler. He was average height with jet-black curly hair that Sharla would have thought was quite attractive seven months earlier. Now all looking at it did was remind her that she was in love with a man who was tall and had an ample amount of luxurious silver in his hair.

Still, Tyler wasn't in her life right now, and despite her reservations, Sharla had to admit she found Denny somewhat charming. He had a sense of humor, and she also liked the fact that even though he'd gotten her number from Lindsey, he'd told Sharla he hadn't intended to call her without her permission.

They met up again on Saturday evening at a seafood restaurant Sharla suggested.

Everything had been going smoothly. No lulls in the conversation, plenty of laughter in the appropriate places. Sharla was proud of herself. For her first venture back onto the dating scene, things seemed to be going extremely well. She'd even called her mother before she left the house to inform her that her daughter had officially renounced spinsterhood and was going on an actual date with a real, live man.

Ida was ecstatic. "Oh, praise God!" she yelled into the phone. "Sharla, you don't know how long I've been praying for this."

"Calm down, mom," Sharla smirked. "He hasn't asked me to marry him."

Secretly, however, Sharla was just as excited, and had murmured a little prayer of her own before getting out of her car to go inside the restaurant. But halfway through the meal, Sharla began to get a sick feeling in her stomach, and it wasn't from the grilled salmon.

It started when, after several minutes of the two of them enjoying their meals in silence, Denny suddenly blurted out to Sharla that she reminded him of his ex-wife.

Sharla was taken aback. She had no idea Denny had been married before and said so. Denny told her it wasn't something he liked to talk about.

Actually, he confessed, the divorce papers had not yet been finalized. His ex, Sheryl, had been granted temporary custody of their 10-year-old son, Marshall. Denny took a photo of his wife and son out of his wallet. Sharla's eyes widened. The resemblance between her and Sheryl was amazing.

His psychiatrist, Denny continued, had suggested he try rearranging his life. Get a change of scenery and start going out with other women as a way to move past his pain. Denny hadn't wanted the separation but when he got saved, things became strained between him and his wife, who was an Agnostic. He tried to make Sheryl see how good it was to know God, but she wasn't interested. His newfound faith in Christ made Sheryl uncomfortable. They argued a lot and eventually, she left. Denny had a nervous breakdown and started seeing a shrink. On her advice, he left Chicago, accepted a job in Agape at the university, and here he was.

As surprised as she was by this new information, Sharla felt for Denny. She knew what it was like to be tossed aside by someone she'd cared about.

When dinner was over, the two stood in the restaurant's parking lot for a while, talking. Denny admitted to Sharla that he didn't want a divorce, that he missed his son and wanted desperately to try to work things out with his wife. Sharla prayed for him.

Afterwards, she told him if he felt there was a chance he could work things out with Sheryl, he should try, but to remember that he couldn't change his wife's heart. Only God could do that.

The following week, Denny didn't show up for choir rehearsal or church. Sharla finally received an e-mail from him with a detailed praise report that said after they'd prayed, Denny returned home and called his wife. They had a long talk in which Sheryl admitted that ever since he'd become a Christian, Denny acted as if he didn't need her now that he'd found God. Denny said he realized maybe the problems weren't entirely his wife's fault, that maybe he'd unknowingly shut her out. Both agreed to be open to possibly giving their marriage another try, especially for the sake of their son.

Two weeks later, Denny showed up at church with Sheryl and Marshall. He introduced them to several people, including Sharla and Lindsey, who remarked on how similar-looking Sharla and Sheryl were. Denny briefly took Sharla aside to tell her he was moving back to Chicago to be with his family.

"I never should have left. I gave in too easily," he confided. "I should have stayed and fought harder for my marriage. God made me see that."

He thanked Sharla for her kindness and prayers, telling her that although she didn't fully understand about his new religion, Sheryl had decided to at least come to church with Denny every once in a while. It was slow going, he said, and things weren't 100-percent, but he could see a change.

Sharla hugged Denny and wished him the best.

Ida was crestfallen. To hear her talk, she was already planning Sharla and Denny's wedding.

"Mom, we only went out once," Sharla reminded her over the phone. "And he was still married."

"I know," Ida sighed. "From what you told me, he seemed so nice."

"He was nice," Sharla agreed. "He just wasn't for me."

"You're not going to stop trying, are you?" There was pleading in Ida's voice.

"Mom, I never started," Sharla pointed out. "It's you all who want to hook me up so badly. I'm okay, really. And to be honest, I really don't want to be with anyone but Tyler."

It was usually at this point that Ida would argue with her daughter, telling her to get her head out of the clouds and stop chasing rainbows. But this time, Sharla's mother was eerily quiet.

Chapter 13:   Paperback Writer (Part I)

S harla could hear the phone ringing as she put the key into the front door lock of her apartment.

"Hang on, I'm coming!" she muttered under her breath as the door opened and she stepped inside the semi-darkness, almost tripping over the throw rug in the foyer.

Groping for the switch to the lamp on an end table in her living room, Sharla scooped up the phone with her other hand, pushed a button and spoke breathlessly into the receiver.

"Hello?"

"Yes, is this Sharla Davis?" A woman with a deep voice asked.

"Yes, it is," Sharla said, removing her purse from off her shoulder and throwing it absently on the couch. "Look, if this is about that video I checked out last week, I'm returning it tonight—"

"Ms. Davis," the deep voice said patiently. "This is not the video store. My name is Marla Kent. I'm a book editor with Red Rock Publishing Company. I read the manuscript you sent us."

For a moment, Sharla's mind was totally blank. Red Rock Publishing… did she send them something?

"Ms. Davis, are you there?"

Sharla was removing her heels, still wondering who in the world Red Rock Publishing Company was. "Huh? Oh, yeah! I, um, I was just trying to remember….you said I sent you a manuscript?"

"Yes…" There was a pause. Sharla could hear the faint shuffling of papers on the other end as she sat down on the coach, raising her legs off the floor and placing them under her, lounge-style. "*Chasing Trevor*, it's called."

At the mention of the manuscript's title, Sharla's eyes became huge and she gasped. Of course! Her story! Duh!

"Oh, *that* manuscript," she said, as if she'd written a million others. "Gosh," she laughed nervously. "I sent that in to several publishing houses some time ago. I didn't expect to…"

Sharla trailed off, catching herself. What'd she been about to say was "I didn't expect to get rejected over the phone."

Instead she paused, then said, "I didn't expect to…hear from anyone personally. I figured you'd send me a letter."

A rejection letter, that is, she thought. *I can put it with the rest of my collection.*

"Well," said Marla Kent, "I always like to call and tell people personally when their story has been accepted by us."

"Oh, I see. Well, thank you anywha—"

Sharla sat up, putting her legs back on the floor. "Excuse me, did you just say you are *accepting* my story?"

"Yes," Marla smiled through the phone. "I read it myself and found it very interesting. A few of my colleagues agree that it could make a good book. Tyler Nicks is hot right now and I think people will appreciate how you've chosen to spoof him. With the utmost respect, of course."

"Of course," Sharla said automatically. She hadn't heard a word after 'I read it myself.'

All that was running through her mind now was: OHMYGOD, OHMYGOD, THEYACCEPTEDIT, THEYACCEPTEDIT, THEY ACCEPTEDIT!!!!!!!!!!!

"….next week to set up the details."

Sharla came back to earth in time to catch the tail end of Marla Kent's sentence.

"Will that be alright?" Marla asked.

"Um, I think so," Sharla said slowly, trying to make it seem as if she'd been hanging on every word. "That sounds good. But could you run that by me one more time, just so I'm clear?"

"Sure," Marla said. "I'd like to talk to you about signing on with Red Rock. I'll be out of town the rest of this week but I'll have my assistant call to set up an appointment. Is that alright?"

The blood felt as if it was rushing to Sharla's head. "Yes! Yes, that'd be fine."

"Good," Marla intoned. "I'm looking forward to meeting you, Sharla. If everything goes well, I think we could have your book in stores by summer."

"Wow, that would be awesome," Sharla said, tears welling in her eyes. "I can't believe it."

"Well, believe it, it's true," Marla assured her. "If this book does as well as I suspect it will, Ms. Davis, you're going to be a very wealthy woman."

Sharla was too overwhelmed to speak.

"Congratulations," Marla said. "I have to go but I'll have my assistant call you."

"Um, sure. Sure thing," Sharla managed. "Oh! And thank you for calling!"

"You're welcome. Good night, Ms. Davis."

"Goodnight."

Sharla placed the phone gingerly on its base. The next few minutes were spent sitting in stunned silence on her red cloth couch, her brain still trying to ingest the conversation that had just taken place.

Finally, she leaned forward in the quiet of her living room and opened her mouth. "Somebody's gonna publish my book," she said to the emptiness. Her voice resounded hollowly back in her ears.

She tried her voice on again for size. "Somebody's gonna publish my book," she repeated, a little louder.

The second time felt better, more natural. After a third recitation, her head seemed to process the information.

Suddenly, Sharla was on her feet screaming at the top of her lungs, "SOMEBODY'S GONNA PUBLISH MY BOOK! SOMEBODY'S GONNA PUBLISH MY BOOK! HALLELUJAH! THANK YOU, JESUS!!!!!!!! AHHHHHHH!!!!!!!!"

Before Sharla realized it, she was jumping up and down, running joyfully from room to room, thanking Jesus and yelling that her book was going to be published.

She was using her bed as a trampoline when the phone rang. Without pause, she stooped down to pick it up and held it to her ear, still standing on the bed.

"Hello, yes?" she answered jubilantly.

"Hey, congratulations," a male voice offered.

"Oh, thank you!" Sharla beamed. Then: "Who's this?"

"This is Ed, you're upstairs neighbor."

Sharla's smile widened. This was unexpected. She didn't even know her upstairs neighbor. They'd only just moved in a few days ago and beyond exchanging names, she hadn't yet had an opportunity to say a proper hello.

"Well, hi, Ed! How are you? Hey, how did you get my number?"

"I'm fine," Ed said sweetly. "You're in the book. Listen, I'm very happy that someone's gonna publish your book. In fact, I would bet that anyone within a 20-mile radius heard and is also happy for you. But could you please keep it down? We just put the kids to bed."

"Oh," Sharla said, lowering herself off the bed. "Oh. Sorry. I didn't realize I was being so loud. Guess I got carried away."

"No problem," said Ed. "My wife says good luck with your book."

"Tell her thanks," Sharla said, blushing.

"No problem."

Sharla hung up the phone, a bit embarrassed by her rowdy behavior, but happy all the same. She quickly shrugged off the embarrassment. So what if the entire apartment complex heard her? After this summer, she might be able to buy the place.

The thought made her laugh out loud….quietly.

Sharla put a hand over her mouth to stifle another scream. When the urge had passed, she got down on her knees on the side of her bed and said a prayer of thanks to God.

"Well, Jesus, we did it," she said. "You did it."

"Now what?"

Chapter 14: (Un)Divine Intervention

A t 6:30 on a cool, brisk autumn evening, Sharla pulled into the driveway of her parent's two-story home on Blue Jay Street and got out of her car.

Coming up the walkway via the neatly manicured lawn, Sharla felt a sense of impending doom but she didn't know why. Something just felt….different.

She usually had dinner with her parents at least once a month but this particular meeting had an ominous feeling to it she couldn't describe.

As she approached the front door, Sharla did something she never did—she rang the doorbell. Her parents knew she was coming and they usually left the door unlocked so she could walk right in, but tonight was different. An owl hooted ominously off in the distance, almost as if he were confirming Sharla's suspicion.

A few seconds later, Ida opened the door a crack and peeked out. When she saw it was her daughter, a strained smile stretched achingly across her face, as if she were in pain and trying her best to hide it.

"Sharla, honey," Ida said, opening the door wider so Sharla could step inside. "Why'd you ring the bell? The door was unlocked."

"I don't know, mom," Sharla answered, giving Ida a quick hug. "For some reason, I just felt like it."

As Sharla entered the house, the inkling inside of her that something was out of whack grew to a high chill. Her parents had asked her over for dinner and yet Sharla smelled absolutely nothing coming from the kitchen. Normally, the entire house would have been full of the aroma of Ida's pot roast or collard greens and fried chicken. But tonight, there was nothing in the air. Except dread.

Sharla looked at the dining table. It wasn't set.

The television blared loudly as sports announcers gave the results of a college football game. Sharla's father came out of the den, his hands in his pockets. He looked nervous.

"Hey, kid!" he said, giving Sharla a kiss on the forehead. "Good to see you."

"Hi, dad," Sharla gave her father a hug. There was an awkward silence as the three of them stood in the center of the living room. Sharla searched both her parents' faces and found they could not look at her. Instead, they looked briefly at each other. Her mother then cast her eyes down at the carpet. Her father continued to stare straight ahead.

"So…" Sharla said slowly. "What's that smell?"

Ida frowned. "What smell?"

"Exactly, mom," said Sharla. "I don't smell anything. What's for dinner?"

"Oh," Ida looked troubled. Her eyes quickly darted to her husband, who refused to meet her gaze. "Umm…Sharla, honey, why don't we all sit down?"

Now it was Sharla's turn to frown. "Mom? What's wrong?"

Her parents took seats next to each other on the sofa. At that point, Sharla's brother, Derek, came out of the den as if on cue. He poked his head in tentatively at first, then came into the living room when Richard gave a signal it was okay. This wasn't lost on Sharla.

"Derek? What are you doing here?"

Sharla hadn't seen her brother in about six months. His new job in Austin didn't allow him much time to come home. And he'd emerged from the den alone. Natalie and the baby didn't seem to be with him, which meant if Derek had come all this way by himself, whatever was going on had to be serious. A lump caught in Sharla's throat as she hugged her younger brother.

"Hey, sis! Good to see you."

"You too. How's my little nephew?"

"He's good. Gettin' big. He and Natalie send their love."

"What are you doing here?" Sharla repeated.

Instead of answering, Derek sat down in a recliner next to the couch and looked at Ida and Richard expectantly.

"Sharla, why don't you sit down? There's something we all need to talk about," Ida said gently.

Sharla clutched her handbag anxiously. "Okay," she nodded quietly, and took a seat in a nearby chair next to her brother. The whole situation was starting to creep her out.

Ida, who seemed to have been elected the official spokesperson, leaned forward and for the first time since Sharla had arrived, looked directly at her.

"Honey," she began gently. "There's a problem and your father, brother and I believe it's time this problem was faced."

Sharla looked briefly at everyone then back at her mother. Fear began to gnaw inside of her. Something must be terribly wrong for them to call a family meeting like this. Someone must be in trouble or worse, sick. Awfully sick. Sharla turned to her father who had only recently given up a 30-year, 2-pack a day cigarette habit. He was a little short-winded but his last doctor's visit had shown he was in relatively good health for a man his age. At least that's what Ida had told Sharla. Had her mother lied to her? Was there really something wrong with Richard and they hadn't known how to tell her and Derek?

Sharla's eyes filled with tears at the thought. "Oh, dad, are you alri—"

"Yes, yes, I'm fine," Richard said with quick indignation. "It's not me."

Well, thank God for that, Sharla thought. "Mom, are you okay?"

"Yes, I'm fine, honey, never been better," Ida smiled.

Now Sharla was really confused. If it wasn't her parents, then….Sharla turned to Derek.

"Don't look at me," Derek shrugged. "Take a look at yourself."

Sharla recoiled as if she'd been slapped. "What? What are you talking about? There's nothing wrong with me."

"That's not what they think," Derek pointed to their parents. "And from what they've told me, I agree."

Sharla's eyes became slits. She looked back at her parents. "What is he talking about? What have you told him about me that you haven't even told me?"

Now Richard leaned forward and spoke. "Sharla, we're all concerned about you."

"Why, dad? I'm fine." Sharla asked through clenched teeth. She didn't like this one bit.

Richard struggled to find the right words. "You know I support you and I've tried to stay out of your personal life but it's this….this Tyler business, Sharla. We think it's gotten out of hand and frankly, we're worried about you."

Tyler! So that's what this was about.

"But dad," Sharla said. "There's nothing to be worried about."

"Honey, we think there is," Ida said seriously. "Ever since that TV show with…what's-his-name….Tyler….started, that's all we hear from you. Tyler this and Tyler that and that would be alright but…." She trailed off, unable or afraid to say anything more.

"….you're taking it too far, Sharla," Richard finished.

Sharla laughed. "Really? And how am I doing that?"

"You really think some guy from the TV is gonna marry you?" Derek blurted. "Sharla, come on, wake up."

"Is that why you're worried?" Sharla asked incredulously. "Because I told you I believe Tyler's going to marry me?"

Derek snorted cynically. A brief silence followed before Richard spoke again. "Sharla, if we thought you were kidding, we wouldn't give it a second thought but you seem to be serious—"

"I am serious, dad," Sharla interjected.

"Let me finish," the old man said. "Since you are serious, we as your family feel it's time to talk some sense into you about this. Now, Sharla, we love you and we want to see you happy but you need to start being realistic. This man, Tyler...."

"Nicks," Sharla said.

"Nicks," Richard echoed. "He's a big star now. You even said yourself he's got women all over the world clamoring for him. He's a rock musician and honey, you know what kind of life those rock musicians lead. But aside from that he doesn't know who you are and you don't know him, not really."

Sharla opened her mouth to speak but Richard put up a hand to stop her. "Now, you may think because you've been following this guy on this show and reading about him on the computer, you know him. But the truth is, all you know is what he presents. And that's not enough basis for this notion that this is the man you're supposed to marry."

Richard paused, but Sharla said nothing. She only sat slumped in her chair looking out in space.

"Sharla, are you listening?" he asked.

"Yes." The reply was short, non-committal.

"He's a fantasy, Sharla, do you understand? This thing you believe, it's not real."

Sharla looked over at her brother. He was looking at her as if she'd lost her mind. They all were.

They think I've gone nuts, Sharla thought. She sighed and looked at her parents. "Dad, I know what I saw. I know what I felt and what I felt was the Holy Spirit telling me Tyler Nicks will be my husband. Now, you always told me that we should never deny the voice of God when we hear it. I know what I heard and I heard God!"

"Are you sure it was God?" Derek asked. Sharla looked at him to see if he was trying to be sarcastic but his face looked earnest.

"Yes, Derek, I'm sure."

"Because the Bible says Satan disguises himself as an angel of light."

Sharla rolled her eyes. Her little brother, the know-it-all. "Yeah, I know but I'm telling you, this was the Holy Spirit, I felt it. And I was given a prophecy about it."

Derek raised his eyebrows. "Yeah? From who?

"My pastor."

Derek chuckled. He was a diehard Catholic. "So you're still going to that Holy Roller church, huh?"

"It's Pentacostal and yes. You should come with me sometime. Maybe the pastor can cast a devil or two out of you."

"Oh, you think you're so funny," Derek sneered. While brother and sister went at each other for a moment, Ida turned to Richard and said, "Maybe it's time to bring in Dr. Carl."

"I think you're right," Richard agreed. Cupping his hand over his mouth, he yelled out, "Dr. Carl, you better come on in here now."

When Sharla and Derek heard that, they both became quiet.

"Who's Dr. Carl?" Sharla asked aloud. The name sounded familiar.

Just then, a short, balding, rotund man in his 50's emerged from the den. He was followed by a camera crew complete with booms and bright lights.

Sharla's mouth dropped. No wonder the name was familiar. It was Dr. Carl Redding, the psychotherapist from the reality drama series *Breaking Habits*, which follows everyday people suffering from addictions. Dr. Carl also had his own nighttime talk show. Then it clicked! On *Breaking Habits*, the show usually began with a family staging an intervention for an unsuspecting loved one in the hopes of convincing them to seek help.

"Oh my GOD!" Sharla shrieked. "Is this an intervention? You were gonna put this on TELEVISION?"

"Sharla, Sharla, honey, just calm down," Ida soothed. "Dr. Carl simply wants to talk to you."

"Talk to me?!" Sharla yelled. "Then why is there a camera crew in the living room?!"

Derek looked at Richard and Ida. "I told you she wasn't gonna go for this," he said, shaking his head.

"Sheila," Dr. Carl soothed, holding out his hands. "We'll edit out anything you're not comfortable with."

Sharla stared at Dr. Carl coldly. "I'm not comfortable with any of it!" Then, to her parents: "I can't believe you would have a complete stranger, some television hack, come in off the street and–"

"Now, hang on a minute, Sheila," Dr. Carl drawled. "Before you go attacking me, let's sit down and talk about this situation. Your family's concerned about you and I just want to help."

Sharla could feel the blood rushing to her face. She couldn't remember when she'd been so angry. "My name is Sharla. You want to help? Get out!"

"Well, *Sharla*," Dr. Carl continued. "I don't think that's your decision to make. This is not your house."

Sharla looked at her parents. Neither spoke.

"All right," she said, grabbing her purse. "I'll leave."

"Sharla, honey, wait," Ida begged, grabbing her daughter's elbow. "Don't leave like this. We love you. We're just trying to help."

"How mom?" Sharla hissed. "By airing my problems on national television without even asking me? By siccing this quack therapist on me?" Sharla pointed at Dr. Carl.

"Little lady, I am not a quack," said Dr. Carl. "I am an Emmy-winning, licensed psychotherapist and don't you forget it."

"Listen, since we're all here, let's all just sit down and try to hash this out like reasonable adults," Richard said.

"I'm not going to talk about anything with him," Sharla pointed at Dr. Carl. "And especially not with them," She pointed at the camera crew.

Dr. Carl sighed. "What if I agreed to turn the cameras off?"

Sharla thought for a moment. "No, no, that's not good enough. I don't want to discuss this. I am not crazy." She turned to her parents. "Mom, dad, do you think I haven't thought about this? Do you think I didn't think the whole thing sounded nuts? I've been agonizing over this for weeks, months! Sometimes, I still wonder if I'm wrong but you know what? I don't think I am. I don't know how it'll happen or when, but God gave me a promise and I choose to believe it."

"You know," she continued, her eyes filling with tears, "I have to wonder if maybe if I was a different kind of girl, this wouldn't be so hard for you to believe."

"What does that mean?" her father asked.

"You know what it means, dad." Sharla sobbed. "If I was thinner and prettier? Maybe the idea of somebody like Tyler Nicks marrying me wouldn't be so preposterous to you."

"Sharla, this has nothing to do with your looks," Richard said. "You're a beautiful girl. I've always said that and I've always meant it. We just don't want you to get your heart broken and we feel that you could be setting yourself up for just that. Have you done anything to get in touch with this man? Does he know how you feel?"

Sharla quietly said 'no.' He had her there.

"If you're really serious about this man, what have you done to go after him? Do you expect God to simply drop him in your lap? It's one thing to have faith, Sharla, but it's another thing entirely to simply wish and hope and dream. This Tyler guy has no idea who you are. You don't even know if he's in a relationship!"

"Sis, dad's right," Derek said, putting an arm around Sharla. "What do you really know about this guy except that he's famous? Is he even a Christian? What does he believe? Sharla, you know how you get sometimes about men."

Sharla couldn't speak. She was too busy trying to fight back tears.

"Sis, I think the trouble is you're too afraid to take a chance on a real guy. When was the last time you went out on a date? I mean, ever since you broke up with Paul, all you've done is work and go to church. It's been almost three years. Maybe it's time to start dating again."

Sharla looked up at her mother. "What? You didn't tell him about Denny?"

Derek shook his head. Ida opened her mouth to speak but Sharla interrupted. "Oh, she tells you about how crazy I am and how pathetic and lonely my life is without a man," Sharla snapped at her brother, "But she doesn't bother to tell you when I do go on a date!"

"Sharla, there wasn't time to go into all that," Ida explained. "Besides, it was just one time and when I talked to you about it you started on Tyler again. What? One date with one man and you're done—"

"Oh, please, mom!" Sharla countered. "You obviously had time to tell Derek I was a nut and he better get down here quick and see about his wacko sister!"

"That's not the way it happened," Richard broke in.

"I never said you were crazy," Ida argued. "But maybe if you could start dating more, it'd take your mind off this Tyler nonsense."

Sharla flinched. Nonsense. That's what they thought it was.

Sharla was deeply hurt; she felt betrayed. She had so wanted her family's support. They claimed to know and trust God but when God had manifested Himself in her life, they'd refused to believe it, believe her. They didn't even see anything wrong with bringing in outsiders to broadcast her problem to the nation. No matter what emotions she may have had for various men in the past, this was different. It wasn't a fixation and it wasn't loneliness and it wasn't mere lust. It was God. And it was real.

"You really think there's no way this could happen with Tyler?" Sharla asked her family.

"I suppose it's not completely out of the question," Richard said. "But if it really is God's plan as you say it is, then it'll happen no matter what we say, right? So, in the meantime, why don't you take your brother's advice and try going out more? You may find that Tyler was just a fixation. How will you ever know, though, if you spend all your life on the computer living vicariously through someone else?"

There was no use arguing with them. They were right, she was wrong. She was crazy, they were sane and there was no amount of reasoning that would make it otherwise. Sharla remembered her pastor once saying that sometimes, when God gives you a vision, don't expect everyone to jump up and shout 'hallelujah' with you about it.

Still, Sharla had not expected such outlandish and inconsiderate behavior from her own family.

She rose to leave. "I'll think about it," was about all she could manage as she headed for the door.

"Well, I believe my work here is done," Dr. Carl announced. "Come on, gang," he said to his camera crew, "Let's pack this baby up."

On her way out, Sharla reminded Dr. Carl she hadn't signed a release form, which meant he didn't have permission to air her face on television. She made it very clear she wouldn't hesitate to sue if she found out he'd used her likeness.

Several weeks later, the segment aired on Dr. Carl's talk show. The subject was "TV Reality Stars and the Women Who Love Them." As promised, Sharla's face was was covered by a filmy cloud. Her voice also was altered to sound like an eerie cross between Kathleen Turner and Barry White. Only the backs of Ida's and Richard's heads were shown. Derek was edited out completely and he *did* sign a release form.

Everyone's names were changed.

Sharla watched the episode in disgust. She had no idea at the time, but she would soon end up showing her face on Dr. Carl's show after all. And that time, he would have no trouble remembering her name.

Chapter 15: Paperback Writer (Part II)

The plane ride to New York was daunting.

Not because of the weather—except for some mild turbulence, it was clear and sunny all the way—and not because of any mechanical glitch. It was the fear of the unknown that worried Sharla, the fear of abandoning where she'd been in favor of where she was headed.

Sharla had no idea when she'd sent in her story, but Red Rock was a huge publishing company, one of the largest on the East Coast. It was considered top notch in the publishing world, boasting offices in the UK and Europe. Some of the most well-known authors of the day were signed with Red Rock, which made it all the more miraculous to Sharla that her manuscript had made it past the mail room, let alone onto the desk of the woman who had been named one of America's most influential book editors of 2002 by the National Book Review.

Had Sharla known any of those things, she never would have sent her story to a mammoth company like Red Rock. She never would have thought she had a shot. But God obviously had other plans.

After the initial shock of her book's acceptance wore off, Sharla began retracing her steps. She fished out an alphabetical list of publishing houses she'd printed out. She'd placed checkmarks next to the companies she wanted to submit to, none of them powerhouses in the industry. Sharla wasn't sure her story was good enough for a major publishing company to consider, especially since she didn't have a literary agent. And remembering her father's admonishment about the hardships of finding a publisher, she'd wanted to start small. As she went down the list using her index finger as a guide, she saw in the "R" section two companies with similar names. One was called

RedHouse Books Ltd. The one directly under it was **Red Rock Publishing**. Sharla was familiar with Redhouse. It was a fledgling little company that published lightweight paperbacks and dimestore novels. She'd put a check next to it.

There was no check next to Red Rock.

I sent my book to the wrong company, Sharla thought with awe. *I must have gotten the addresses mixed up.*

What's more, Sharla, a chronic pack rat, had kept every single rejection letter she'd received from various publishing houses over the past few months. She discovered that when she compared the source of each letter to her checkmarked list of about 20 companies, she'd received a rejection notice from every one of those companies except Red Rock, and she hadn't meant to send her story to them in the first place!

Sharla folded up the list and placed it and the rejection letters in a wooden chest that housed all her special mementos, wondering as she did so who was the nitwit that said God didn't have a sense of humor?

The next few days were filled with activity as Sharla corresponded with Marla Kent's assistant about traveling to Red Rock's main headquarters in New York. Sharla made arrangements to take a personal day the following Friday so she could arrive in New York Friday morning. A driver would meet her at the airport and take her to her hotel, where she could relax for a bit before being taken to Red Rock for a two o' clock meeting with Marla. Afterwards, if nothing came up in her schedule, Ms. Kent had left word she'd like to take Sharla to dinner. After dinner, Sharla would be driven back to her hotel. She would be back in Agape by Saturday evening.

Marla's assistant told Sharla not to worry about anything. Red Rock would arrange her flight and hotel accommodations, as well as take care of all her travel expenses. Everything was going to be first class.

Sharla spent a good deal of time on her knees during this period, asking God for wisdom and direction. She was scared to death this whole thing was a dream from which she would undoubtedly be awakened, trembling and mournful that she could not go back to sleep.

She told almost no one of her impending meeting, but did finally break down and call her parents, whom she hadn't talked to since the intervention fiasco almost three weeks earlier. Her mother had tried reaching out to her, leaving several messages on both her cell phone and her home answering machine. Sharla was too angry to answer them. The only person she could calm herself enough to talk to was Derek, who'd called twice shortly after the incident.

"I told mom and dad you'd never go for it," he said of the dreaded intervention, adding that Sharla had her family all wrong. No one believed she was crazy, just obsessed. Somehow, Sharla sarcastically told her little brother, that didn't make what they'd done much better. In fact, the more she replayed the incident in her mind, the more certain Sharla became she'd never speak to her parents again. She started having a recurring dream in which she and Tyler, now married, were on a tour bus surrounded by legions of fans. Richard and Ida were in the crowd outside, banging wildly on the bus windows as Sharla stared out at them without the faintest hint of recognition, wondering out loud who in the world that wild-eyed, crazy couple was that kept tapping on the windows? Tyler would shrug and say he didn't know. Every now and then, her brother would poke his head over her shoulder like a Jack-in-the-box and say, "I told them you'd never go for it," and then she'd wake up.

It wasn't until she was praying one night for Tyler and the upcoming book deal that she felt a strong conviction in her heart to forgive her parents. At first, she dismissed the thought, but found that she could not go on praying when she tried. After a few more attempts, Sharla sat back on her haunches and exhaled deeply. Maybe it was time, she thought reluctantly. Her book was about to be published, her spirits were higher than they'd been in years. Perhaps time had dissipated her anger. Then the words of Jesus from the book of Matthew, Chapter 6, came to her mind: *For if you forgive men their trespasses, your heavenly Father will forgive you. But if you do not forgive men their trespasses, neither will your Father forgive your trespasses."*

Sharla immediately leaned forward on her knees again and asked God to forgive her. How stubborn and stupid she'd been. It didn't matter if an appropriate amount of time had elapsed in order for her to forgive her parents. It didn't matter if what they'd done happened two-and-a-half weeks ago or two years ago or two minutes ago! She simply needed to forgive, and that was that.

Despite what they'd done, Sharla had to accept that they were still her parents, and they had been supportive of her writing. They deserved to hear the good news.

"Well, hello, kid!" Sharla's father said when she called her parents a few minutes later. There wasn't a hint of anger in his voice. He just sounded happy.

"I knew you'd come around eventually," Richard said with a smile Sharla could hear. "I told your mother, 'Just give her some time. She'll cool down.'"

Both Richard and Ida was ecstatic to hear of Sharla's publishing deal, although Ida was quite a bit more ecstatic simply to hear her daughter's voice. Sharla apologized for being so hardheaded, an inherited trait she playfully blamed on her mother, and Ida admitted that maybe calling in the media to help deal with a family issue wasn't the wisest thing she'd ever done. The two made up over the phone and made plans to go to lunch before Sharla left for New York in a couple of days.

Sharla also called Lindsey, who cried with glee and tried to convince Sharla to notify the church so they could pray for her before she left, but Sharla refused. After some coaxing, Lindsey promised not to say anything to anyone, including Roxy and Diane.

"I don't want a lot of people to know," Sharla explained over the phone. "Not until there's really something to tell."

"But there *is* something to tell!" Lindsey exclaimed. "A major company is going to publish your book! You don't think that's something to tell?"

"But what if I get up there and the deal falls through?" Sharla countered. "What if they decide they don't want to publish me after all and I've told all these people they would?"

"Sharla, that won't happen," Lindsey assured. "Why would they be willing to fly you to New York first class on their dime and put you up in a five-star hotel if they had no intention of signing you?"

Sharla was quiet. Lindsey did have a point.

"I think maybe you're being a little paranoid," Lindsey sighed.

"You're probably right," Sharla agreed, "But I have to go with what I feel in my spirit, and I feel that I'm supposed to sit on this until I get back. It's like, the timing's not right. It's not for me to announce. It's for God to announce."

Now, Sharla was sitting in first class, reclining comfortably in the plush, leather seat of an airplane, sipping orange juice at 30,000 feet and looking out the window at the white, powdery clouds as they zipped past, feeling like David going out to meet his Goliath. Only instead of a slingshot, she was carrying a manuscript.

●————————————————————————————————●

Red Rock Publishing's offices were just as grand as the company's reputation.

True to its name, the building was six stories of rich, deep red brick, located in the heart of downtown Manhattan's posh business district.

The outside was designed in a 1930's Art Decco style that Sharla found tasteful and pleasant to the eye. Inside, however, the offices were completely state-of-the-art, with plush, red carpets that made Sharla feel as if she was walking on freshly cut grass. There were nouveaux Cubist paintings on the walls, and the faint yet persistent background hum of copiers, printers and fingers clacking softly against keyboards. All the women Sharla passed looked elegant in their chic, business-like dresses or expensive, crisply pressed pantsuits, making Sharla feel underdressed in her dark-blue power suit she'd bought off the rack at K-Mart.

The receptionist's area smelled like fresh paint.

"May I help you?" a young woman with stylishly-framed glasses and dark hair pulled back in a tight bun asked.

"Yes," Sharla replied in her most business-like tone. "I'm here to see Marla Kent. We have a meeting."

"Your name?"

"Sharla Davis."

The receptionist looked down briefly at something Sharla couldn't see from her vantage point.

"Uh….yes," the receptionist said. "I see that Ms. Kent is expecting you. If you'll just have a seat…" She pointed to some oversized chairs across from her. "…I'll let her know you're here."

"Thank you," Sharla nodded. She took a seat, clutching her imitation leather briefcase that contained her manuscript and her Bible tightly to her chest.

"Lord," Sharla silently prayed, "I have no idea what I'm doing in this gargantuan place. But You know, so I'm asking You to please give me the right words as I go into this meeting. Give me wisdom on how to negotiate."

Just then, Sharla remembered Exodus 14:14: *"The Lord will fight for you, and you shall hold your peace."*

Okay, Jesus, Sharla smiled, relaxing a little. *I didn't want to handle this anyway.*

"Ms. Davis?"

Sharla jerked her head up at the receptionist, who was walking towards her. "Yes?"

"Marla's running a little late. She said to go ahead and show you to her office. If you'll just come with me…"

Sharla followed the receptionist down a long corridor into a huge, brightly lit office with thick, cherry wood double doors. The receptionist motioned for Sharla to have a seat in one of the chairs opposite Marla's desk, then asked Sharla if she'd like something to drink while she waited. Sharla told her water would be fine.

Looking around the office, Sharla noticed that behind Marla's desk and to the right was a bookcase full of literary awards. On the other side, the wall was covered with photos of a lady Sharla assumed was Marla accepting many of the awards that now sat on her bookshelf. There were also pictures of her with presidents, spiritual leaders, rock stars and a few familiar literary faces: Stephen King, John Grisham, Amy Tan, Alice Walker, Truman Capote.

A few seconds later, an older, exquisitely dressed woman who looked to be in her mid-50's entered the room in a rush, whisking past Sharla, the aroma of her perfume wafting in the air as she plopped down into the large, swivel chair at the desk.

"My goodness, what a day!" the older woman gushed. "This place has been a madhouse since 9 a.m."

Sharla recognized the woman as being the same one in the photographs, but even without visuals, Sharla knew immediately from the sound of her dark, husky voice who she was.

"Now, where are my manners?" the woman said, smiling at Sharla. She arose and stretched out a hand. "I'm Marla Kent, managing editor of Red Rock Publishing. You must be Sharla."

"Yes," Sharla said, shaking hands. Marla's grip was firm but not intimidating. "It's nice to finally meet you."

"Same here," Marla affirmed. "Please, sit down. Would you like something to drink?"

As if on cue, the receptionist reappeared with a tray of cold bottled waters and some glasses.

"Thank you, Connie," Marla said. "You're a gem."

Connie nodded and smiled and left the room.

"So," Marla began, grabbing one of the waters. "How was your flight?"

"It was good," Sharla admitted. "I'd never flown first-class before."

Marla leaned in and flashed a knowing grin. "Feels good, doesn't it?"

Sharla chuckled nervously. "Yeah, it did."

"And your room. Did you have any problems checking in?"

"No, no. It's beautiful, thank you."

"Good," Marla leaned back. "This your first trip to New York?"

"Second," Sharla replied. "I came here once for a weekend with my high school choir."

"Oh, well, I know you won't be here long this trip, but perhaps some other time you can get yourself reacquainted with the city."

"Sure," Sharla said.

"So, I guess you want to know why I flew you out here all the way from Texas, right?"

Sharla grinned. She liked Marla's no-nonsense way of putting things. "Well, yes, that would be nice."

"Alright. I like people who like to get right to the point. Red Rock Publishing would like to publish your manuscript," Marla said, her voice going into pat business mode. "We're prepared to offer you the standard deal we negotiate with most first-time authors, which is a $25,000 advance plus 15% of the royalties from sales of your book."

Marla paused, waiting to see Sharla's reaction. At this point, most new writers' eyes tended to bug out at the mention of a $25,000 advance. But Sharla remained poised, almost unaffected. She'd been prepared for this and merely nodded as Marla spoke.

"Since you don't have a literary agent....?"

"No," Sharla said. "I don't have an agent."

"…Then you won't have to worry about sharing any of that advance. But don't get too comfortable," Marla warned, wagging a manicured finger. "If you want to continue in this business, you need to get yourself an agent. I can help you with that if you'd like."

Sharla leaned forward in her chair and cleared her throat. "Um, Ms. Kent—"

"Please, call me Marla."

"Marla," Sharla hesitantly continued. "I'm very grateful that you flew me out here and I'm really happy you want to publish my book. But I have to ask…why?"

Marla looked at Sharla quizzically. "I don't think I follow you," she said.

Sharla took a swig of her water. "I mean, this place, this company…" she gestured around Marla's office. "It's huge. It's gorgeous, don't get me wrong but you obviously deal with some big names…" she looked in the direction of Marla's wall of fame. "…Red Rock is a giant in the publishing industry and I can't help wondering what made you decide to take on a no-name like me who doesn't even have formal representation?"

Marla didn't speak right away. She simply looked at Sharla as if she was trying to figure her out. When she finally did speak, it was to ask a jarring question.

"You're used to being rejected, aren't you?"

Sharla sat up. She felt as if she'd been punched in the stomach. Oddly enough, her first thought was of Paul. "Wha-what do you mean?"

"Well, it's clear to me you've experienced a lot of rejection," Marla said, getting up and walking to the window that overlooked a scenic view of the Manhattan skyline. She turned around and looked at Sharla. "Let me guess. You probably sent your story in to a 100 publishing houses and they all said 'no.' So, here a big company like Red Rock comes along and says 'yes,' and you don't know how to accept it. You've gotten so used to hearing 'no' that you can't even recognize when someone's saying 'yes.'"

For a split second, Sharla thought Marla had somehow seen into her past, into her soul. But she was only speaking of book publishing.

Wasn't she?

Marla was still standing at the window, her arms crossed. "You know how long I've been in this business, Sharla?"

"No, ma'am."

"Too long. Long before you were even a thought, that's for sure." She walked back to her desk and took a sip of water. "I didn't get all these awards you see here for not being good at what I do."

She came around her desk and sat down in the chair next to Sharla. "You're right," she went on. "Red Rock Publishing is a well-established, major publishing house. And normally, I wouldn't even look at a manuscript that was submitted by an unknown, first-time author who doesn't have a literary agent and no notable writing credentials to speak of. But you know what? I liked your story. I think it has potential. And I like you. I want to help you. Don't ask me why, but I do! I think you've got something, and I'd like to help you bring it out."

Marla smiled at Sharla, a warm, caring smile that quickened something in Sharla's spirit. She felt at peace, as if God Himself was talking through Marla. She could sense His favor all over this.

"So, do you want your book published or not?"

After a moment's silence, Sharla smiled back and said, "Of course! I didn't fly all this way to hear 'no!'"

"Now, that," Marla Kent said. "Is what I like to hear!" She went back to her desk, sat down, took a pair of reading glasses out of an embroidered case and put them on.

"Here is a copy of the contract we have all of our clients sign." She handed the contract to Sharla. "You don't have to sign it now. You can take it back home with you and have an attorney look it over if you'd like. There's no high-pressure tactics here, although I must say that the sooner you sign the sooner we can have your book in stores."

"Which stores?" Sharla asked.

"We do business with all the major chains: Barnes & Noble, Borders, Waldenbooks, websites like Amazon. I can give you a list."

"What about the packaging?"

"We'll handle all of that. You may have some input on the jacket designs our team comes up with but ultimately, Red Rock has final say on all aspects of marketing, design, etc. It's in the contract. We have one of the finest marketing and design teams in the industry, so not to worry. As far as the editing, which will be minimal, Candice will handle that."

Sharla frowned. "Who's Candice?"

Marla was about to answer when the phone rang.

"Excuse me," she said. She picked up the phone without saying 'hello' and held it to her ear. After a short pause, she said, "Okay, tell her to come up," and placed the phone back on its base.

"You're about to find out." Marla said.

Just then, a wispy young lady in her early 20's with short, strawberry blonde hair dressed in a crème-colored top with a matching short skirt entered the room. She walked over to Marla and gave her a hug and a kiss on the cheek.

"Candice," Marla said, gesturing towards Sharla. "I'd like you to meet Sharla Davis. Sharla, this is my niece, Candice."

At the mention of Sharla's name, a huge smile appeared on Candice's face and she eagerly stretched out her hand. "Hi."

"Nice to meet you," Sharla replied.

"Candice is working with me right now," Marla explained. "She decided she wants to become a book editor like her illustrious aunt and I've agreed to let her shadow me. I guess you could say she's my protégé." Candice and

Marla exchanged smiles. "In addition to watching my every move, Candice also has the job of reading many of the submissions that come through this office. She was the one who told me about your manuscript."

"Oh?" Sharla looked at Candice.

"Yes," Candice said. "I really liked it. I think it's well-written, it's funny and it's timely. Plus, I like Tyler Nicks. See I've been after Aunt Marla to kind of break with tradition. Bring in some fresher writers, start publishing material that's a little more cutting edge..."

"...And your story is fresh," Marla added. "America's Next Big Star is definitely...what's the word they're using these days?.....Dope? Is that it?"

Candice blushed and looked away. "Aunt Marla!"

"I just love embarrassing her," Marla winked, then looked at her watch. "Well, sorry to break this up but I've got another meeting across town I've got to attend. Sharla, it's been lovely talking to you, sorry I'll need to run. I'll call you about dinner this evening. Candice, would you mind walking Sharla out? I've got to make a phone call."

"Sure, no problem."

"So, how long have you been working with your aunt?" Sharla asked as she and Candice walked through the corridors of Red Rock.

"Well, really, all my life. I come from a long line of bookworms. You can't be around that stuff all the time and not have it rub off on you. But technically, only for the last six months."

"And you like Tyler Nicks?"

"Oh, yeah," Candice nodded. "Me and my boyfriend are huge fans. We both voted for him like, a cajillion times!" Both women laughed as they stood waiting for the elevator. "My boyfriend's from Georgia and he sings, so he felt kind of a kindred spirit with Tyler."

The elevator doors opened and Candice and Sharla stepped inside.

"In fact," Candice offered. "It's really because of my boyfriend that I even saw your story."

"Really?"

"Yeah. He's good friends with one of the guys that works down in the mailroom."

"Uh-huh…" Sharla was getting a tingle down her spine, though she had no idea why.

"Don't spread this around," Candice muttered, "But our mailroom staff is trained to automatically disregard any material that wasn't submitted through a literary agent," Candice went on.

"Really?" Sharla nodded. She wasn't surprised.

"Yeah. But this friend of Steven's, that's my boyfriend, he liked the title of your story and he started reading a little of it. He knew we'd never look at it, so he took it home for his wife to read because she likes Tyler too. Well, his wife read the entire story and raved about it!"

"Are you serious?" Sharla gasped.

"Well, this is what my boyfriend told me later," Candice said as they stepped out into the main lobby. "But he told me that his friend's wife was like, 'You have *got* to get this to Candice, she has got to see this!'"

"Right," Sharla had her hand over her mouth.

"So, Steve brought me the story. I read it, I thought it was good and I showed it to my aunt. I mean, it wasn't easy. She's set in her ways but when she saw that it really was good, she wanted to sign you just as much as I did. I guess every now and then, God makes an exception."

Sharla stood frozen. "What did you just say?"

"What?"

"About God….making an exception."

"Oh!" Candice laughed. "It was something my granddad used to say." Her face clouded in a frown. "You know it's weird, but I hadn't even thought about that saying in years. Funny, it just popped out when I was talking to you. Hey, you okay?"

"Yes," Sharla nodded, tears leaking from the corners of her eyes. If she hadn't been sure God was in this before, she was positive of it now. She swiped at her eyes with her hands. "I'm just a little overwhelmed. I'm in New York and I'm about to have my first novel published…"

What was happening was so much more than Sharla ever could have expected.

"Well, hey," Candice said, taking Sharla's hand. "You deserve it. You're very talented."

"Thank you so much for your help."

"Sure, no problem." Candice walked over to the welcome counter and grabbed a few tissues from a box sitting on the corner.

"Thank you," Sharla said, taking the tissues and dabbing at her eyes with them. "I'm normally not this emotional."

"You don't need to apologize," Candice smiled. "I've got to head back but it was nice meeting you. Maybe I'll see you at dinner tonight."

"That'd be nice," Sharla sniffed and smiled.

Candice got back in the elevator. Sharla waited until the door had closed and Candice was no longer in view before she walked over to the welcome counter and asked the counter person to please call for her driver.

Look at me, she thought. *Asking for my driver.* The Lord was so good!

Sharla decided to walk outside and wait. She looked up into the crisp, blue sky and sighed.

Sometimes God makes an exception.

Chapter 16: Nobody Told Me There'd Be Days Like These

***

The following week, Sharla was working late covering a livestock show about 45 minutes outside of Agape when her cell phone rang.

She was in the middle of an interview with Bobbi Duncan, a spunky, freckle-faced 10-year-old girl whose pet bull, Clancy, had just won first place.

Bobbi was espousing about the ins and outs of preparing a bull for competition in the cute way that only a child's vocabulary could as Sharla jotted down quotes in her reporter's notebook. But the darn phone buzzing in her pocket was making it hard for her to concentrate. Her editors knew she was covering an event, and it was well before the evening deadline.

Great. Maybe there's been a huge industrial accident or a 15-car pile-up, she thought irritably.

"Hey, Bobbi," Sharla said, cutting into the kid's monologue. "Listen, my phone's ringing and I have to take it, okay?"

"Okay," Bobbi shrugged, popping her bubble gum.

"Hello?" Sharla answered the phone.

"Sharla!" It was her editor, Ray, and he didn't sound happy. "Where are you?"

Sharla frowned. Ray knew where she was. He was the one who'd given her the assignment.

"I'm at the Livestock Show, " Sharla stammered. "You sent me to cover it for tomorrow's local section, remember?"

"Well, wrap it up and get back here now!"

"Why? What's happened?"

"That's what we'd like you to tell us!" Ray barked and hung up.

Sharla snapped her company phone shut and slowly put it back into her pocket. She'd never heard Ray so angry.

"Miss, are we through?"

Sharla turned to see Bobbi staring up at her under thin little lashes.

"Um, yeah," Sharla said. "I think we are."

"Is this gonna be in the paper?"

At this rate, Sharla didn't know if *she* was still going to be at the paper, but she managed a smile for Pembrook County's first-prize bull owner.

"It certainly is," she told the little girl. "Be sure to look for it tomorrow."

"Sweet!" Bobbi exclaimed. "I'm gonna go get my picture taken with Clancy. Bye!"

Sharla smiled and waved as the little girl, ponytail bouncing jauntily atop her head, sauntered off to find her bull. For a second, Sharla wished she could go with her.

Or at least be 10 again.

The drive back to the paper seemed endless as Sharla's mind replayed the short conversation with Ray. Her first thought was that perhaps someone was threatening to sue the newspaper over something she'd written, which happened to reporters from time to time. But the newspaper had lawyers for that. It didn't seem likely that would be Ray's beef. And he'd said tell *us* what was happening. What the heck did that mean? Who was us?

By the time Sharla pulled into the *Agape Gazette* parking lot, she had a gnawing feeling in the pit of her stomach, which only got worse when she walked into the newsroom and saw all three of the assistant night editors and the managing editor huddled around the conference table in the center of the room. It was way too late for a budget meeting. Something had happened. Something big.

"There she is!" Sharla heard someone say and looked in the direction of the voice. It was Jeff, the managing editor. He looked serious.

"Sharla, come on over, we need to talk," he said, beckoning her.

Slowly, Sharla walked to the conference table as one headed for the guillotine.

"Hey, everybody," she said, trying to sound chipper. "What's up?"

"Sharla," Jeff asked in a let's-just-get-straight-to-the-point tone of voice. "Why didn't you tell us you'd written a book?"

Sharla closed her eyes and sat down. She'd known this moment was coming. She'd planned to have a talk with Jeff shortly before *Chasing Trevor* came out, but she hadn't figured it would be like this. She'd only just signed the contract with Marla shortly before she left New York. She hadn't even had time to deposit the $25,000 cashier's check that had come certified mail the day before into her savings account. The book's cover hadn't been finalized. There was still some last-minute editing to be done. The only people who knew she'd accepted Red Rock's deal was her family. She hadn't even told her best friend yet, so how did Jeff find out?

"I didn't think it was a big deal," Sharla answered cautiously. "It wasn't a conflict of interest and I wrote it on my own time." Then, after a moment's thought, she asked what she really wanted to know: "How did you know I'd written a book?"

"Channel Four sent us a fax," Ray said. He almost sounded hurt, as if he were offended Sharla had kept this from him. He dramatically plunked the fax down on the table before her with the same fervor as those actors on cop shows who throw the evidence in front of the suspect and calmly advise them to confess their guilt.

"We also got calls from the other two local news affiliates," Jeff said. "And there's a small wire story on the AP that says you recently inked a deal with a publishing house."

"What?!" Sharla exclaimed. Marla hadn't said a word to her about there being any sort of press release.

"Is this true, Sharla? Are you publishing a book?" one of the other assistant editors asked.

"Well….yes, but I didn't want to say anything until I was sure the book was going to print."

"The AP says the book's already been released on the Internet."

The Internet! Sharla's mouth flew open. She hadn't agreed to anything being published online!

"This is news to me," she said earnestly.

"It's news to us too," Jeff said. "And that's the problem, Sharla. You work for the *Agape Gazette* as a reporter and yet we, your employer, were the last to know that you were about to be a published author. Apparently, your book's getting a lot of buzz and our competitors picked up on it before we did. How do you think that makes us look?"

Sharla was dumbfounded. She didn't know what to say.

"Those jerks from Channel Four have been calling to interview you for the last hour," Ray said. "We've been stalling them until we could talk to you, find out if this was true."

"That's not all," another editor said. "Somebody with TMZ.com, an online gossip magazine, called asking to speak to you, Sharla. Then in a teasing tone: "They want to know if you know Tyler Nicks personally.""

Sharla rolled her eyes.

"I have a feeling it's not going to stop there," Jeff sighed. "Now, Sharla, you're right. What you do on your own time is your business. But this book has become news, which makes it our business. We need to do some damage control and we need to do it right away. It's not gonna look good for this newspaper if we don't have some type of an exclusive on you in the paper ASAP. You work for us and we should have had this story before anybody else."

"But I didn't know it was going *be* a story!" Sharla threw up her hands in exasperation, then put them down again, realizing it wasn't going to do any good to be argumentative.

"You're right, Jeff," she finally said, her voice calm. "I should have told you sooner. I'm sorry. What do you want me to do?"

For the first time since she walked in, Jeff's face softened. He even managed to crack a little smile. "You want to make this up to me? Give us an exclusive."

Jeff turned to Ray. "Where's Carl?" Sharla assumed they meant Carl Wilcox, the features reporter.

"I think he's gone for the day," Ray said.

"Call him, get him in here," Jeff ordered. "Or better yet, if he's got his laptop, he can interview Sharla over the phone. I don't care, as long as we get a story in before tonight's deadline."

Sharla's heart fell down into her intestines. "You want Carl to interview me now?

"Of course!" Jeff said. He was looking at Sharla as if she were insane. "We need to get this out for tomorrow's paper. The TV stations already have it, we can't do anything about that. But what they don't have is an interview with the author and that's where we'll get the jump on 'em!"

With that, Jeff practically leaped out of his seat, a new spring in his step, as he bounded for his office. The minute he jumped up, the other editors followed suit, leaping from their chairs like flies alighting from around a dung heap.

"Nobody go to dinner, I'll order pizza!" Jeff yelled as he passed through the newsroom. "We've got an extra story we'll need to make room for tonight."

His announcement was met with some resentful sighs and murmurs from the copy desk.

"What about my livestock story?" Sharla cried out to no one.

"We're bumping it," Ray said, walking to his desk. "Carl's feature on you will go on the front page of the local section. Just write a quick blurb, no more than eight inches on the livestock story, and we'll move it somewhere in the back. But hurry. As soon as we get a hold of Carl, I want you to talk to him."

Sharla sat down at her desk, took out her notebook and began to write her livestock story. She did it all as if in a dream. Somewhere in her mind, she thought regretfully of little Bobbi Duncan waiting anxiously to see her name in print.

In the midst of the pandemonium, Mona, one of the older ladies on the copy desk, came up to Sharla and congratulated her on her book. Sharla thanked her suspiciously. Apart from the occasional 'hello,' Mona had never said much to her.

"I guess you won't be working here much longer," Mona chuckled. "Looks like you might have a bestseller."

Sharla swiveled around in her chair. "No! Really? You think?"

"Well," Mona shrugged. "I got to see an excerpt of your book online and I liked it. Then again, I'm a huge Tyler Nicks fan."

"Really?" Sharla said. "I didn't know you liked America's Next Big Star. Roxanne and I used to talk about it and I don't ever remember you saying anything."

"Oh, well…" Mona said, bending down to talk more confidentially. "It's kind of a closet thing with me. Some of my friends think it's lame, so I kinda keep it to myself."

"Oh," Sharla nodded. "A guilty pleasure."

"Yeah, you could say that."

There was an awkward silence as Mona continued to stand over Sharla. It was making her nervous.

"Well, I've got to talk to my publisher about this online thing," Sharla frowned, hoping to get rid of her newfound fan. "I didn't agree to my book being published on the Internet."

"I don't think it's the whole book," Mona said. "I think it's just some excerpts. If you didn't agree to online publication, somebody must have leaked it."

"Where did you see these excerpts?"

Mona looked around guiltily to make sure no one was listening. The way she was leaning into Sharla, anyone walking by would have thought the two were passing government secrets.

"Don't laugh," Mona said. "On the ANBS website. They have a message board."

"Are you serious?" Sharla's mouth flew open, something it seemed to be doing a lot of lately. The ANBS boards! Unbelievable. Had this not been happening to her, Sharla would have found the whole thing laughable. It was like the plot of some bad sitcom.

"Someone put my book on the ANBS boards?"

Mona shrugged noncommittally. "I guess."

Now she really did need to talk to Marla. Sharla began digging in her purse for her address book. She had Marla's cell phone number somewhere…. maybe she'd inputted it into her own cell phone, she couldn't remember. Where *was* her phone?

As she hunted for the number, Sharla felt hot breath over her neck. She looked up to see Mona still staring down at her.

"Did you need something else, Mona? I really need to make a call."

"I was just wondering," Mona said coyly. "*Do* you know Tyler Nicks?"

Sharla gave Mona an are-you-serious look. Mona didn't budge. Obviously, she was serious.

"No," Sharla finally said. "I don't know Tyler Nicks."

Mona's shoulders fell disappointedly. "Oh," she said flatly. "That's too bad."

"Yeah."

"Well, listen," Mona went on, clearing her throat. "If...and this is just IF you do happen to meet him, would you give him this for me?" She tried to hand Sharla her *Agape Gazette* business card, but Sharla was too busy looking at Mona as if she'd lost her mind to take it. Not at all phased, Mona simply sat the card in the space bar of Sharla's keyboard so that it stood at attention in front of her.

"You've got to be kidding," Sharla said.

"He's a real hottie," Mona reasoned. "You never know," she winked, and went back to her desk.

Sharla picked up the card and stared at it. What nerve! This woman, who was probably around the same age as Sharla's mother, had hardly said two words to her in the two years she'd worked there, yet now she was looking to Sharla to hook her up with Tyler?!

Take a number, girlfriend, Sharla thought, and tossed Mona's card in the trash can under her desk. Just then, Sharla's desk phone rang. She picked it up absently, still searching for her address book with her free hand. "Newsroom, Sharla Davis," she answered.

"Sharla, finally! Girl, I've been trying to get you for two hours! I called your house, I called your cell..." It was Roxanne. She was panting heavily into the receiver as if she'd just run 10 miles with wild dogs chasing her.

Sharla stopped digging in her purse and turned her attention to the breathless voice on the other end of the phone. "I had to work late. Roxy, what's wrong? You sound exhausted."

"Yeah, I figured you had to still be at work, that's why I called you up there," Roxanne said. "Sharla, girl, your book is all over the Internet!"

Sharla put a hand to her forehead and sighed. "Yeah, so I've heard." Then: "Wait. What do you mean 'all over?' Isn't it just on the ANBS boards?"

Roxanne laughed. "Sure. About two hours ago. Now it's on just about every Tyler website that has a forum and parts of it are up at Grey Brown."

Sharla sat bolt upright. There were scores of Tyler forums now. And the Grey Brown website, which derived the first word in it's title from an allusion to the color of Tyler's hair and the second word as a reference to Tyler's affinity for James Brown, was the most trafficked Soul Squad site of all. Originally started as a blog to track and discuss Tyler's progress on *America's Next Big Star*, it had become *the* place to obtain the latest and most accurate information on all things Tyler. Hoards of people flocked to it daily.

If Sharla's story had been posted there, it was no wonder the Associated Press and TMZ.com had picked up on it.

Sharla sank in her chair. "Oh my God," she moaned.

"Exactly!" Roxanne gushed. "Congratulations, honey, you must be so happy!" Then, in a more serious, chastising tone: "So, when were you going to tell your friends you'd published an e-book?"

I'm dreaming, Sharla thought wildly. *I'm dreaming and I'm having a nightmare.* She pinched herself. Hard.

Over at the night editor's station, Sharla overheard one assistant editor say to another that Channel 8 was calling to talk to her.

"Tell them 'no comment' and hang up," Ray stiffly replied.

"Sharla, you there?" Roxanne asked.

Sharla took the receiver away from her ear. She wondered briefly what would happen if she just let herself go and started screaming. When the urge passed after a few seconds, she put the phone back up to her ear.

"Roxanne," she said, "I didn't publish my book online."

There was dead silence for about 10 seconds. Then: "You didn't? But if you didn't, then how—"

"I got a publishing house to publish my book."

"You did? When?"

"A few days ago. Look, Roxy, it's a long story and I can't talk about it right now," Sharla said. "It looks like somebody leaked my book. All hell has broken loose here, I feel like I'm losing it, and I need to get a hold of my publisher and find out what's going on."

"Oh, I know what's going on," Roxanne said confidently. "You just said it yourself, all hell has broken loose. This is the enemy, Sharla. This is the work of Satan, honey. He's trying to stir you up, get you feeling afraid and confused."

"Well, he's doing a pretty good job right now."

No sooner than the words came out of her than Sharla wished she could stuff them back in. She knew what was coming next.

"Oh, DON'T YOU TALK LIKE THAT!" Roxanne yelled, almost blowing out Sharla's eardrum. "Have you forgotten who you are? Well, let me remind you. You are a child of the Most High God, daughter! You are MORE than a conqueror!" she thundered. "Don't you know that NO weapon formed against you shall be able to prosper? No! When the enemy comes in like a flood, the Lord shall raise up a standard against him…" her voice took on a preacher's cadence. "…You've gotta stand firm in the day of evil, honey, with the belt of truth buckled around your waist and with the breastplate of righteousness in place, halleLUjah!"

Out of the corner of her eye, Sharla could see Ray motioning to her from his desk. She put a hand over her phone and looked at him. Ray held up his phone and mouthed, "It's Carl!"

Sharla nodded and put up an index finger as if to say, 'Just a minute.' She put the phone back up to her ear. Roxy was on a roll.

"…gotta look the devil in the face and say, GET thee behind me, Satan!.."

"Roxy—"

"…for I KNOW my Redeemer lives and I'm covered in the blood! Oh! Hallelujah!…"

"Roxy—"

"…because greater is He that is in ME than he that is in this world…"

"Roxy, I—"

"…Lord, I ask that you re-BUKE the devourer for my friend's sake—"

"ROXY!" Sharla shouted.

Several heads in the newsroom turned in Sharla's direction.

"What?!" Roxanne answered, sounding highly annoyed.

"I have to go."

"But I'm trying to pray for you."

"I know, but my editors says there's a phone call for me and I have to take it."

"Alright," Roxanne replied reluctantly. "But just remember, I'm praying for you, honey. You're not alone."

"I know," Sharla smiled. "And I appreciate it."

"Okay, I'm a prayer warrior, you know that," Roxanne admonished. "You can beat this. Remember, you have the victory, you can do all things through Christ who strengthens you. I don't want to hear no more defeatist talk."

"You're right, I know, I know," Sharla said. "I gotta go."

"Okay, call me tomorrow."

"I will."

The two exchanged goodbyes and hung up. After taking a moment to collect herself, Sharla signaled for Ray to transfer Carl to her. Her phone rang almost instantly. Sharla exhaled and picked up the receiver.

Chapter 17: Strange Days Indeed

It was nearly midnight when Sharla finished her interview with Carl and spoke to a few local media outlets.

Jeff insisted she answer all the media's questions as vaguely as possible until Carl's story had gone to press, which turned out to be easy. The news stations were mainly interested in how Sharla's book got leaked and how it had grown so popular so quickly online, both questions for which she did not have an answer.

After reading a proof of Carl's feature to check for accuracy, Sharla checked her company e-mails. She found a message from Mona. The subject line read, "Pass This On." Her curiosity got the best of her and Sharla clicked on the message. Upon opening it, she saw a picture of Mona in a belly-dancing outfit. Underneath the photo was a caption: "Please Give This to Tyler."

Sharla deleted the message and logged out for the night never to return, though at the time, she didn't know it.

The power of the Internet and Tyler's popularity had made Sharla's book one of the hottest online topics, and she quickly became one of the most Googled women on the planet. After her story broke in the paper over the weekend, the floodgates flew open.

Sharla awoke to discover she had over 1,000 e-mails, most of them penned by Soul Squad members from all over the country.

She walked out of her apartment to get her mail and walked into a war zone. There were people standing around she'd never seen before thrusting printed excerpts of her book and a pen in her face, asking for autographs. Several news vans were parked out on the curb and at the sight of Sharla, a few reporters—writing pads in hand—jumped out like clowns out of little novelty cars at the circus and stampeded towards her. Flashbulbs started popping in Sharla's face and she had to quickly run back inside and lock the door.

By mid-week more than 100 self-professed Nicks Chicks (some from right around the corner and some from as far away as Canada) had already made a trek to Sharla's apartment just to meet her, and more importantly, find out if she'd gotten her analysis of Tyler straight from the singer's mouth.

With news hounds and onlookers camped outside her door, Sharla realized she was going to need some time to sort out the bizarre situation in which she suddenly found herself. She had some sick days reserved at work and decided to use them. Meanwhile, Sharla's parents were calling every hour on the hour to make sure she hadn't been shot or kidnapped.

"Do you need me to come over there?" Sharla's dad offered.

"No," Sharla said. "My landlord's already called the police and they're patrolling the grounds. He wasn't too happy about all the attention at first but I think he made a deal with one of the Channel 8 camera guys that they could shoot footage of the apartments as long as they made sure to get the place's sign in every shot."

"Free publicity," Richard said with disdain. "Oh, he sounds like a real gentleman."

"Honey, the story they did on you in the paper was nice," Ida commented. She had been listening on the other extension. "But that picture they used of you was terrible. You look like you just got out of prison."

"It was my work I.D. badge," Sharla said. "I was having a bad hair day that day."

"Couldn't they have used something else?"

"Well, mom, I didn't have my Glamour Shots picture with me and they needed something right then," Sharla explained. "If I'd known I was going to a photo shoot instead of my job, believe me, I would have brought a better picture. As it is, I wish they hadn't printed anything, period." She peeked outside her window at the crowd of people still milling around.

"I feel like a freak, holed up in my apartment like this."

In the midst of all the chaos, Sharla was finally able to get in touch with Marla, who regretfully admitted that the book leak was an inside job. A college intern at Red Rock, who happened to be a big Tyler Nicks fan, leaked the excerpts to several online Tyler fansites. Marla apologized profusely and assured Sharla the situation was being handled. The intern had been fired and Sharla was promised that Red Rock Publishing's attorneys were in the process of drawing up 'cease and desist' orders, which would be sent to any website found displaying excerpts from her book without permission.

"The bright side of all of this," Marla said, "Is that this leak is actually going to help sales of your book. We couldn't have asked for better publicity!"

Sharla had a hard time seeing it that way but Marla was right. By the time *Chasing Trevor* came out in stores several weeks later, Sharla Davis was already a household name...at least among followers of Tyler Nicks and *America's Next Big Star*, which Sharla quickly assuaged was a fairly large number.

After a mere three weeks in bookstores, *Chasing Trevor* sold 300,000 copies and shot to the top of the *New York Times* Bestsellers List. Sharla was suddenly sought after by everyone. Her phone began ringing off the hook, and it wasn't merely calls from local news affiliates. There were calls from NBC, CBS, CNN, RAM and ABC, all asking for interviews. The voice mailbox on her cell phone became overloaded with messages, and Sharla eventually had to change both her home and cell phone numbers.

As for her job, Sharla had initially asked for a leave of absence. But when it became apparent that *Chasing Trevor* was a runaway hit, Sharla realized she would have to leave the newspaper. Disguising herself in a frilly blonde wig, large-framed sunglasses and an oversized floppy hat, Sharla managed to climb out the back window of her apartment while some neighbors distracted the media so she could see Jeff to personally announce her resignation.

"You look like a blonde Jackie O.," Jeff laughed when Sharla walked into his office wearing her garb.

"I wish I could say I didn't see this coming," he chuckled, referring to her resignation. "But I'm proud of you, Sharla. You've done what most writers only dream about. Go. Enjoy your success. The *Agape Gazette* wishes you the best."

"You know," Sharla reasoned. "There's always the possibility this book was a fluke."

"Are you serious?" Jeff asked. "I think that blonde wig's gone to your head."

But Sharla told Jeff she wasn't taking anything for granted, not even her success. When all the hoopla died down, she said, she might be back, but Jeff wouldn't hear it; he had better foresight.

While Sharla was sneaking around in disguises questioning her career, Marla was seizing the moment. She helped Sharla find a good agent, who scheduled her for a whirlwind booksigning tour and press junket that included appearing on several major talk shows including *Oprah, The View, Live with Regis and Kelly, Larry King Live* and, in an ironic twist, Dr. Carl's night time talk show, *Up Late with Dr. Carl.*

Sharla and everyone close to her was stunned by the momentum of her success. The situation became a testament to the real friends in her life. Her closest girlfriends, Lindsey, Diane and Roxanne, all remained supportive. But other people Sharla had known for years suddenly started treating her differently, as if she were some oddity they no longer knew how to react to. Her extended family, many of whom she hadn't had close contact with in years, began calling her 'just to talk,' which usually led to them asking her how much money she'd made and could she lend a few dollars until payday; or possibly help out cousin so-and-so who was trying to get a treatment of his movie read by Spielberg?

But the most stinging jolt was the isolation she suddenly felt from people at church. Pastor Mike continued to be warm and caring, and he never stopped treating her like he always had—no better and no less than anyone else. And while being a bestselling novelist had seemed to help her become more attractive to the men in the church, a few of the ladies, especially her fellow choir members, began treating Sharla coldly. They still smiled and acted polite towards her, but the camaraderie she'd shared with many of them seemed to have vanished and she wasn't sure why.

Sharla also noticed that the married women seemed to hold on to their husbands just a tad tighter than they used to when she came around. Conversations suddenly became shorter, curt. To Sharla, it didn't make sense. Aside from the fact that she'd lost some weight and gotten herself a facial, she was still the same person she'd been before she'd published a book.

One Sunday after church, Sharla happened to be passing by on her way to the restroom when she overheard a group of women in the choir saying that it just wasn't right, someone like her having so much success.

"You see her strutting around in her new clothes like she's so cute," one woman mocked. "Trying to show off, I guess, because she wrote a book. Big deal. *I* could write a book!"

There were murmurs of approval.

"...all the men just watching her with their eyes bugged out. I told my husband, 'don't you look at that Jezebel.' She ought to be ashamed. Coming into the house of God looking like a painted up tramp."

"She didn't even write a Christian book!" another woman replied acidly. "I guess it just goes to show how some people who only show up to church on Sunday seem to prosper while others, who are here every time the doors are open, have to suffer on in faith," to which the others in the group nodded their heads and mumbled 'amen' and 'I know that's right,' under their breath.

Tears welled in Sharla's eyes. A painted up tramp? She didn't wear any more make-up than she'd always worn. How could they say that about her? Up until a few months ago, those women had treated her like their friend. How dare they judge her? They didn't know anything about her! They didn't know the nights she'd sat up crying and praying for revelation, for God to give her a breakthrough, for God to heal her broken heart. They didn't have a clue of how the Lord Himself had given her the unction to write. They knew nothing of her relationship with Him and it was obvious none of them had read one word of her book for if they had, they would have known that her female protagonist was a Christian, and quite a vocal one at that.

And what was wrong with the way she dressed? It wasn't like she was coming to church wearing micro-skirts and low-cut blouses. Wasn't she entitled to a few new outfits? Wasn't she worthy of being blessed?

"Sharla, you can't pay any attention to those women," Veena, Pastor Mike's wife told her. She'd noticed Sharla coming out of the bathroom, dabbing at her wet eyes with a tissue. After some coaxing, she'd gotten Sharla to tell her what she'd overheard.

"They're jealous of you 'cause you're looking good and you're a threat to them."

"A threat?" Sharla laughed bitterly. "Me?"

"Yes," Veena said. "Because you're walking in prosperity."

Sharla frowned.

"Look," Veena continued, her petite, regal frame sitting squarely in the middle of the sanctuary pew as she and Sharla talked. "When you were down on yourself and overweight and you had about as much going for you as they did, they could afford to like you. Why not? You were all in the same boat. But the minute you get out of the boat and begin to put your faith and your feet to the pavement, I promise you, you will have opposition. Jesus had it. His own followers turned against Him. The very people He came to save crucified Him."

Sharla was quiet. She was taking in what Veena was saying.

"I know it's hard but you should feel sorry for those women," Veena said, extending her arm in the direction of the lobby where Sharla's critics had stood moments earlier. "Pray for them. They're whitewashed tombs. And until they change their hearts, they will never see any more of God than what they come to church for because they don't expect to."

"And you…" she said, gently poking Sharla's shoulder. "You're going to have to get used to people saying things against you because God's got so much more in store for you, I can see that. That's not to say it won't hurt when people talk, I know. When Mike first started out preaching, we had some awful things said about us by people who didn't want to see our ministry prosper, but we endured and we made it by the grace of God. Now those same people…." She waved her hand around to illustrate the huge sanctuary they sat in…."Want to try to take credit for what God has built."

Veena took Sharla's hands and looked at her.

"Daughter, you've got to remember who you are in Christ and that He knows your heart. When you decide to walk with God on a higher level, it can be lonely. But it's worth it because when God blesses you, nobody can *un*bless you!"

Sharla hugged Veena and thanked her. She knew everything she'd said had come directly from God. From then on, she no longer cared what the other church ladies thought of her. There wasn't time. Once she began her book tour, Sharla had to take to having her own private sessions with the Lord. Of course, she'd known the overall response from the Soul Squad regarding *Chasing Trevor* was positive. But what Sharla didn't expect was how much the critics seemed to enjoy the book.

The *New York Times* called it "Gutwrenching. A must-read for the postmodern single woman of the 21st century."

There were other favorable reviews, all of which Sharla kept in a scrapbook:

"You won't be able to put it down." –*USA Today*

"You've heard of the feel-good movie. This is the feel-good book of the year." –National Book Review.

One critic called it "an instant literary classic," while another deemed it "a masterpiece of feminine ingenuity."

"Thoroughly moving and thought-provoking," said *Time* magazine. "A clever read."

"Davis is a new author with promise," the *London Standard* raved. "Trevor Reams is the new archetypal every man."

But the review that really cracked Sharla up was one written by an Oxford literary critic which stated that *Chasing Trevor* was "a smooth read that like William Mann's review of the Beatles' "Not a Second Time," embodied a word structure that was of an Aeolian cadence tinged with pandiatonic clusters."

Sharla had no idea what it meant, but she liked it.

Still, in the midst of all her success, Sharla had yet to hear from the one person for whom the book had been her inspiration. She was anxious to know what Tyler thought about the story, but neither he nor anyone from his camp had even so much as sent her an e-mail.

Did he like the book? Did he find it funny or offensive? There'd been no talk about his personal feelings on the subject in any web forum. The book had been on the bestseller list for going on two months. Surely, he'd heard about it by now. Someone had to have told him about it, at the very least.

When Sharla was asked in interviews if she'd heard from Tyler or what he thought, all she could do was shrug her shoulders and say, "No" and "I don't know,' which was the most daunting thing of all. In spite of everything, not even being a bestselling author could quell the feelings Sharla still had for Tyler. She still thought about him, still cared about him. He remained in the forefront of her every thought. All the success and the perks that were coming with it would have paled in comparison to hearing what he had to say.

If Tyler didn't like the book, then it didn't matter how much the critics raved about it. After all, if not for Tyler, there would have been no Trevor Reams. The fact that he was remaining silent began to concern Sharla.

Paranoia started to creep in. She began to think that perhaps his lack of comment on the book was his way of silently voicing his displeasure with it. Sharla wondered if she should try to get in touch with him but then thought better of it.

Instead, she turned to God.

"Lord, I don't care what Tyler's response is," Sharla prayed. "I just want to hear from him. Even if he says he hates the book, at least I'll know he read it."

Several weeks later, Sharla got her answer.

Chapter 18: Flower Power

●————————————————————————————————●

L indsey, Sharla and Roxanne were having lunch on the patio of Sharla's new condo—one of the few luxuries Sharla had allowed herself since her book's release— when the doorbell rang.

Sharla was busy bringing some homemade quesadillas to the table so Roxanne offered to answer the door.

She returned a few minutes later carrying a large, ornate glass vase with an arrangement of yellow and red roses so huge, they covered Roxanne's face, forcing her to poke her head out to the side to see where she was going.

"Hey, I need some help here!" she cried out.

Sharla and Lindsey turned around, saw the flowers and quickly rushed over to help Roxanne, with each woman grabbing a corner of the vase and sitting it down on the kitchen counter.

"Geez, that vase didn't look that heavy when I took it from the delivery guy," Roxanne said, sitting down with a sigh.

"Wow!" Lindsey remarked, then whistled. "Who are these from?"

"I don't know," Sharla said, gently easing her nose into the bouquet. A sweet floral aroma immediately began to fill the room.

"Is there a card?" Roxanne asked.

"Let's see." Sharla began turning the vase clockwise. After a few turns, she found among the flowers a white envelope with the words *"CONGRATULATIONS"* written in fancy silver calligraphy on the front. She plucked the envelope from its small, transparent perch and opened it.

Sharla's eyes had only briefly scanned the card's contents when she let out a startled yelp and put a hand to her mouth.

"What? Who's it from?" Lindsey asked, half amused, half concerned.

Sharla dropped the card and let it flutter to the floor, where Lindsey grabbed it and picked it up. She read it aloud:

> *Dear Sharla,*
> *Congratulations on your book.*
> *I just finished reading it and thought it was*
> *sweet and funny. If imitation is the sincerest*
> *form of flattery, than I must say, I'm flattered.*
> *Your friend,*
> *Tyler Nicks*

Lindsey's eyes grew huge as she read Tyler's name.

Roxanne gasped and let out an involuntary scream. "Tyler Nicks?! Oh my God, Sharla!" She got up and went to hug Sharla, who was paralyzed with shock.

"Well, Sharla," Lindsey surmised, her hands on her hips and a huge smile on her face. "You have officially arrived."

Roxanne snatched the card from Lindsey excitedly. "Lemme see that."

As Roxanne studied the card, Lindsey put a hand on Sharla's shoulder and squeezed gently. "Tyler liked your book," she said softly.

Sharla heard but could only nod. She was still too surprised to talk.

"Well, aren't you gonna say anything? This is great news!" Lindsey said.

"I-I…don't know what to say," Sharla stammered, gazing at the flowers as if she'd never seen flowers before. "I can't believe he responded. I'd kind of given up that I'd ever hear from him."

"He's probably been busy," Lindsey reasoned. She reached out to gently bring a rose to her nose and sniff. "I figured you'd hear from him eventually."

"I'm just glad he said he liked the book." Sharla sat down at the kitchen table with Roxanne. "He did say he liked it, right? I can't remember."

"Actually, what he said was that he thought it was sweet and funny and he's flattered," Roxanne corrected, her eyes skimming the card.

"And he called you his friend," Lindsey added, raising her eyebrows on the word 'friend.'

Sharla smiled but consciously tried not to make it too huge. Inside, though, she was doing cartwheels. She wanted to be Tyler's friend very much.

Putting her hand over her heart, Sharla leaned back in her chair and squeezed her eyes shut dramatically. "Oh, thank God," she exclaimed. "I was afraid he hated the book."

"You need to stop being so paranoid," said Lindsey.

"Why would he hate it?" Roxanne chimed in.

"I dunno," Sharla sighed. "It's like Lin said, I'm paranoid."

"Well, he didn't hate it," Lindsey said, "And there's the proof." She pointed to the flowers.

"They are gorgeous, aren't they?" Sharla asked, beaming. "That was sweet of him to send flowers. Then with a huge, heartfelt sigh: "Then again, Tyler's a sweet guy."

Roxanne and Lindsey exchanged knowing looks; Sharla caught it.

"What?" she asked.

Neither Roxanne nor Lindsey volunteered to speak.

"No, really," Sharla pressed. "What? Why are you two looking at each other like that?"

"No reason," Roxanne said, trying not to smile. "You're just...so cute when you go on about Tyler."

"Yeah, you're like a lovesick teenager," Lindsey agreed, smirking.

"Oh, please," Sharla rolled her eyes. Her face was turning a bright shade of red.

"No, but it's really sweet," Roxanne assured her, patting her hand. "We're not laughing at you, we just think it's nice to see you so happy."

"Exactly, it's a good thing," Lindsey replied. "Don't mind us, we're just jealous, aren't we Roxanne, 'cuz we don't have anybody to gush about?"

Roxanne frowned and waved Lindsey off. "Please, girl, speak for yourself."

"Oh, yeah?" Lindsey countered. "Well, I don't see you getting any flowers from anybody lately."

"Honey, I can get flowers anytime I want."

"From who?"

Roxanne paused, looked first at Lindsey then at Sharla and said: "From the funeral home down the street from my house. The funeral director likes me. He said he'd give me a discount."

The three of them busted out laughing.

"No, thanks," Lindsey howled. "I don't need flowers that bad!"

"Hey, let me see the card, Roxanne," Sharla asked, holding out her hand. She read it again, slowly, then began turning it over and over in her palm.

"What are you doing?" Lindsey finally asked.

Sharla stopped playing with the card and placed it on the table. "There's no return address or a phone number," she said disappointedly. She looked hopefully at Roxanne. "Hey, Roxy, did the delivery guy give you anything else, like an invoice to sign, anything?"

Roxanne thought for a moment. "Yeah, he had me sign some form on a clipboard, but I didn't pay any attention to it and he didn't give me a copy."

Sharla must have looked upset because Roxanne reached a hand out across the table to her. "Sharla, I am so sorry. I didn't think about asking him for a copy of the invoice."

"That's okay," Sharla mustered a smile. "It probably didn't have anything on it anyway."

"You can always call the shop the flowers came from and ask them," Lindsey said.

"Yeah, I suppose I could." She picked up the card again and studied it. "It doesn't even have the shop's name on it."

She tossed the card back on the table. "Those flowers could have come from anywhere."

Sharla looked hopefully at Roxanne once more. "Roxanne, please tell me you saw the logo on the delivery van."

Roxanne shook her head slowly. "No, I didn't."

Both Lindsey and Sharla sighed.

"Look, you two, I'm just not as observant when it comes to that type of stuff," Roxanne whined. "I'm not a reporter like you, Sharla, I'm an accountant. I pay attention to numbers."

"The delivery guy must not have been very cute then, because you definitely would have remembered that," Lindsey joked.

"Fine," Roxanne said, crossing her arms over her chest. "From now on, you answer the door!"

"It doesn't matter," Sharla said, waving a hand in the air.

There was a moment of silence before Sharla spoke again.

"Well," she sighed, "At least he liked the book."

"At least?" Lindsey teased. "This is great!" She put an arm around Sharla. "Tyler liked your book!" Then with a wink: "Now you can sleep at night."

Sharla chuckled. "Yeah."

"Hey!" Roxanne exclaimed, pointing at Sharla. "You know, you could get the phone book and call all the flower shops. I'm sure he had to have ordered these locally," she said, gesturing toward the arrangement.

"Oh yeah, that's a great idea," Lindsey said sarcastically. "There's only about 100 or so floral shops in Agape."

Roxanne sat back, deflated. "Oh, I forgot about that."

"BUT," Lindsey added. "You're kind of a celebrity now yourself, Sharla. Maybe you could have your people..." she used the first two fingers on each hand to signify quotation marks on the word *people*.... "do some research for you. I'm sure if someone does a little digging, it wouldn't be too hard to find out where he got the flowers from. And how he got your new address."

Roxanne and Sharla looked at each other.

"Come to think of it," Sharla mused, "How *did* Tyler get my new address? I just moved in last week. Half the house is still in boxes."

"He's got....*people*," Lindsey replied, using the quotations gesture again. "Once you become famous, you can get access to almost any kind of information. It comes with the territory. It's like, part of a celebrity's job description."

"You say that as if you speak from experience," Sharla smirked.

Lindsey smiled and shrugged confidently. "Hey, I watch *Extra*!"

"So, that means Tyler had to go to some trouble to find you," Roxanne giggled, nudging Sharla in her side. "You're right, Sharla, he is sweet. And kind of romantic."

"Either that or he's a stalker," Lindsey said, giving the roses another sniff.

"I highly doubt that," Sharla said, getting up to go to the refrigerator. "He's probably the one *being* stalked, I'm sure." She took out a pitcher of lemonade and walked back to the counter with it. "And as for romance," she continued. "He sent me some 'thank you' flowers, that's all. Let's not read any more into it."

"Sharla, you're not fooling anybody, you know," Roxanne said. "You want that man!"

"Roxy!" Sharla gasped, embarrassed. "Sure, I wouldn't mind if it turned romantic but I'm not going to blow the fact that he sent me flowers all out of proportion. The guy didn't even leave a phone number so what does that say?"

"I dunno," Roxanne shrugged. "That he's a forgetful romantic?"

Both Lindsey and Sharla laughed.

"You're crazy, Roxanne," Sharla chuckled.

"Yeah, crazy and hungry!" Roxanne rose from her seat. "Let's get to those quesadillas."

"Amen!" Lindsey agreed, following Roxanne out to the patio. Sharla stopped her for a moment.

"Have you said anything to Roxanne?" she whispered.

Lindsey looked confused. "Said anything about what?"

"Tyler. You know, what I told you?"

Recognition dawned on Lindsey's face. "No, you know I wouldn't do that. I promised I wouldn't and I haven't."

"She seems to know," Sharla said. Both women looked briefly at Roxanne, who had just stepped onto the patio and was digging in her purse.

"You guys seen my cell phone?" Roxanne called from outside. "I want to call Diane. She is gonna freak when she hears about this. Of all the times for her to be out of town!" Then: "Oh, nevermind, I got it."

"Sharla, you don't hide your feelings for Tyler very well," Lindsey went on. "Anybody with eyes can see you're crazy about him."

"Okay," Sharla sighed. "Just as long as you haven't said anything."

"Not a word." Lindsey held up her right hand. "Scout's Honor. And I certainly haven't told anyone you think Tyler's your husband."

"Do you still have doubt?" Sharla asked, gesturing at the flowers. "Even now?"

Lindsey looked briefly at the floral arrangement then back at Sharla. She put her hands on Sharla's shoulders and looked her squarely in the face.

"Sharla," she said soberly. "They're flowers, not an engagement ring. Let's just say….the jury's still out," she smiled and went to join Roxanne.

Sharla stood in the middle of her spacious new kitchen, speechless.

"Sharla! You coming?" Roxanne yelled from the patio.

"In a minute." Sharla stepped over to the kitchen counter and grabbed the cordless phone. "I'm just gonna call my parents and let them know I heard from Tyler. They'll be tickled."

"Bring the phone out on the patio. I want to hear their reaction."

"I'll be there in just a minute."

"Well, don't be too long." Roxanne motioned to the flowers. "Oh! And be sure to get your camera and take some pictures of this arrangement so when the flowers die, you'll still have the memory of them."

Roxanne closed the patio door behind her and disappeared out onto the deck, leaving Sharla alone with her new, beautiful floral arrangement.

I won't need a camera, she thought. *I couldn't forget this day if I tried. Thank you, God, for answered prayer.*

At least one answered prayer, anyway. The promise was still pending, but...

Sharla smiled to herself and touched one of the roses with the tip of her finger.

...this was a good start. Even if the jury was still out.

Chapter 19: Say It Isn't So

———————————————————•———————————————————

"Hey, maybe after Christmas, we should all take a vacation. Just us girls."

Sharla made the suggestion to Lindsey as she stood in her kitchen mixing peach smoothies in a blender. The book blitz had died down, although Sharla had committed herself to write another two books for Red Rock Publishing within the next two years. But for now, she was done promoting *Chasing Trevor*, and savoring the break.

She and Lindsey had been milling around Sharla's new home of three months for the better part of the evening, gearing up to watch *America's Next Big Star*, which was already well into it's fourth season. Sharla still wasn't too sold on the show. She'd mainly watched it last year because of Tyler, but Lindsey enjoyed it, so Sharla didn't mind seeing who's head was on the chopping block this year.

"I think maybe around the latter part of January or early February," Sharla yelled over the hum of the blender. "You think you could get time off then?"

"Probably," Lindsey yelled back. As a pharmaceutical rep, Lindsey basically set her own hours. "Where would we go?"

"I was thinking about maybe New Mexico or Colorado," Sharla replied. She turned off the blender and resumed a normal speaking tone. "Some place where we could go skiing. I've never been skiing."

"Yeah, but Diane hates the cold," Lindsey shook her head. "She probably wouldn't go for it."

"I dunno," Sharla shrugged, getting two glasses out of the cabinet. "It might be fun. Diane's such a stickler about always doing the same old stuff. We need to try to get her out of her comfort zone."

"Speaking of getting out of comfort zones," Lindsey smiled. "Have you gotten in touch with Tyler yet?"

Sharla frowned. "If you mean did I try to investigate where the flowers came from, no. I thought about it but…it just didn't feel right."

"But what about calling him?" Lindsey pressed. "Couldn't your friend, Marla, get his number? She knows a lot of big name people."

"Yeah, but what would I say if I did call him?" Sharla grimaced.

"How about 'hi, I'm Sharla, I'm madly in love with you and you and I are supposed to get married. What are you doing Saturday?'"

Sharla chuckled. "Just like that, huh?"

"Yeah, just like that."

"With come-on lines like that, I see now why you're still single," Sharla teased. Lindsey rolled her eyes.

"Call me old-fashioned," Sharla said. "But I still like it when the guy makes the first move. And you know, I figured the reason this book took off the way it did was because that was how God wanted me to meet Tyler. So, after the book came out, I kept expecting to hear from him or maybe run into him at a dinner party or something but it hasn't happened yet."

She shrugged. "I don't know what God's up to."

"Maybe He's waiting for you to do something," Lindsey offered.

"But if I get in touch with Tyler myself, how would I ever know it was really God and not just me doing something in my own power?"

Lindsey was silent. She didn't have an answer.

"What about Jamaica?" she suggested, changing the subject.

"For what?" Sharla asked.

"For our just-us-girls vacation," Lindsey said. "I betcha nobody'd complain about going there."

Sharla stopped in her tracks and thought a moment. "Yeah, Jamaica might be nice."

Lindsey got up from the kitchen table and headed for the living room. "It's almost time for the show," she said, looking at her watch. "I'm gonna turn on the TV."

"Okay," Sharla said absently.

"Hmmm," she mused aloud. "Jamaica sounds like a great idea," she called out from the kitchen as she poured the smoothies. "The four of us could go on a cruise. Maybe do the Caribbean, see all the different islands. Let's run it by Roxy and Diane tomorrow. I am dying for a vacation!"

"Uh, Sharla…"

"But if we go there," Sharla continued excitedly, not paying attention, "Then we should go, say, in March. That should give everybody plenty of time to ask for time off, and the weather would be good…"

"Sharla!" Lindsey interrupted. "You better get in here, NOW!"

Lindsey's voice sounded urgent, strained.

Sharla picked up the smoothies and trotted into the living room. Lindsey was standing in front of the television set looking pensive.

"What's wrong with you?" Sharla asked, handing Lindsey a glass.

Lindsey took the glass and immediately set it down on the coffee table without taking a sip.

"What's wrong?" Sharla repeated, growing concerned.

"There's something on the news…" Lindsey said, pointing towards the set. "About Tyler."

"What?" Sharla managed after a second. It felt as if all the air had left her body.

On television, a newscaster for *Entertainment This Evening*, a popular entertainment news program, was in the middle of saying Tyler's name. In the upper right corner next to the newscaster's head was a smiling photo of Tyler. Under the photo were the words: BREAKING NEWS in large, capital letters.

"….stunning news is making headlines around the country tonight," the newscaster was saying. "And nowhere has the shocking revelation of Tyler Nicks' marriage been more resonant than in the music industry—"

Sharla let out an involuntary scream as she stared at the television. She couldn't believe what she'd just heard. Did he say MARRIAGE?

Lindsey grabbed the remote control and turned up the volume. She took a seat on the couch while Sharla remained standing.

"*Entertainment This Evening* was the first to break the story this afternoon that America's Next Big Star winner Tyler Nicks recently married Venice Dupree, an up and coming young starlet…."

A picture of a very pretty, young blonde flashed across the screen.

"….Dupree is the daughter of record mogul, Lawrence Dupree," the newscaster said as other photos of the smiling young woman were displayed. "Nicks recently signed a mult-million dollar deal with Dupree's record label, Saturn Records. Dupree's career as a Grammy-winning producer spans 40 years and includes collaborations with artists such as Aretha Franklin, Tyrone Davis, Otis Redding, Lionel Richie, and Usher."

"He married the daughter of his boss's record label?" Sharla asked incredulously. She shook her head in disbelief. "That just doesn't sound like Tyler."

"Hey," Lindsey said. "It happens. Didn't you once tell me one of the Jackson 5 married the daughter of the president of Motown, er, what's-his-name…."

"Barry Gordy," Sharla said absently. "Jermaine Jackson married Barry Gordy's daughter."

Old photos of Lawrence Dupree with famous R&B singers was being shown on TV.

"Well, there you go," Lindsey shrugged, pointing at the television. "This is one of those deals."

Sharla still couldn't believe it. The girl was beautiful, though. And thin. And young.

Damn her, Sharla thought.

"It's being reported that Nicks and Dupree wed in a secret ceremony in Las Vegas about two weeks ago. The two are rumored to still be on their honeymoon in an undisclosed location. Neither of the couple's publicists have been able to be reached for comment."

Anger from a place she knew not where began to rise up in Sharla. She began to pace furiously, clenching and unclenching her fists.

This made absolutely no sense! She checked into the Tyler forums every day and she'd heard nothing, *nothing* about him getting married. Not even a flicker of a rumor about it. Tyler's every move had always been tracked so meticulously. The people that ran those sites knew when he so much as sneezed! How could they have missed this?

Lindsey turned around to see Sharla pacing behind her. "Would you stop that and come sit down? You're gonna wear a groove in the carpet."

Lindsey changed the channel only to find a reporter for a local news affiliate who, armed with a photo of Tyler's new bride, was interviewing people on the street to get reactions about the singer's surprise marriage.

Most of the men didn't care.

"I don't know who Tyler Nicks is," one elderly man commented after viewing Venice's photo. "But his wife sure is a looker."

"He's a lucky man," another male said. "I need to get me a record deal."

There were a few bystanders who said they wished Tyler the best.

"You know, if he's happy, I'm happy," said one chubby older woman with horn-rimmed specs. "He seems like he's a good boy. I wish he'd married my daughter."

One couple agreed it was good he'd finally settled down. But the single women told a different story.

"I'm devastated, just devastated," a young woman who looked to be in her mid-20s said. "It's just such a shock."

Another young girl who looked to be about 15 was standing outside the local Tower Records next to a picture of Tyler in the window. She was holding a homemade sign that said **Say it Ain't So, Tyler** and crying profusely.

"I can't believe he did this!" she sobbed. "It's like.....the end of an era or something."

"Are you upset that it's not you?" the reporter asked.

"Well, yeah, of course," the girl sniffed. "Sure I would have liked to have been the one. I mean, what's this Venice got that I don't got?"

Cut back to the reporter in the studio. "I'm told a group of 'Nicks Chicks', as the singer's female fans call themselves, will hold a candlelight vigil at Ferris Park later tonight, where fans can gather to mourn the passing of Nicks' eligibility as a bachelor."

Sharla gasped. "Ferris Park? That was right around the corner from where she used to live!

Cut to the serious face of a redheaded woman in her 40s as the reporter's voice- over said, "Darla Thornberg is the president of the Texas chapter of the Tyler Nicks Fan Club based here in Agape."

"You know, for many women, Tyler Nicks has been the epitome of the perfect man," Thornberg said in a soft-spoken, clipped tone. "And so, although we his fans are happy to see that he's found true love, there are many women who are hurting about this and it's very serious to them. So, I wanted to have some type of gathering where those who need to can vent their frustration. Tyler's now officially off the market, I know it'll be hard for some women to accept that. We're also looking into starting a Tyler Nicks support group."

"Good Lord!" Lindsey exclaimed.

Information about the vigil came on the screen. Lindsey flipped to other channels. The story seemed to be on every station. CNN was doing a brief segment on how the news of Tyler's marriage was affecting different parts of the country. Clips of women collapsing, screaming and crying hysterically seemed to be the norm in nearly every city in America. Bookings at counselors' and psychiatrists' offices were said to be through the roof. Sharla had never seen anything like it, although she'd heard women reacted in a similar fashion after hearing of Paul McCartney's first marriage in the late '60's.

After watching a few seconds of a clip on a woman who refused to eat until Tyler married *her*, Sharla had had enough.

"Turn it off," she said exhaustedly. "I can't watch anymore."

Lindsey pushed a button on the remote and the television went dark. She and Sharla sat for a few moments in silence. Finally, Sharla took a deep breath and put her head in her hands.

"Wow," Lindsey whispered.

"Yeah, wow," Sharla echoed, her voice muffled in her hands.

"And they're gonna hold a vigil here, like somebody's died," Lindsey continued. "That's...that's just....odd."

"Yep," Sharla said dryly. Her head was still buried. She thought a vigil was appropriate, in a way. This was the death of something—the death of her hope.

She squeezed her eyes shut. *I guess I didn't hear God after all.*

That thought brought the tears. They came suddenly, as a flood overtakes a dam.

She hadn't wanted to cry in front of Lindsey, not in front of anyone. But now she'd started, she couldn't stop. All she could do was hide her face as deep into her cupped hands as they would allow her. Pain, deep and penetrating, enveloped her. Humiliation, embarrassment, anger, shock, they all ganged up on her.

Sharla never felt so empty in her life.

Lindsey was a little surprised to see Sharla so upset. She'd heard Sharla say she loved Tyler, but not until she looked at Sharla's shaking shoulders as she cried into her hands, slumping further and further into the sofa as if to make herself small, did Lindsey see how much Tyler really meant to Sharla. The revelation broke her heart.

Without a word, Lindsey took Sharla in her arms and hugged her. Sharla's sobs wracked her entire body as she shook uncontrollably with disappointment and shock.

"I'm s-s-sorry," Sharla cried, holding onto her friend.

"*Sshhh*," Lindsey soothed. "You don't have to apologize to me. I'm your friend. Just let it out."

There were no more words for a while. Sharla simply cried on Lindsey's shoulder until she didn't seem to have any tears left. When the flood had subsided, the two stopped hugging. Sharla leaned back on the couch, wasted and limp.

"You know what?" Lindsey said softly. "Tyler Nicks is a fool."

Sharla looked at her friend quizzically. "What do you mean?"

"I know you love the guy," Lindsey said, "But I read your book and yes, it's funny, but you poured your heart out for Tyler in it. If he couldn't see how you felt about him, then he's a fool. And you just need to tell yourself that, okay?"

"Yeah, maybe," Sharla managed a frail smile. "You're sweet."

"I didn't say it to be sweet." Lindsey's eyes were full of sympathy and hurt for Sharla. "I mean it. He's a fool."

Sharla sighed. "This…this just doesn't make sense! I don't understand what happened."

"Do you want me to stay over?" Lindsey offered. "We can have a little slumber party. You know, drink hot cocoa and talk."

"You have to work tomorrow," Sharla said, sitting up some. "But thanks for the offer."

"I have a few sick days I haven't used," Lindsey said. "I could take tomorrow off and stay up with you if you want."

Sharla was touched. She hugged her friend again and said, "No, I'll be alright. I just need to be alone some to think. I need to pray."

Lin searched Sharla's face to see if she was telling the truth. After a quick scrutinizing, she decided it would be safe to leave her alone.

"Okay," Lindsey sighed. "But I want you to call me if you need me. I don't care what time it is."

"I will, I will," Sharla promised. Then: "There is one thing you could do before you leave."

"Sure, what?"

"Could you pray for me?"

Lindsey smiled. "Of course."

Taking Sharla's hands in her own, Lindsey closed her eyes, bowed her head and said: "Father, my sister is hurting dearly right now. I know her heart is aching and I ask You to please give her peace and heal her hurt. Lord, we don't always understand why some things happen the way they do, but I ask that you give Sharla the grace to accept this situation, and make her see that Tyler's marrying another woman is no reflection on how beautiful she is in Your eyes."

That last statement made Sharla open her eyes briefly and look at Lindsey. Sharla had been thinking she wasn't beautiful.

"I ask this in Jesus' name, Amen."

Both women opened their eyes and stood up.

"Thank you, Lin, that was nice," Sharla said, grabbing a paper towel in the kitchen to wipe her eyes with.

"Sharla, I'm worried about you," Lindsey frowned.

"I'm fine." Sharla pepped up. "Really. I'll be alright. Go home, please."

Lindsey picked up her purse and began walking slowly towards the door. "Okay," she said hesitantly. "But remember, you call me if you need me. I don't care what time it is!"

"I promise, I will," Sharla said.

Lindsey opened the door and stepped out. "Sharla, you probably don't want to hear this right now, but this too shall pass."

Lindsey was right. Sharla hadn't wanted to hear that right now or ever.

"I know," Sharla nodded.

Another brief hug, then the door closed and Sharla stood in the hallway of her new home alone.

Her eyes locked on a framed version of the Lord's Prayer on the wall. She stared at the prayer intently for several minutes as the hurt welled up in her again. It started in her feet and quickly rose through her midsection up into her chest until it was in her throat and she found it hard to swallow. She tried her best to keep it down but it was like a bad meal that simply refused to be digested. She could feel the acrid, bitter taste of the hurt in her mouth, making her lips quiver. Then the hurt was in her eyes, making them sting and fill with tears. The hurt forced her to open her mouth and let out a silent wail of pain that grabbed her and made her sink to her knees in a heap on the hardwood.

"Oh, God," she cried soundlessly, and thought about the candlelight vigil just around the corner from where she used to live.

Chapter 20: Ain't No Way

The phone kept ringing.

People leaving her messages, asking to talk to her, was she alright, pick up, pick up…

Why couldn't they just leave her alone?

Sharla opened her eyes and stared up into the darkness of her bedroom. She had no idea what time it was. The clock on the nightstand was facing the other direction, its red digital numbers hidden. The shades in her room were drawn, as they were all over the house, but it looked dark outside. Could be early morning, could be evening. Sharla wasn't sure. It didn't matter anyway. Nothing mattered.

"Sharla," her answering machine echoed from the living room, "It's Marla…" her voice seemed hesitant. "Listen, dear, I need for you to call me. Your agent said she hasn't been able to reach you for over a week. Your mother called me yesterday. She said she hasn't heard from you. She wouldn't tell me what was going on but she asked me to call…" hesitancy again.

"Sharla, if you're there, please pick up the phone. Your folks are worried about you. *I'm* worried about you…" a pause. "Look, whatever's happened, you can talk to me about it. If not me, someone. I know a very good therapist…" another pause followed by a sigh. "Well, I guess either you're really not there or you're not going to pick up. Call me on my cell if you need to. I'm here if you want to talk. Bye."

There was a click followed by a loud beep.

Sharla squeezed her eyes shut in the darkness, tears streaming down her face.

Marla was right. She should at least call her parents, let them know she was still alive. But it seemed too much of an effort to raise the phone to her ear. She was too tired, too disgusted, too distraught, too ashamed….

She'd been sleeping on and off—but mostly on—for days. Ever since she'd heard about Tyler's marriage, it was all she had the strength for. Aside from going online shortly after hearing the news and finding out that the marriage was true, Sharla had had almost no contact with the outside world for nearly two weeks. She'd deliberately isolated herself from everyone, refusing to answer the phone or even walk outside to get her mail. Eventually, she knew she would have to talk to people, especially her literary agent. She needed to discuss the deal she'd signed to write two more books. But the way she felt right now, Sharla didn't care if she never talked to anyone at Red Rock Publishing again. They could sue her if they wanted. The money meant nothing to her, it never had. She'd written *Chasing Trevor* for one reason: to express her feelings for the only man she felt she'd ever really loved.

Now that man had married someone else.

Sharla continued to cry silently in the dark and pounded her fist into the pillow. Tyler read her book but he hadn't read *her*. Maybe the message was too veiled. Maybe she'd hidden herself too deeply behind humorous words.

Or maybe she'd just been plain dumb.

Sharla hiccupped a sob; her bladder was full. Reluctantly, she raised up from her bed, felt around with her toes for her house shoes, slipped her feet into them and went into the bathroom. When she came out, she went into the living room and turned on the CD player. The first melancholy notes of a piano followed by a soft, equally mournful tenor saxophone introduced Aretha Franklin as she sang "Ain't No Way." Sharla grabbed a bag of chips from the pantry (she was going to have to go shopping pretty soon, her food supply was dwindling) and laid down on the couch, holding one of the sofa pillows to her chest as she munched and listened to Aretha in the dark:

"Ain't no way..." Aretha sang... *"for me to love yooo...If you won't let me..."*

> *It ain't no way...*
> *for me to give you all you need*
> *If you won't let me give all of me!*

Sharla clutched the pillow tighter and cried harder. Aretha continued her lament:

> *I know that a woman's duty*
> *is to help and love a man*
> *And that's the way it was for them*
> *Oh but how can I*
> *how can I how can I*
> *Give you all the things I have*
> *If you're tying both of my hands*
> *Ohhh, it ain't no way!*

As Aretha cried that it ain't no way and the backup singers echoed the same, Sharla's heart was torn afresh as she thought about Tyler.

Now, there really was no way.

She stuffed some more chips in her mouth. Tyler's new wife really was beautiful, Sharla thought. Way more glamorous than she could ever be. Sharla twisted her body on the couch in frustration. She was so stupid! How could she have ever dreamed Tyler would want her?

But he didn't even give me a chance! Sharla screamed in her head, crying harder. He hadn't seemed like the type who was so hung up on looks. Maybe what she'd heard on the Internet about the marriage being merely a career move was true. But again, that didn't seem like Tyler. None of this seemed like him. How could she have so greatly misjudged his character? How could she have so greatly misjudged what God had shown her?

The thought made her cry harder as she hugged the sofa pillow tighter to her chest, continuing to fuel her heartache with Doritos.

What an idiot she was! This wasn't supposed to happen! She'd promised herself she'd never get so emotional over any man ever again, let alone one that didn't even know who she was. Maybe she did need a shrink.

Or a lobotomy.

A sudden, loud knocking startled Sharla and made her jump up from the couch. She used the stereo remote to turn off the music and stood motionless in the dark. The knock came again from the front door, louder.

"Sharla, open up, I know you're in there!"

It was Lindsey.

Sharla's shoulders sagged.

"Go away!" she yelled back gloomily. She hadn't spoken much in days and her voice sounded raspy and thick in her ears.

The knocking returned, more persistent.

"Sharla, I'm not leaving till you open this door."

"I said go away, Lin," Sharla walked to the kitchen to get some bean dip. "I don't feel like company right now."

There was a pause, then: "Sharla, I brought the police."

Oh, great! Sharla rolled her eyes.

Picking up the bean dip, she angrily shut the refrigerator door, walked over to a window and peeled back the curtain. Outside, it looked to be about dusk. Sharla could just make out the figures of Lindsey and Pastor Mike standing with a police officer on her porch. And there were two other people, who upon closer inspection, Sharla realized were her parents. A police cruiser was parked across the street.

Sharla let the curtain fall back into place and walked back into the living room. They could stand out there all night for all she cared. She wasn't letting anyone in.

There was brief silence outside, then Sharla could hear murmuring voices and feet shuffling.

Another heavy knock at the door.

"Ms. Davis," an authoritative man's voice said. "Ma'am, could you please open the door?"

Sharla slowly backtracked to the door, the sound of her shuffling house shoes echoing throughout the quiet house.

"What do you want?" she demanded wearily.

"My name's officer Trent Shelby. I'm with Agape P.D. I need you to open the door."

Sharla was about to tell Officer Shelby exactly what he could do with her door when she got a very clear vision of herself being carted off in handcuffs to the Agape County Jail for assaulting a police officer. Her mug shot—nicely framed by her bedhead hairdo, crooked frilly pink chiffon bathrobe and deadpan, washed out expression that would make Nick Nolte's mugshot look like it should be on the cover of *Vogue*—splashed on the front page of every newspaper and rag mag in the country. She even saw the headline: **Texas Author Goes Ape on Cop**.

Sharla sighed heavily. After another moment's hesitation, she reluctantly unlocked the front door but left the chain on the link. She opened the door a crack and peeped out. A tall police officer with steel gray eyes was peering back at her. Behind him stood Lindsey and Sharla's parents.

"Evening, ma'am," the officer nodded. "Could you please open the door? These people..." he gestured behind him... "want to see that you're alright."

With great hesitancy, Sharla unhooked the chain and slowly opened the door.

"Okay," she sighed, holding the door open wide. "You've all seen me. Now, please—"

She went to close the door but her father quickly wedged himself in the doorway.

"Pastor!" he yelled, grimacing as he tried to keep the door open while Sharla pushed in the opposite direction to close it. "Help me here!"

Pastor Mike quickly came running up and the two of them started pushing the door open as Sharla, emotionally spent and no match for two determined men, stepped back in astonishment. She could see out of the corner of her eye that Officer Shelby also looked surprised.

"Dad, go away!" Sharla cried, almost in tears again. She ran a nervous hand through her disheveled hair. "I don't want to see anybody."

She backed into the house like a frightened animal being backed into a corner as her friends and family flooded their way inside.

"Well, we want to see you," Richard shot back, trudging inside, huffing and out of breath from the door struggle. Officer Shelby followed, looking at Sharla with concern.

"Ma'am, do you want these people in your house?"

"Why didn't you ask me that 30 seconds ago?" Sharla said disgustedly. She kept her head down and her eyes averted. A brief, slightly amusing vision of everyone being loaded into a paddy wagon flashed before her. "They're in here now!....Yes, just.....yes, it's fine."

The scanner on Officer Shelby's hip loudly began to squawk. He picked it up, spoke some police jargon into it and politely excused himself.

"It's so dark in here," Lindsey replied. "Let's turn on some lights." She flipped the switch next to the front door and the hallway was instantly illuminated.

Sharla moaned and reflexively put her hand over her eyes, squinting like a vampire who's just been exposed to the sun.

Ida turned on the living room and kitchen lights. The kitchen looked like a disaster area. Dishes were piled up in the sink, the remnants of various foods that were now dried out and crusted still clinging to some of them. Empty Diet Coke cans lay askew on the counter. The trash was overflowing.

The living room didn't look much better. There were CD's—most of them of Blues and Soul artists Lindsey had never heard—strewn on the coffee table, the stereo and the floor. Lindsey picked up one of them. Who in the world was Johnny Taylor?

She flipped the jewel case over in her hand then put it down absently. Reaching down to pick the fallen sofa pillows up from the floor, Lindsey accidentally stepped on the stereo remote control, which went off and began to play Little Milton's "Walkin' the Back Streets and Crying" somewhere towards the middle of the song:

"...that's why I walk the back streets and cry!" Little Milton wailed.
You know it hurt me so bad
to hear my baby say goodbye...!

Lindsey went over to the stereo and turned it off.

"This is real uplifting stuff you've got here, Sharla," she stated, smiling. "No wonder you're in such a good mood."

Sharla held up a hand. "Don't start, Lin," she warned. "Just don't start."

With that, she retreated to the living room, suddenly afraid all of her CDs were about to be thrown out. Lindsey was looking at a Miles Davis album when Sharla came up to her and grabbed it out of her hand.

"Don't you touch Miles!" she snapped and clutched the CD protectively.

"I was just gonna put him right there," Lindsey said softly, pointing to the coffee table. Her tone was slow and cautious, as if she were talking to a highly unstable individual.

Now that she was standing so close, Lindsey was able for the first time since she'd walked in to get a good look at Sharla, whose tear-streaked face looked wan and pale. Her eyes were swollen and puffy from crying and there were dark circles under them. Her hair was a mass of tangles, her pajamas and bathrobe hanging drunkenly off her small frame. Her slippers were on the wrong feet and her breath smelled like stale Doritos.

No wonder she hadn't wanted the lights on.

Lindsey briefly turned her head away from her friend, tears of compassion now beginning to fill her own eyes. She couldn't speak but tried to place a comforting hand on Sharla's back. Sharla flinched slightly at the touch but then relented, her shoulders shaking as she broke down into fresh tears.

"Sharla, could we pray for you?" a kind voice behind her asked. It was Pastor Mike.

Pray. That was the one thing Sharla hadn't done in weeks. She had been too shocked and angry at God to pray. She felt mislead, betrayed. But as Pastor Mike gently reached out to touch her and her family gathered around her in a circle, she suddenly felt the calm, reassuring touch of Jesus on her and it made her ashamed for yet another reason.

She was ashamed of her thoughts towards God.

As Pastor Mike began to entreat the name of Jesus and her family and friends joined in muttering prayers under their breath, their eyes closed, Sharla continued to weep bitterly. It felt as if she had a 2-ton weight on her shoulders.

"Please, everyone," she said, breaking away from the circle. "I know you all mean well, but I just want to be alone. You can stay up here and pray if you want, but….but I have to go…"

She ran back into her room and closed the door.

Lindsey and Ida started to go after her but Pastor Mike instructed them not to follow.

"She needs to talk to you," he said, looking at Richard. "She needs to hear from her father."

———————————•

Sharla lay in a heap on the bed, her face buried in a tightly-clutched pillow. The waves of her sobs wracked her small frame, making her shoulders shake and the mattress rumble softly underneath her.

Richard walked into Sharla's bedroom and turned on the beside lamp. He sat down on the edge of the bed, his back to his daughter.

Richard was never good with tears. He'd cried only twice in his life: once as a child when his dog was hit by a car and killed instantly, and again only a few years ago at his own father's funeral.

His son, Derek, wasn't a weeper but Sharla, his precious daughter, was different. She had always been sensitive. Apt to cry at the drop of a hat, and he'd never been able to handle it. Usually, he'd let Ida take care of the situation, then come in to console with soothing hugs and promises of ice cream after the water works had dried up. But this time, Richard knew it was different. He'd heard it in the Pastor's tone, but even without that, he'd been feeling inside of himself for a while that perhaps it was time he and his daughter had a heart-to-heart. He knew he'd been sent to talk to her now, and that he was supposed to be the one to dry her tears.

Noisily, he cleared his throat, just in case Sharla hadn't noticed he was there.

"Sharla?"

No answer. Only the continued sound of her muffled sobs.

"Sharla, honey....it's your dad." Richard's voiced sounded small and shaky. He looked down at his hands nervously and cleared his throat again. Reluctantly, he got up and moved closer to Sharla on the bed, placing a gentle hand on the small of her back. The poor thing was shaking like a leaf. It made his heart ache to see her like this.

"Sharla....sugar....I want to talk to you."

Sharla stopped crying and lay perfectly still, her face still buried in the pillow. Her father hadn't called her "sugar" in years. It was his pet name for her whenever he wanted to get her to do something she didn't want to do. Sharla was glad to hear her dad call her by that name. It made her feel close to him. Special.

She felt his hand resting gently on her back.

"What is it?" her voice was thick with tears.

"I want to talk to you about Tyler."

Sharla could feel the emotion beginning to well up within her again and closed her eyes tightly to try to keep the tears from seeping out.

"I don't want to talk about it right now, dad," she said, her fists clenching and unclenching on the bed.

"I know you don't, sugar, but you need to right now. It's important."

"I already know what you're going to say," Sharla replied angrily, jerking her head up from the pillow. "You should have known better, Sharla," she spat in a high-pitched mocking I-told-you-so tone. "You should have listened to your family. We told you not to take this thing with Tyler so seriously. We told you!"

Then, in a voice filled with dawning fear, "Oh, daddy, what have I done to myself? What have I done?! I was so sure this was God. How could I have been so wrong? How could I have been so wrong?!"

Sharla was crying again harder than ever now, her last few words almost unintelligible through the bitterness of her tears. She let herself collapse into the arms of her father, her body heaving with sobs.

Richard received his daughter and hugged her to him tightly.

Sharla was so angry and ashamed. Angry that even though she was now a 30-something-year-old woman, she still wanted and needed her daddy's shoulder to cry on; and embarrassed at her lack of self-control in front of him.

Here she was, crying with such reckless abandon like a child who has lost its favorite toy, but she couldn't help herself. Her heart was broken. It seemed there was no depth to her sorrow, no way to put into words the hurt she felt.

Richard simply continued to stroke his daughter's back, like he used to sometimes when she was little, and let her cry for a while. Ida poked her head in the door in time to see father and daughter embrace, but the look in her husband's eyes told her not to enter, not yet. Reluctantly, Ida eased the bedroom door closed again, her lips pursed together in a thin line of concern.

When it seemed the worst of Sharla's sobs had momentarily subsided, Richard spoke.

"Sugar, I didn't come in here to tell you 'I told you so'."

Sharla pulled away from her father and looked up at him. "Could you hand me that box of tissue on the nightstand, please?" she sniffed.

"Sure." Richard reached around, took the box off the nightstand next to him and held it out to Sharla. She slowly pulled a few tissues from the box and used them to dry her eyes and blow her nose, all of which had turned a bright crimson red.

After a good facial wipe down, Sharla frowned and said, "So, if you're not here to tell me what a fool I've been, what about Tyler do you want to talk about?"

Richard briefly closed his eyes and prayed silently for God to give him the strength to say what he needed to say.

"Sugar," he said slowly, "Did it ever occur to you that maybe you misinterpreted what you thought you heard God say?"

Sharla's brow furrowed deeply as she covered her mouth with a tissue. She thought about the question for a long moment then said, "No, no, I know what I heard in my spirit, dad. I know what God told me."

"He told you that you would marry Tyler."

"Yes, yes," Sharla bobbed her head up and down adamantly. "I know what He told me. I know Tyler was meant to be my husband."

"And yet," Richard went on, very aware that he was treading on dangerous ground. "Tyler's married someone else."

Richard thought he saw a momentary look of hatred for him flash in his daughter's eyes. But when he looked again, whatever he thought he'd seen was gone. There was only Sharla staring at him wide-eyed, her face red and raw from her tears. The truth of her father's words stung her as if she'd been slapped.

"Yes," she swallowed, trying to hold back another fresh flood of tears.

"Sharla, listen to me," Richard went on. "You know God cannot lie… right?"

Sharla looked at her father with suspicion, wondering just where he was going with this.

"Yes."

"So, if God cannot lie, and He told you Tyler was going to be your husband, then Tyler will be your husband."

"But he's married to someone else!" Sharla nearly screamed, the tears feeling as if they would again overtake her at any second.

"I know, I know," Richard soothed, taking his daughter's hands in his own. "But what I'm telling you is that if you truly heard from God, it doesn't matter who Tyler's with now, he'll end up with you."

Sharla looked at her father, studying his eyes. He was serious.

"Do you really believe that?" she asked him.

Richard nodded. "I believe God. And if God has said something is going to happen, then I believe God that it will. Now, I know we've all given you a hard time about this guy, but that was only because we didn't want you to put all your hope in what seemed an impossibility. We didn't want you to get hurt. But sugar, I've seen such a change in you. A positive change. We all have."

Richard shifted slightly on the bed and put an arm around his daughter's shoulder.

"Ever since you discovered Tyler Nicks, it's like you've become a different person. He's brought out something in you that I don't think even you knew was there. From the moment you began talking about how he was meant for you and how God had shown you he was your soul mate, you began to be more….more…."

Richard struggled for the right word.

"Out-going?" Sharla offered.

Richard paused. "Well, yes, but that's not the word I'm looking for. You started to be more….uh.."

"Confident?" Sharla tried again.

"That's it! Confident!" Richard nodded. "Sugar, it's like that man brought you out of a shell that no one, including your family, had been able to crack. Just thinking that he was going to marry you made you want to be…better!"

"Really? You think so?" Sharla asked.

"Of course! My gosh, just look what you've accomplished in just two short years. Because of him, you wrote a book, Sharla, a *book*! My baby girl wrote a book! And not just any book but a bestseller! Do you know how proud that made me? Sugar, do you know how proud we all are of you?"

Sharla shrugged, still battling sniffles. "I guess so."

"You guess," Richard chuckled. "You guess. Sharla, you're a best-selling author. A year ago, you never would have thought you could write a book."

Sharla thought for a moment. Her dad did have a point. A year ago, just finishing a grocery list would have been a major feat.

"And look at how beautiful you've become," Richard continued. "Not that I ever thought you were ugly because you're not. But Sharla, you glow now. You smile all the time and you never used to smile much before. Don't take this the wrong way, sugar, but you always used to look like you were on your way to a funeral. Probably your own."

Sharla tried to conceal a giggle but it came out anyway.

"See?" Richard said. "Lookit that, there that smile is. You've lost weight, you're taking better care of yourself, you're more open to people. Sharla, just think at what having something to build a hope on has done for you. You're successful, you're healthy, you've got good friends and family who love you. For the first time, you're really standing on your own two feet. Sugar, I look at you now and I see the woman that God always intended for you to be. And all because of a promise you think God made to you."

Richard squeezed his daughter's hand and looked squarely into her eyes. "Sugar, I know you think you did all of this for a man, but the person who's benefited from it is you. I know you're looking at what's happened and you're asking, where is God? But I'm telling you that even if Tyler doesn't marry you, look what you've accomplished for yourself. Doesn't that alone show you the hand of God in all this?"

Sharla shrugged but remained silent.

"Which brings me back to my original question. Do you think, just think now, that perhaps you misinterpreted what God told you?"

Sharla opened her mouth to object but Richard interjected.

"Now, before you go off on me again let me just say that I've been watching how you've been running after this fella. How you've been trying in your own power, to have him end up with you. And I just want to throw this out there to you—you do what you want with it—but don't you think that if God gave you this prophecy, God would be the one to fulfill it, not you?"

To Sharla, the question seemed utterly ridiculous.

"Well, of course, dad, I expected God to fulfill it. He's the one that spoke it."

"Exactly," Richard said. "So why haven't you turned this problem over to God to solve instead of you trying to solve it?"

Sharla tried to speak but then snapped her mouth closed again. Had she been trying in her own power to make Tyler see her?

"You know, sometimes, we can get in the way of God and when we do, we can end up blocking the blessings He intended for us," Richard chided.

"I have to admit, when you first started going on about Tyler this and Tyler that, I was skeptical. It didn't seem possible. But as time went on and you began to grow and change and blossom into the Godly, confident, beautiful woman you've become, I began to think that any man who could influence my hard-headed daughter in the positive way Tyler Nicks has influenced you, well, he just could be the right one for her. Any person who encourages you to be better than you are is a good person to have around."

"So I say, if God said this is the man for you, he is. Looking at what you've become, I can honestly say that any man would be lucky to have you for his wife. But maybe what God is waiting for on your part, is the complete and total trust in Him that *He* will bring the right man into your life, *when* it's meant to be."

"Sharla," Richard sighed, "Turn Tyler over to God. I know this is very hard on you, but you need to wish Tyler well and let him go."

"Dad—"

"No, listen to me. If Tyler's meant to be with you, it'll happen. But you've got to stop trying to make it happen and let God be God. Don't surrender everything you've worked so hard to achieve because this man married someone else. Give him to God. Cry if you still need to. Get all the tears out but don't give up on yourself. I believe God used this man to help you see the truth about yourself. That you're beautiful and valuable. So don't now turn around and make God out to be a liar by reverting back to what you were. Stand firm. Get on with your life. Give Tyler to God. Surrender all to Him and let Him work this out in His time. God cannot give you what you refuse to let go of."

Sharla was crying again but not because of the pain she felt over Tyler, but because she knew her father was right. She had to let Tyler go. If it was meant to happen it would. If not, then it wasn't God. Tyler had married someone else, so maybe it hadn't been God. Either way, she was going to have to get on with her life.

At that moment, a Bible verse came into Sharla's mind: *I have given you the power to choose life or death. Choose life.*

Sharla knew then what she had to do.

With great care, she reached up and kissed her dear old dad on the forehead and hugged him close.

"Thank you, Father," she whispered into her dad's chest.

"You're welcome, sugar," he said.

Sharla smiled a wry smile. That comment hadn't exactly been directed at Richard.

"Dad," Sharla said. "If you don't mind now, I'd like to be alone for a little bit."

Richard looked at his daughter, concerned. "Are you sure?"

"Yeah, I'll be fine, daddy, really," Sharla replied. "I need some time to pray."

Understanding lit across her father's weathered face. "Okay," Richard said, standing up and stretching for a minute before heading to the door. "We're in the living-room if you need us."

"Dad?" Sharla said.

"Yeah, sugar."

"I love you."

Richard smiled at his precious eldest child. Now it was his turn to try to hold back tears.

"Not half as much as I love you, kid."

And then he was gone, leaving Sharla to stare at her closed bedroom door.

Chapter 21: Blinded by the Light

After staring at the door for what seemed an eternity, Sharla kneeled down on the side of her bed and prayed with her head bent to her clasped hands. No sound came from her except for a few inadvertent whispers as her lips moved silently, stray tears running down her cheeks.

She prayed like that for a quite a while, until her knees felt numb from staying in the same position. But when she finally said "amen" and got up, she felt better. Her soul was right again.

Reaching under her mattress on the other side, she got out her journal, sat on the bed and wrote:

> Well, it's done.
>
> I took my dad's advice and gave Tyler over to God...
>
> It was very hard and I think I've cried enough to fill a large basin but I feel better now that I've prayed...
>
> I suppose, dear journal, you'd like to know what I prayed for.
>
> I prayed for Tyler mostly. I prayed that God would bless him and take care of him and that he would be happy with his new bride.
>
> That part was hard to get out. The new bride part, I mean. But I said it, and after a few times of saying it, I came to mean it. I love Tyler. I know that in my heart I've loved him almost from the moment I saw him and no matter what, that love outweighs the hurt I'm feeling right now. Tyler doesn't know me so he doesn't know I'm hurting. But God knows. And I believe God has shown me that He cares.
>
> I'm not sure what I'm going to do now. It's not going to be easy to move forward without thinking of Tyler every waking moment...I imagine

I will still weep and mourn for months to come. But one thing I realize I cannot do is stop living my life. Dad was right about that. If Tyler is not the one, then I know that God has reserved someone for me. I just have to be patient and wait.

I only wish I really understood why all of this happened the way that it did. But the Bible says that God's ways are not the ways of man, that His ways are higher than man's ways. So maybe I don't have a right to question. I don't know. All I know right now is that my heart is broken.

Maybe no one is to blame. Maybe sometimes, things just happen and there is no explanation for the why. In any case, I sincerely wish Tyler the best. Maybe one of these days, I'll run into him and his wife so I can congratulate them both in person.

Sharla looked up from her journal and thought a moment. A snippet of "Your Luck Ran Out" was playing in her head.

She poised her pen over the page again and added:

But not right this minute.

Chapter 22: Redemption

A few nights later, Sharla was listening to music and trying to drown her sorrows in a pint of Ben & Jerry's ice cream when she saw the preacher.

She was sitting on the couch watching television with the sound down and listening to Otis Redding sing "The Happy Song."

"Gonna sing this song y'all", Otis cried, *"Singin' it for my baby…"*

> *She's the only one can bring me joy*
> *That's why I sing these happy songs*
> *They go*
> *dum, dum, deedle dee,*
> *dum dum…*

A lump caught in Sharla's throat. This wasn't working. All it did was make her think of Tyler. Everything made her think of Tyler, especially music.

Sharla sighed and turned off the CD player. Otis usually cheered her, but tonight, "The Happy Song" wasn't living up to its title.

Sharla turned up the volume on the T.V. She turned to CNC, the Christian Network Channel, and saw that W.L. Groves, one of her favorite preachers, was on. A dynamic speaker, Groves was pacing methodically back and forth along the altar of his large Texas-based church. According to the caption on the screen, today's message was entitled, "Waiting on God."

Waiting on God, Sharla wryly thought. *I feel like I could give a sermon on that!*

She grabbed her ice cream and got comfortable on the couch. The program was almost over.

".....but what do you do," Groves was saying, "when you've been faithful, you've done everything just the way you were supposed to and God *still* hasn't shown up?"

Affirmative shouts from the congregation.

"It's easy to praise God when everything is going well," Groves said. "I know how to lift up the Lord when He says 'hold on' and they're just about to cut off the electricity and the Lord shows up at the last minute...."

He paused for emphasis.

"...But what do you do when they've cut off the lights and you're sitting in the dark...and it looks like....God...didn't...do...what...He promised?"

Yeah, what do *you do?* Sharla thought.

"You're alone. In the dark," Groves went on. "Seeking. Asking God 'why?' I thought I was gonna get the job, and I didn't. I should have gotten that promotion and I didn't. My next door neighbor won the lottery and they're a bunch of HEATHENS! They don't even believe on you, Jesus!"

Sharla sat up, absently putting down her ice cream.

"But me, I've been faithful, God. Why?"

Then turning to the camera, Groves looked into it and said, "And God says, 'Why not?'

Ooh and aahs from the television audience.

"Why shouldn't I test you? Why shouldn't I see if you'll still serve Me when you're in the dark? Why should I not find out if you will trust Me when it looks like everything around you is black and you can't see My face?"

Sharla frowned.

"The Bible says, *Count it all* JOY *when you fall into various trials.* It says in first Peter, *'Beloved, do not think it strange concerning the fiery trial which is to try you, as though some strange thing happened to you! But rejoice to the extent that you partake of Christ's sufferings, that when His glory is revealed, you may also be glad with exceeding joy.'*"

"Remember, beloved," Groves went on, "This is only a test. God is faithful and He will come, but not in your time, in HIS time! And what He gives, He gives with a peace attached to it the world knows nothing about."

Groves turned back to the camera. "So the next time you feel like asking God, 'Why me?' Ask instead, 'Why not?' Then: "I need to say something. There's somebody out there, somebody watching this program, I don't know who you are, but you're in the dark right now. God promised you something and it's looking like it's not going to happen but I'm here to tell you that what God spoke to you *will* happen…"

Sharla dropped her spoon. More shouts and applause from the congregation.

"God is going to birth out of you that which He spoke into you," Groves commanded, pointing into the camera. "That thing in your life, that promise that looks dead, God is about to resurrect it and you WILL see it come to pass! Oh, I don't know who I'm talking to, but God said to tell you, 'The prophecy is not dead but had to be birthed out of you! Oh, Jesus! See…see God had to see if you would trust Him…"

He was half singing, half talking now.

"…He had to see would you still praise Him in the dark. If He didn't come on your time, would you still be with Him on *His* time…Would you get out of the way and let Him work! Oh, yessss! I feel the Spirit of God in this place!"

The television congregation was on its feet, cheering and shouting and worshipping God as Groves began pacing once again back and forth, shouting praise and admonishment.

"Let God be true and every man a liar!" he exclaimed. "If God spoke it, He's gonna do it! Don't give up. You may be in the dark but don't STAY in the dark. Get in the light! Get in God's light! Get out of His way and LET…HIM…MOVE!"

With that, the program faded out and a promo for next week's message came on the screen. Sharla didn't notice. She was on her feet, tears streaming down her face.

Her dad's words came back to her: *Sometimes, we can get in the way of God and when we do, we can end up blocking the blessings He intended for us.*

Sharla got on her knees, resting her elbows on the edge of one of her sofa cushions and prayed, "Thank you, Father, for this message. I hear Lord, and I'm willing to move out of your way."

With that, Sharla got off her knees, threw away the ice cream and wrote Tyler a letter, one she intended to send.

———————————————————————————

The following morning, Sharla awoke with the premise for her next book. This new story would not be a parody, but a fictional account of a young woman, who with the help of her newfound faith in Christ, overcomes many obstacles—including leaving an abusive relationship—to triumph over her fears and become a missionary in China, where she meets the man she falls in love with and marries. Sharla believed God had already given her the book's title: *Beauty in the Ashes.*

Once she sat down at her computer to begin, Sharla found it hard to stop. She wrote from morning until night almost non-stop, barely leaving her house (let alone her study), where she would wake up, grab a cup of coffee and hunker down at her desk to write. Her family was concerned about her, thinking Sharla had lapsed back into a state of depression. But she assured them she was far from depressed.

"Mom, really, I'm the happiest I've been in a long time!" Sharla told Ida during a brief phone conversation. "This book is so Spirit-driven. It's practically writing itself."

The best part was that when she was writing, she wasn't thinking about Tyler. As Sharla immersed herself in the progression of her work, the thoughts of him became less and less, until he became a faint but pleasant memory in the back of her mind. When she did think about him, it was always with a sad fondness and a sincere desire for his happiness. But the thought was usually brief, stealing in like a raindrop that runs down the side of a window and quickly dissipates.

It seemed that Sharla had finally gotten Tyler out of her system and that God was preparing her to move on. She was just beginning to settle into the acceptance of her fate when the sound of the phone ringing one morning wrenched her out of a deep sleep.

Reluctantly raising her head off the pillow, Sharla opened one bleary eye and looked at the digital clock: 7:30 A.M.

She dropped her head back on to the pillow with a thud and released a deeply annoyed sigh. Blindly, she reached out for the phone, grappling to pick up the receiver.

In a voice thick with sleep she answered, "Whoever this is, this better be good."

"Sharla!" Lindsey shouted excitedly, making Sharla jerk straight up in bed. That girl had a voice that could wake the dead.

"Turn on the TV, they're interviewing Tyler."

Sharla shut her eyes and swallowed hard. She slumped back onto the pillow. Then, sighing into the phone: "Is that what you woke me up at 7:30 in the morning for? That's nice, Lin, but I really don't—"

"I know, I know, you don't care," Lindsey finished. "But you will when you hear what Tyler has to say about his so-called marriage."

Sharla had a vision of Tyler and his new blonde bride, sitting together arm and arm and gazing into one another's eyes as they both expressed to Diane Sawyer how deliriously happy they were.

"No, thanks," Sharla replied. "I'm really not interested."

"Sharla, please," Lindsey pleaded. "I wouldn't have called you this early if I didn't think it was important. Hurry, he's on Good Morning America after the commercial."

Sharla began to grow alarmed. "Is Tyler okay?"

"Oh, he's more than okay," Lindsey said with a smile in her voice. "He's not married."

Sharla froze, her hand clutching the phone. "What did you just say?"

Lindsey repeated the sentence, slowly emphasizing each word. "He's—not—really—married."

Sharla rose up on her elbow. "What? Did they get a divorce already?"

"No!" Lindsey said with awe. "They were never married to begin with! That girl, Venice, she made it all up."

"You're kidding," Sharla whispered.

"No, it's true! Get up and see for yourself!"

Sharla's paralysis broke and she was up like a shot running towards the living room and the remote control, the cordless phone held tightly to her ear.

"What channel is Good Morning America?" she screamed.

"Channel 5," Lindsey said. "Hurry, he's on!"

Sharla was so flustered, she dropped the remote control twice before she was able to get a steady enough grip to turn on the television. After a few seconds of channel surfing, she was staring at Tyler, who was talking to, of course, Diane Sawyer.

Tyler looked handsome as always, dressed in a dark suit and white, open-collared shirt. Sharla could tell he was tired and seemed a little tense. Judging from the scenery, he was outside somewhere, maybe sitting on the terrace of his hotel suite, the early morning sky a dark backdrop behind him. A small curly wire hung from the back of his left ear.

Diane was explaining that Tyler, who was being shown on a huge, widescreen monitor in the *Good Morning America* studio, had agreed to speak on the program via satellite from Los Angeles, where he was in town for a children's charity event.

"Wow, it's got to be about what? 5:30 where he is?" Sharla spoke into the phone.

"Yeah, something like that," Lindsey said. "I think California is two hours behind us."

"He looks good," Sharla commented, mainly to herself. "A little tired but good."

"Tyler, good morning," said Diane. "Thank you for agreeing to speak to us so early and under some rather bizarre circumstances. I understand you just flew in last night from the Bahamas where you were vacationing to address these circumstances?"

"Uh, good morning, Diane." Tyler nodded and smiled, taking a moment to adjust the wire in his ear. "Yes, that's true, I did just fly in only a few hours ago, but I had to be back in LA in a few days anyway."

Diane: "I know there's a three hour time difference between New York and LA. I imagine you must be tired."

Tyler, chuckling: "Yeah, a little. I'm a little jet-lagged but I got to sleep some on the plane."

"Well, Tyler," Diane said, moving forward in her chair to begin the real interview. "I understand that part of the reason your vacation was cut short is because you only just found out it is being reported you are married and that is not true. Is that right?"

"Yes, Diane," Tyler nodded emphatically. "I'm not married, never been married." He then held up his left hand to the camera, wiggled his fingers and smiled. "See? No ring, folks."

Sharla inadvertently let out a deep sigh mixed with relief and astonishment.

"Tyler," Diane continued. "I'm sure you're aware of what widespread news your supposed marriage has become over the last few weeks. The news devastated women everywhere. I've even heard some women have joined convents in protest. What's your take on all of this? How did a rumor like this manage to get so out of hand?"

"Diane, your guess is a good as mine," Tyler shrugged. "I really don't know much about how this happened. As for women joining convents, I wouldn't know anything about that, but it sounds a little sad, actually."

Both he and Diane shared a laugh.

"Well, what about the young lady involved," Diane said. "The one you were said to have married, Venice Dupree? We know that she is the daughter of Lawrence Dupree, who is the head of your record label. It's being reported that she is the one who leaked the news you two were married."

At this, Tyler's face became serious, his tone respectful. "I do know Venice but not well. I don't want to say too much about her but I will say that this whole thing has been a misunderstanding and we are not married."

"So, the report that you and Venice were married in a private ceremony in Las Vegas and that you gave her a heart-shaped 12-carat diamond ring…."

"All false," Tyler said with a small sweep of his hand. "Very elaborate, but false," he smiled.

"What about the rumor that Venice's father, who was not at the wedding, was furious when he found out and insisted the marriage be annulled because you're not Catholic?"

Tyler's eyes widened for a moment and he shifted in his chair amusedly. "Wow, I hadn't heard that one. Uh, no, completely untrue."

"Have you talked to Lawrence Dupree since you got back?"

That serious look again. "Yes, we have talked and like I said, this has been a big misunderstanding. He knows that."

"He is the president of the record label you're signed with. Do you think this will affect your working relationship with him?"

"No, Mr. Dupree and I get along very well. That hasn't changed."

"Have you spoken with Venice?"

"No," Tyler said firmly. Then, in a more polite tone: "But even if we had I wouldn't discuss it."

"Is Venice the one who started this rumor?" Diane pressed.

"You know, Diane, I don't want to point fingers," Tyler replied. "I'm still learning how this all got started myself."

"He's just trying to be nice," Lindsey chimed in through the phone. "That girl started it. I read it online. She's been telling anybody who'll listen she and Tyler are married."

Sharla smiled. Tyler, ever the diplomat.

"Now, you were out of the country when this was first reported. How did you find out?" Diane asked.

"Right. I hadn't really had a real vacation since I won America's Next Big Star," Tyler explained. "So I decided to take some time off. How I found out I was married, it was kinda funny, actually."

Tyler smiled, snapping back into a more jovial mood. "I was in the Bahamas and some reporter called asking me to comment on my marriage and how the honeymoon was going, and I was like, 'what are you talking about? I'm not married.' And he said 'yes you are,' and I kept saying 'no, I'm not!' We went back and forth like that for a good while and he kept insisting that I was married and I finally had to tell him, 'Look, man, I'd know if I was married!'"

"He insisted you were married?" Diane asked incredulously.

"Yeah," Tyler said. "I thought it was a joke till some photographer showed up where I was staying and shouted he wanted a picture of me with my wife. After that it just got....crazy. I had reporters and photographers literally hanging off my balcony and...it was just crazy."

"When did you find out?"

"What? That I was married?" Tyler laughed.

"Yes."

He hesitated. "Uh, about three days ago."

"So, was it a matter of 'I have to get out of here?'"

Tyler put a hand up to scratch the back of his head, something Sharla noticed he did whenever he was thinking of how he was going to answer a question.

"Yeah, in a way," he said. "But I had known about this charity fundraiser for some time. It's a children's charity called Kid One Transport that transports kids from poor families to hospitals and doctors appointments who have no way to get there otherwise. It's a cause that's always been near and dear to my heart and I wanted to be here to support it. So, I had been thinking about flying back anyway but this whole marriage situation just kinda…cemented my decision, you know?"

"Tyler, you're very popular, especially with the females," Diane continued. "Are you at all worried that this kind of publicity has negatively affected your relationship with the fans?"

Tyler shook his head. "Not at all, Diane. I have a great relationship with my fans, the Soul Squad, they're just a great bunch of people. If it weren't for them, I wouldn't be sitting here talking to you right now. My fans, the people who have been behind me since day one, I have no doubt will still be behind me. You know, I believe they're with me through thick and thin. This was an unfortunate misunderstanding, I believe the fans will come to realize that. I wanna just, you know, put this whole thing behind me and take my music to the next level."

"Are you seeing anyone right now?"

Tyler grinned a wide Cheshire Cat grin and again scratched the back of his head. "Uh, well, Diane, lemme just say that right now, I'm keeping my options open."

Sharla frowned. She didn't like the sound of that.

"So, there's no one in particular in your life right now?"

"No, no one in particular."

"Well, Tyler, I know your time is limited," Diane said. "Thank you for speaking to us and good luck with the charity event."

Tyler smiled. "Thank you, Diane, I appreciate that. It's been my pleasure."

"Incidentally, your new album is due out when?"

"I go into the studio next month and I should have something ready by the fall, hopefully."

"Great, I'm sure all your fans will be looking forward to the new album."

Tyler pumped a fist and said, "You bet. Wooo! Soul Squad!" before his monitor went blank.

"Well, ladies," Diane said into the camera, "There you have it. Tyler Nicks is still very much single. Good news for many, I'm sure. And now, here's a look at the weather...."

Sharla was barely aware of hitting the "off" button on the remote control. She sat in stunned silence, the phone still held to her ear. She might have stayed that way the rest of the day if Lindsey's voice hadn't broken in.

"Hey, they're talking about it on the Good Day Sunshine show," Lindsey said. "Channel 8. Sharla, are you there?"

"Yeah, I'm here," she blinked. "I'm just...I don't know what to say. I can't believe it."

"I know. Isn't it bizarre? Poor Tyler," Lindsey said. "Can you imagine being on vacation and getting hit with some news like that?"

"No," Sharla hoped she didn't sound as happy as she felt inside. A huge grin surfaced across her face. "It must have been awful for him."

She went to the kitchen to get a cup of coffee.

"You said you heard this girl made it up. What did you hear?"

"I read an article—well, I skimmed an article online that said what's-her-name...um, Venice, bragged to some of her friends she and Tyler had secretly been seeing each other for months and that they'd eloped in Vegas. She told people the wedding had to be secret because her dad hated Tyler and didn't approve of him."

"What?" Sharla frowned. She couldn't imagine anyone not approving of Tyler.

"Yeah," Lindsey went on. "She was going around running her mouth and flashing a ring and somehow, the tabloids picked up on it and then the mass media and it just blew up."

"Wow," Sharla said. "And the whole time, Tyler was in the dark about it?"

"Apparently. You saw him. What was your impression? I mean, maybe he's a really good actor but he seemed genuinely shocked."

Sharla took a sip of her coffee. "Yeah, he did."

"Well....." Lindsey said in a teasing tone. "I bet you're happy."

"Why do you say that?" Sharla asked, perhaps a bit too defensively. "This is awful. I feel terrible for Tyler. My heart goes out to him."

"Mm-hmm," Lindsey smirked.

Sharla rolled her eyes. "No, really, it does!"

"Hey, you don't have to convince me," Lindsey laughed. Then, in a come-on-you-know-you-can-tell-your-best-friend voice: "Can you honestly say you're not still in love with the guy? That you're not jumping up and down inside about this?"

Sharla lowered the phone for a few seconds and closed her eyes. It was sometimes frustrating how good Lindsey was at reading her thoughts. Reluctantly, she raised the phone back to her ear.

"Yes, I will admit that I'm happy to hear Tyler isn't married..."

She could hear Lindsey take in breath to reply and quickly went on. "BUT....I am also truly sorry to hear that he has apparently been the victim of a cruel prank."

"Uh-huh. Yeah," Lindsey said flatly. "Come on, Sharla, It's me, Lin. I know you."

Stony silence on Sharla's end.

"Look, it's okay to admit you still have feelings for him," Lindsey said softly. "It's only natural. I know you couldn't have gotten over him in just a couple of weeks."

Sharla bit her lip. "Alright," she said. "I still have feelings for him. Are you happy now?"

"Are *you* happy?"

The question stung Sharla, causing the coffee mug she'd been about to bring to her lips to freeze in mid-air.

"What does that mean?" she asked.

"It means have you really been happy?" Lindsey said matter-of-factly. "For the last few weeks you've been talking about how you've given Tyler to God, trying to act like this whole thing doesn't bother you anymore, but I can see you're still frustrated. You're obviously still crazy about the man. Now you might have a second chance, I know inside you've got to be thrilled. The question is, what are you gonna do?"

"I don't know," Sharla sat down the mug and pushed it away from her in frustration, hot coffee sloshing out onto the counter. "I only just found out the man's still available! And anyway," Sharla complained, lightly kicking a bottom cabinet with her house shoe, "I don't think he's interested in me."

"He sent you a nice thank you card when your book came out. And those flowers were gorgeous," Lindsey reminded.

"Yeah, but, he didn't leave a number or a way to get in touch with him," Sharla pouted. "Seems to me that if he was interested, that would have been the time to say something, you know?"

"Well," Lindsey sighed. "If you really feel in your heart that this is the guy for you, maybe you should try to get in touch with him again. Who knows? He might be in a different place now. Things seemed to have slowed down in his life. Maybe he wasn't ready then."

"Hmmm, maybe," Sharla shrugged. "I did write him a letter."

Lindsey gasped. "You did? When?"

"Oh….not too long after you and the gang came over to pull me out of my funk. About two…two-and-a-half weeks ago now, I guess."

"Did you send it?" Lindsey asked suspiciously.

"Yes, I did," Sharla said proudly.

Lindsey whistled. "Wow. I can't believe it. What did you say to him?"

Sharla hesitated. She loved Lindsey and trusted her like a sister, but what she'd had to say to Tyler was personal. Sharla wanted to keep it to herself.

"Well, not much," she slowly answered. "Just basically wished him well in his life and his career."

"You might hear back from him," Lindsey mused.

"I don't know," Sharla said, glancing in the direction of the television. "Looks like he may have his hands full right now."

"Just pray about it, see what God says."

"I will."

"Well, friend," Lindsey teased, "I need to be getting off to work."

Sharla looked at the time on the microwave. It was almost 8:00.

"Okay. Thanks for the early wake-up call."

"You're welcome. I'll call you later. Bye."

As Sharla hung up the phone and laid it thoughtfully on the counter, Lindsey's words rang in her mind:

The question is, what are you gonna do?

Sharla looked up at the crown molding in her kitchen and said aloud, "I don't know. What *am* I gonna do?"

The crown molding didn't answer back.

Chapter 23: Why Does Love Got to Be So Sad?

The marriage hoax was the lead story on just about every news and entertainment program in the country.

Sharla couldn't get away from it. The newspapers and Internet were suddenly flooded with information, while Tyler forums became filled with angry fans demanding to know just how that 'no-good, lying tramp' had managed to pull the wool over their adoring eyes. Or better yet, how was it that no one who had inside information on Tyler bothered to comment before now?

The people that ran the sites, some of whom were thought to have personal connections to Tyler, were sticking to their guns, explaining that their websites only reported facts not rumors, rendering the information in their minds, pointless.

Tyler had been out of the country for well over a month. He'd been on the go non-stop for over a year. The man was exhausted and needed to rest. No one had wanted to bother him with something so blatantly unsubstantiated as a marriage rumor, nor stir up trouble in the forums. There was a tacit admission, however, that looking back in hindsight, perhaps Tyler's PR team could have paid more attention to the buzz. But apparently, Venice Dupree's reputation within the industry for telling a few whoppers was as legendary as her father's status as a hit-making producer, so insiders ignored it. It wasn't the first time Tyler had been falsely linked to someone. And anyone who really knew him knew he wasn't married. But the rumor had spiraled out of control and before anyone could do damage control, it had gotten back to Tyler via the paparazzi hanging precariously off the edge of his hotel balcony. In the meantime, a general statement had been issued asking the public to please respect Tyler's privacy as he and his team worked to set the record straight.

Now Tyler was out on another kind of promotion: the "I'm Not Married, Give It A Rest" tour, which given the way things were going right now, Sharla figured would soon be coming to a city near her.

Deciding to take a rare break from her writing one afternoon, Sharla flipped to the entertainment section of the newspaper. There, front and center of the entertainment section, was an article about the whole marriage fiasco, along with a picture of Tyler inserted near the top of the story. The headline read:

NICKS: 'I'M NOT MARRIED'

Singer sets the record straight about his alleged new bride
By Rita Dylan
Associated Press

LOS ANGELES, CALIF. — The American Dream has temporarily become a nightmare for Tyler Nicks.

Facing a flurry of press as he hurriedly made his way through Los Angeles International Airport, the soul-singing sensation who recently won the coveted title of *America's Next Big Star* returned to the U.S. on Sunday amid allegations that he had secretly wed the daughter of one of the most powerful music moguls in the country.

Dressed in khaki pants, a white polo shirt and lowering the brim of a black baseball cap over his eyes, Nicks stood before a sea of reporters to address rumors he had married Venice Dupree, daughter of record producer, Lawrence Dupree, in a private ceremony in Las Vegas nearly six weeks ago.

"It's not true," Nicks, 31, said. "I'm not married to anyone. I'm just trying to get my music on track. That's the most important thing to me right now."

Nicks, who was vacationing in the Bahamas when he learned of the marriage hoax, decided to cut his trip short in an attempt to put an end to the rumors.

"I'm just as shocked about this as everyone else," Nicks said, adding with a smile, "Believe me, the rumors of my marriage have been greatly exaggerated."

News of the gray-haired stunner's alleged nuptials a month ago has sent shock waves through the music industry, plunging many female fans into a widespread state of mourning that has not been seen since Paul McCartney married photographer Linda Eastman in 1969.

Nicks admitted during the impromptu press conference that he and Dupree, 25, went out only once, adding that it was more of a casual business meeting than a date.

"Her dad was there," Nicks said. "We talked for a little while, then he left and she and I got to talk some. She seemed like a nice young lady but we did not take it any further than that one meeting."

But according to associates of Venice Dupree, she did take it further, telling friends she and Nicks were madly in love.

Anne Gable, a former classmate and longtime friend of Dupree's, said she was not surprised when Dupree called her two months ago and said she and Nicks had begun dating. Gable said Dupree's interest in Nicks bordered on obsession.

"Tyler was all Venice talked about," said Gable. "She's had a huge crush on him ever since *America's Next Big Star.*"

According to an article in the *New York Post*, Dupree told friends she and Tyler eloped to Las Vegas, where they were married in a quickie ceremony at an all-night wedding chapel. The service was reportedly attended only by the bride and groom, two chapel employees as witnesses, and a minister/ Elvis impersonator who conducted the ceremony.

"It was very romantic the way Venice described it," Gable said. "The only thing she said she regretted was that her dad wasn't there."

According to Dupree, her father, Grammy winning record producer, Lawrence Dupree, 60, was vehemently opposed to Nicks' relationship with his daughter, forcing the lovebirds to wed in secret.

Nicks is currently signed to Dupree's music label, Saturn Records.

On Monday, Dupree released a statement on behalf of his daughter in which he apologized to Nicks and called the events of the last few weeks "a terrible misunderstanding."

"I am very sorry this happened," Dupree said in the statement. "I like Tyler very much and look forward to working with him. He is an upstanding young man and a fine talent. I sincerely hope the actions of my daughter will in no way affect our musical partnership."

Dupree also revealed in the statement that his daughter suffers from manic depression and a psychological disorder that "makes her prone to stretching the truth."

"She's a good girl, really," he said. "She just has a problem."

Sharla closed the paper and put it aside. She went back to her study to resume working on her book, but thought she'd check her e-mails first. Once in her mail, Sharla saw she'd received a Google Alert for Tyler Nicks and pondered even reading it. She'd meant to turn that Google-thing off a while back but it kept slipping her mind. She clicked on one of the links and found an online article regarding Tyler's bogus marriage:

———————————————————

Tyler Nicks says he holds no ill will towards the young woman who, early last month, made up an elaborate story in which she claimed she and the Soul crooner were married.

Venice Dupree, 25, daughter of legendary record producer, Lawrence Dupree, 60, was admitted to a private psychiatric hospital on Wednesday to begin treatment for manic depression and a compulsive lying disorder, which her father said caused the young woman to lie about having married Nicks in a hush-hush wedding ceremony.

"My heart goes out to Venice," Nicks said. "I hope she gets the help she needs."

In a statement released on Sunday, Lawrence Dupree, who recently signed Nicks to his Saturn Records label, apologized to the singer for his daughter's behavior and said he hoped the current events would not affect their musical partnership. Dupree said Nicks has not spoken to Venice, but did send her a small jewelry box that plays music as a get-well present.

"We talked and [Tyler] understands, he's been nothing but sympathetic about this situation," Dupree said. "This has been very hard on Venice, on all of us. It's not easy to talk about publicly, but I'm hoping that by doing so, it might help someone else who's battling a mental disorder."

Friends of Venice Dupree said she sent postcards from Las Vegas after having made up a story that she and Nicks were married at an all-night wedding chapel there.

Childhood friend Marshall Tucker recalled how Dupree showed up at a party about a month ago sporting a huge diamong ring on her left hand.

"She told me Tyler had proposed," Tucker said. "She was so happy. We were all happy for her."

When asked if he thought it strange no one had ever seen Nicks and Dupree together, Tucker said it did cross his mind but he didn't think much of it.

"Venice was always kind of secretive about her boyfriends," he said. "She told everyone Tyler was away on business."
In reality, Nicks was out of the country taking a much needed break from his whirlwind tour of duty as *America's Next Big Star.*

"The first people I called when I found out [about this] were my parents," Nicks said. "I told my dad it wasn't true and he was glad."

He then joked, "Mom was upset that I didn't invite them to the wedding."

Myra Mann, a former teacher who privately tutored Dupree as a child, said Dupree has always had a problem with telling the truth.

"I really think she's a pathological liar," Mann said.

"She was always saying things that weren't true, always making things up. And when you confronted her, she'd just shrug it off. She would lie all the time. I don't think she can help herself."

━━

Sharla's eyes climbed back to the middle of the story:

Nicks...did send her a small jewelry box that plays music as a get-well present.

Sharla thought that was so sweet. Instead of being furious (as he had every right to be) and blasting this woman in the press, Tyler was showing such compassion towards her. No wonder he hadn't wanted to comment about her on *Good Morning America*. The girl was obviously sick and he'd probably known it.

Pushing her chair back from her desk, Sharla took off her glasses and rubbed the bridge of her nose thoughtfully.

A pathological liar. Wow.

It was truly terrifying how a person could become so fixated upon another that they would actually trade in the truth for a fantasy, especially when it came to celebrities. Sharla guessed that for some people, any kind of escape was better than the dead life they were living. She frowned and wondered if perhaps she and Venice weren't that different from each other. After all, she had been pining for Tyler for almost two years now, even going so far as to write a book about it.

But I would never go to the lengths this poor girl went to, Sharla thought, biting her lip. *I couldn't have* lied!

Sharla closed her eyes and said a brief, silent prayer for Tyler and for Venice. She thanked God that by His grace, she had not fallen under a delusion, but had His promise vested in her heart. A Bible verse came to her memory, something found in Hebrews: *Without faith, it is impossible to please Him, for he who comes to God must believe that He is, and that He is a rewarder of those who diligently seek Him.*

Sharla finished her prayer, then rose to get up but sat back down again as if she'd just remembered something.

Closing her eyes tightly, she clasped her hands together and murmured under her breath, "Lord, please help me to always see the truth."

Chapter 24: The Age of Good Feelings

xactly six months to the day after she'd first sat down at her keyboard, Sharla typed the last sentence of what was to become her second novel.

She hit "save" and wearily removed her glasses from her face. Taking a deep breath, she pushed her chair back from her desk and called Marla to let her know *Beauty in the Ashes* was finally finished.

"Catchy title," Marla quipped. "I like it."

"Good," Sharla smiled. "I'll e-mail you the manuscript."

A week later, Sharla got a reply from Marla which read: "Congratulations. I haven't read it all but it looks like you've got another bestseller. I'm already looking into scheduling you for a book signing tour. Get ready. Marla."

By coincidence, an article about Sharla came out the same day she finished her book. The story, which appeared in *Bookends*, a major literary magazine Sharla subscribed to, alluded to her as a one-hit wonder.

"…there is little question that Davis' first attempt as a published author was commercially and (in most literary circles) critically successful," the article's writer proposed.

"…but quantity does not always beget quality. Granted, Davis' book was funny and even a tad poignant in a schmaltzy sort of way, but does that mean she has what it takes to be a writer or any great merit? It has been a year since Chasing Trevor *shook the literary world, but we have yet to hear again from this reclusive new author. I, for one, wait*

anxiously to see what kind of tale will come flowing next from Ms. Davis' proverbial pen. Perhaps she'll right another spoof about this *year's America's Next Big Star. Maybe she can start a book franchise on the subject. Personally, I think her first novel was beginner's luck, which isn't exactly a rare commodity in this business, but it can only take one so far. In any case, whatever true writing potential Sharla Davis has remains to be seen..."*

Such scathing criticism a year ago would have crushed Sharla and confirmed her own worst fears about her talent. Now all it did was make her angry. Of course she had it in her to be a writer of great merit! And she felt sure that with this next book, she would be able to prove that. For Sharla, the article was a sign that her upcoming book was exactly what God wanted her to write. She was anxious now more than ever to show her critics she was no fluke.

The public seemed to agree. Sharla had been slightly worried that the same people who bought *Chasing Trevor*, most of them Tyler fans, would stay away from *Beauty in the Ashes*, which was far more serious and had nothing to do with their idol, but that wasn't the case. A marketing research study showed that in addition to a newer demographic of readers attracted to such books, the same majority of people who were members of Tyler's Soul Squad were also Christians hungering for a good, God-based storyline. Even though the book wasn't slated to hit stores until Christmastime, advanced orders were already through the roof. It was as if an entire section of Sharla Davis fans had been patiently watching and waiting for her to come out of her funk.

Sharla was extremely grateful. She was so thankful to God that neither He nor her family and fans had given up on her, even when it seemed she had given up on herself.

To mark the launch of her new book and also recognize the current period in her life she jokingly referred to as the "Age of Good Feelings," Sharla threw a celebratory bash at her home with her family and friends.

For the first time in a long time, Sharla threw caution to the wind and splurged, hiring caterers and a live band. She had the entire back yard decked out in a Hawaiian theme, complete with tropical paper lantern covers, wide brimmed sun hats and grass skirts. A beautiful, flowing lighted fountain was brought in and placed in the center of the yard, and a large white chocolate cake was made with the words 'Congratulations, Sharla' written in cheesecake icing across the top.

Just about everyone Sharla knew or thought she'd ever met was in attendance. She felt like she was in an episode of *This is Your Life*. Some of her former co-workers from the *Agape Gazette*, including her old editor, Jeff, came to the party; Pastor Mike and Veena and some other friends from church; Lindsey, Roxy and Diane, and a few old friends from school Sharla hadn't seen in ages. Candice and Marla flew in from New York, along with Sharla's agent and publicist. Even Derek made a surprise appearance with his family. Sharla ran to greet them, scooping up her little nephew and smothering his small round face with kisses.

Sharla briefly walked up to her new housekeeper, Ines Allende, whom she'd hired only a few weeks earlier, and asked if everything was going okay.

"*Sí, señora*," Ines nodded, placing more hors d'oeuvres onto a tray. "Everything is going....how you say?.....okey-dokey."

Ines made the O.K. sign and flashed a winning smile at Sharla, who couldn't help smiling back. Ines had a smile that was infectious.

A native of Juarez, Mexico, Ines was a woman in her early 40's who had legally immigrated to the United States with her family four years ago. She had only recently become born again and was attending Sharla's church. Her husband, the sole bread winner in the family, had been seriously injured on the job and was unable to work. The family had no insurance and her husband's job didn't offer workman's compensation. Pastor Mike mentioned in passing after church one day that Ines needed a job. And though she hadn't been too keen on the idea of a housekeeper at first, Sharla was immediately taken with Ines and felt impressed by the Holy Spirit to hire her. Now Sharla couldn't see how she'd ever gotten along without her.

"You know, Miss Sharla," Ines said in her thick accent that still struggled sometimes with the English language, "You are so blessed. Jus' look aroun' you…"

She made a sweeping gesture with her hand at the partygoers which included Ines's husband and three children, who were playing a game of hide-and-seek with Jeff's kids and Sharla's little nephew.

"…You got so many people that love you."

Sharla gently squeezed Ines's shoulder and nodded. "You're right, Ines. You're absolutely right."

"God is good, *verdád*?"

"Yes, He is."

"*Gloría a Tí, Señor*," Ines whispered. She picked up the hors d'oeuvres tray and walked out onto the deck.

A few minutes later, a server announced dinner by ringing a loud bell. When everyone was gathered, Sharla took center stage. After saying a prayer that was followed by a brief speech about how lucky she was to have such good friends and family in her life, everyone sat down to eat. Later, the band started up again as Sharla, with the help of Ida and Roxanne, served cake. Behind her in the house, the phone was ringing. Sharla turned to walk inside but Ines beat her to it.

"Hello, Davis residence?" she answered.

Sharla went back to serve and became engrossed in a funny conversation with Candice's boyfriend, Steve.

Meanwhile, Ines was walking outside with the phone to her ear. "*Un momento*," she spoke into it, then gently called Sharla's name, but the band was loud and there was so much commotion that she finally had to tap Sharla on the shoulder to get her attention.

Sharla half-turned towards Ines, still laughing at something someone had just said, a cake spatula in her hand.

"Miss Sharla," Ines said. "I sorry to interrupt, *pero* there's somebody calling for you."

Ines held out the cordless phone to Sharla but Sharla waved it away absently.

"Just take a message, Ines," she said, licking some icing from her fingers. "I'll call 'em back later."

"Si, señora," Ines nodded and went back into the house with the phone.

"And come have some cake!" Sharla yelled after her, although she wasn't sure Ines heard. Her ear was already to the phone as she stepped inside the patio door, closing it behind her.

When the party was finally over, Sharla was exhausted but happy. Most of the guests had left save for Sharla's parents and brother, her three closest girlfriends and Marla, who was somewhere in the back of the house on the phone. Sharla was sitting on the living room sofa with a cup of coffee. She sighed good-naturedly and smiled at Lindsey and Roxanne, who were gathering up used plates and cups.

"You guys don't have to do that," Sharla said.

"We know we don't have to," Lindsey agreed, taking a stack of plates to the kitchen. "But we want to. It's the least we can do since you set this entire shindig up by yourself."

"Okay," Sharla shrugged. "But just put the dishes in the sink for now. Ines can load the dishwasher in the morning."

"Well, this was a great night!" Ida observed, sauntering over with arms open wide to hug her daughter. "One for the record books."

She squeezed Sharla tightly.

"Glad you enjoyed it, mom," Sharla said, patting her mother warmly on the back. "It's the calm before the storm, I think."

"Why do you say that?" Ida asked, sitting down.

"I don't know," Sharla answered honestly. "Just something I can feel, I guess. I'm supposed to be going on a press junket for this new book soon and if it's anything like the one for *Chasing Trevor* was, that's going to be pretty tiring."

"It could also be fun," Ida said, raising an eyebrow. "Who knows? Maybe Mr. Right is out there waiting for you to sign a copy of your book for him."

Sharla laughed and rolled her eyes. "Maybe."

"I know you think I'm a nag when it comes to this subject," Ida said, tapping her daughter's thigh, "But I am definitely sensing a man in your future."

"Did somebody say 'a man?'" Diane came and plopped down unceremoniously between Sharla and Ida. "Who? Where?"

"Diane, you have bionic ears, you know that?" Sharla teased. "I thought you were still outside."

"I was outside but I came inside," Diane said dryly. "And when it comes to men, yes, God gifted me with incredible hearing. Now…" she looked at Ida then Sharla. "What is this about a man? Do you have one and does he have a debonair, independently wealthy older brother?"

Sharla thought hard for a moment, scratching her head for effect. "Uh, no and….no."

"Oh," Diane flatly replied and rose from the couch. "Then this conversation's over. I'm going for some water. Anybody want water?"

There were several 'no's throughout the room as Diane passed Lindsey and Roxanne coming out of the kitchen.

"I don't want water but what's this about a man?" Roxy asked, sitting on the loveseat.

"Nothing," Sharla said. "Just Diane being Diane. She and mom were teasing me about being single. Again."

"I wasn't teasing," Ida objected. "I'm serious. You're a pretty girl, a successful writer, you've got a lovely new home, money....any man would be jumping at the bit for you."

"Come to think of it," Sharla said slowly. "I have been getting calls from men lately."

All the women leaned in. "Really?" Lindsey asked. "From who?"

"Well, let's see...." Sharla said, using the tips of her fingers to count. "There was the cable guy when my cable went out last week, I just interviewed a landscaper—he was cute, although the gold band on his left hand and the picture he showed me of his five kids made me think he might not be available—then there was Ned, the 70-year-old plumber who came by when my upstairs toilet overflowed, and oh yeah, a man called yesterday asking if I was happy with my long distance service. At least, I think it was a man. It's hard to tell sometimes over the phone."

Sharla looked directly at her mother as the other women sat back in their seats again, amused but deflated. "So, you're right, mom, I am having to beat the men off with sticks."

Just then, Ines, who had come from outside and caught the latter part of Sharla's monologue, walked up and announced in a loud voice that got everyone's attention:

"Oh! Miss Sharla, that remind me, some man, he call for you tonight."

Ida was instantly all ears. Sharla looked around the living room. Her father and brother had paused their conversation when Ines spoke but had quickly gone back to talking, but the other ladies were looking at Ines expectantly.

"Oh?" Sharla finally said. "Who was it?"

Ines opened her mouth to speak, then stopped and began patting herself down and digging in her apron pockets.

"I not sure," she said, still searching her person. "He lef' his name. I write it down. It's here somewhere..." she walked over to the dining table, her eyes scanning its surface. "I find it for you *pero* I think I remember his first name." She closed her eyes to concentrate then opened them wide a few seconds later.

"Teeler!" she said with glee. "Teeler! That what he say was his first name!"

Sharla looked openly blank at Ines.

"Teeler?" she repeated.

"Sí, Teeler!" Ines nodded.

Sharla searched the eyes of her friends and her mother before putting them back on Ines. Teeler was an unusual name and she didn't know anyone that went by it. Then it struck her that perhaps Ines was saying "Taylor" but it was coming out "Teeler" because of her accent.

"Ines, do you mean Taylor?" Sharla asked. "Somebody named Taylor called?"

Ines was about to speak but Lindsey interrupted her. "Sharla, you don't know anybody named Taylor, do you?"

"No," Sharla said. "Maybe it was a wrong number."

"Hope he at least sounded cute," Diane quipped.

"Taylor....Taylor...." Ida mused aloud. "Why does that name sound familiar?"

"Mom, do you know someone named Taylor?" Sharla frowned.

Ida thought a second then shrugged. "I don't think so." She looked at her daughter, puzzled. "But the name sounds vaguely familiar for some reason."

"I think I went to school with a Taylor...but that was a girl," Sharla thought aloud. "Mom, you remember Taylor Reed from third grade? The one that stole Iris Matthew's lunch and told the teacher I did it...?"

"...and I had to go down there and straighten that teacher out, you bet I remember," Ida added. "I told her, my daughter does not steal—"

"Señora!" Ines broke in. "It was not Taylor. He say *Teeler.*"

"Are you sure, Ines?" Sharla said. "Because I don't know anyone named Teeler."

"Sí, señora, I positive."

"Maybe it was a fan that got your number," Roxanne offered.

"How? My number's unlisted?"

"Or...." Diane said, leaning forward as if she'd just discovered the secret to the universe. "Maybe what she's saying....is *Tyler.*" Diane turned and looked at Ines. "Is that who called? Was his name....Tyler?"

"Sí, sí! *Teeler*!" Ines said, nodding her head emphatically.

There was a dead hush in the room. Sharla knew of only one person with that name. She and Lindsey exchanged brief but significant glances before Sharla stood up, her voice calm.

"Did he leave a last name?"

Ines frowned, still searching around her. "Sí, I look for it, I wrote it down..."

She went into the kitchen where some shuffling could be heard then returned a few seconds later with a piece of paper.

"Here it is!" she said, reading it. "His name Teeler...." she squinted, fishing in her pocket for her bifocals. After fixing them on her face, she held up the paper again... "Neek."

She took off the bifocals and smiled triumphantly at Sharla. "Teeler Neek. That his name."

Sharla looked around and saw that everyone, including her father and brother, had stopped talking and were looking directly at her. Every person in the room knew, albeit in varying degrees, of her history where Tyler was concerned and each face looked to be in various degrees of shock. Sharla had never seen so many people at one time with their mouths hanging open. It was as if an announcement had just been made the Rapture would take place in five minutes.

Sharla took the piece of paper from Ines and examined it. Sure enough, it said "Teeler Neek," just the way Ines pronounced it. It was blank otherwise.

"Did he leave a phone number?" Sharla asked.

"No, *señora*," Ines answered. "I ask him to but he say he would call back."

Lindsey grabbed the note and looked at it. "He didn't leave a number?"

"No, just his name," Sharla said.

"What about a message?"

Sharla looked up, startled to see that that question had come from her father. It was directed at Ines.

"No, *señor*, he not leave a message or phone number, nothing. He just say he call back."

"When did he call?" Derek jumped in.

"Tonight, during la fiesta," Ines said, slightly flustered. She looked at Sharla. "Señora, I ask you if you want to talk but you said take a message, remember?"

Sharla thought for a moment. Things had been so crazy for her during the party she could barely remember what happened five minutes ago. But no one had called. Practically everyone she kept in close contact with had been here tonight. Ines must be mistaken—

Then it came to her. Sharla could see in her mind's eye Ines handing her the phone and her refusing to take it.

Just take a message, she'd said. *I'll call 'em back later.*

Sharla closed her eyes. She felt slightly light-headed. "Yes, I remember," she sighed regretfully.

Meanwhile, the note was being passed about and had temporarily landed with Roxanne. "Did he say when he'd call back?" she asked.

Ines shook her head. "No, he don't say when. All he say is he call back."

"Oh, my God, this is unbelievable!" Ida exclaimed. The note was now in her possession. She held it as if it would disintegrate in her hand at any second.

"Sharla, this is what you've been waiting for!" She started jumping up and down like a woman who's just been told she's won the lottery.

"Yeah, but there's no number on there," Richard added, his voice slightly raised. The atmosphere in the room was heightening. "What kind of guy doesn't even leave a phone number?"

"One that obviously doesn't want to be called back," Diane replied. "He's real mysterioso, huh?"

"Wait a minute, wait a minute!" Derek announced. Everyone turned in his direction. He pointed at the phone. "The caller I.D." He walked grandly over to the phone and picked it up. "If he called, his number has to be on the caller I.D."

Sharla rolled her eyes. She couldn't believe how everyone was acting. The same people who a year earlier had chided her for acting so cornball over somebody from the television, the same people who'd staged an intervention to get her to stop obsessing over Tyler Nicks, were now falling all over themselves in a frenzy because he might have called. Supposedly sane people were standing in her living room oohing and aahing her little brother and patting him on the back as if he'd just discovered fire.

The first line of a Doors song came into Sharla's head: *People are strange...*

Derek pushed a button on the phone. It beeped and lit up.

"What's it say?" Lindsey asked anxiously over Derek's shoulder.

Derek's exuberance quickly turned flat. "It says 'out of area.'"

There was a collective moan as he sat the phone back on its base.

"Well, now what, Sherlock?" Sharla said, folding her arms. This was actually kind of fun, watching everybody scramble.

"Whaddya mean, 'now what?'" Derek frowned. "Why are you being sarcastic? I'm just trying to help you."

"Help me?" Sharla couldn't believe what she was hearing. "Didn't you tell me Tyler Nicks was a fantasy, Derek? I seem to remember you saying that to me. Now you want to help me?"

Derek threw up his hands. "Hey, if you don't want to talk to the guy… fine. Sorry."

"Back in my day," Richard said, "If a man wanted to talk to a lady he left a phone number."

"Dad, it's not a big deal," Sharla sighed. "He said he'd call back. I'm sure he will."

"After all the heartache you've been through, you tell me it's not a big deal?" Richard asked. "I can't believe that."

"Well," Sharla hugged herself. "I'm sorry I missed the call but…what's done is done. If it's in God's purpose, he'll call back."

"Sharla, you are being so calm about this," Roxanne said, patting Sharla on the shoulder. "I'm really impressed. If it were me, I'd be freaking right now."

Sharla shrugged. Maybe she was in shock.

Actually, Sharla was surprised herself at how calmly she was handling the situation and was about to say so when she realized something was wrong. Someone was crying, she could vaguely hear it underneath all the chatter. She left the living room and followed the gentle sobbing, which got louder as she approached the kitchen. It was Ines. She was standing at the work island in the center of the kitchen, dabbing at her eyes with a paper towel.

"Ines?….Ines, what's wrong?" Sharla approached her and draped an arm around her shoulder.

"Miss Sharla," Ines sniffed. "It's my fault, it's all my fault!"

"What's your fault?" Sharla asked.

"That everybody so mad," Ines cried. "It's my fault but I didn't know, I didn't know. You said take a message and I tried but he no want to leave a message. He say he call back." Ines blew her nose into the paper towel and added: "Nex' time he call I *demand* a message!"

Sharla smiled a little and stuffed down the urge to laugh. Not at Ines but at how ridiculous the events of the last few minutes had become.

"No, Ines, that's okay, you don't need to demand anything."

"But everybody so angry," Ines insisted. "And I only did what you asked—"

"Exactly," Sharla affirmed. "You did what I asked, Ines. You didn't do anything wrong."

Ines looked at Sharla with an unsure, searching expression, large tears falling from her eyes.

"Really," Sharla said, hugging Ines's shoulder. "You didn't do anything wrong."

"But…everybody so mad…"

"Oh, don't pay any attention to them," Sharla waved off. "That's just how my family is. They're all crazy. I'm the only sane one in the bunch."

Seeing that Sharla was joking with her, Ines smiled, but only a little.

"You and your brother," she observed. "You were fighting."

"Derek and me?" Sharla shrugged. "That's just how we get along. We argue."

As if on cue, Derek entered the kitchen.

"He knows I love him," Sharla added, looking directly at her brother.

Derek smiled and the feud was over. There was a pause, then: "Hey, mom wants to know if Tyler—"

Sharla immediately hushed him with a deadly serious look and some hand waving gestures behind Ines's head that said "zip it!"

"What?" Derek asked, raising his hands.

Sharla said nothing but continued to give her brother the look.

"Okay," Derek shrugged, shaking his head in a way that said he'd never understand women. "Forget it." He turned and left the kitchen.

"This man, Teeler," Ines went on. "He somebody special to you, yes?"

Sharla thought for a moment. Ever since she'd written Tyler, she'd felt freer, as if by wishing him well she'd somehow released him from her system. Finding out he wasn't really married had been nice but Sharla had become so immersed in her book that she hadn't really allowed herself time to think about whether or not a relationship with him was something she still wanted. Ines' question prompted her to the conclusion that it was probably was.

"He was somebody special to me," Sharla finally answered. "I suppose he still is, yeah."

Ines had stopped crying but she still looked distraught.

"But you didn't know that," Sharla quickly added. "I didn't tell you and there's no way you could have known, so don't beat yourself up about this. It's not your fault. He and I, we just…missed each other, that's all."

"He did say he call back," Ines said hopefully.

"Well," Sharla sighed and shrugged. "Maybe he will. If he called once…. right?"

"Sí," Ines nodded.

"Listen, it's been a long night," Sharla said, stretching. "I think I'm gonna kick these people out of my house and go to bed. Why don't you go home too? Get some rest."

"Oh, no, Miss Sharla, I still have to get the table cloths—"

"That can wait till tomorrow," Sharla insisted. "Take the morning off, sleep in and just come in tomorrow afternoon and we'll do the rest."

Ines rose and smiled. "Thank you, Señora."

Sharla hugged Ines. "You're welcome, sweetie."

"What's all the hubbub in the living room?" It was Marla.

Sharla and Ines broke their embrace. Ines grabbed her purse and said goodnight. Sharla's parents also said their goodbyes, followed by Derek, then Roxanne, Diane and Lindsey. When everyone was gone, Sharla answered Marla's question.

"Tyler Nicks called me," she said.

A huge smile lit across Marla's face. "Did he? Good! I was wondering if he would. Did you talk to him?"

"No, I missed the call but he said he'd call back." Sharla frowned. "What do you mean you were wondering if he'd call?"

"Well, when I passed on your number to him, I wasn't sure if he'd call right away. I know he's been terribly busy, what with that whole marriage scam and his new album."

Marla was poking her head in the refrigerator. She opened the freezer, grabbed a glass and got some ice. "That girl that made up that story has a real problem, let me tell you. I've known her father for years. Nice man, Larry. Tough but fair."

Sharla, in the meantime, was dumbfounded. "You gave Tyler my phone number? When?"

"Well, I didn't give it to him directly, dear," Marla explained, opening a Coke and pouring it into the glass. "I passed it on to a friend who knows a friend." She winked and took a long swig of her drink.

"And you were going to tell me this....when?" Sharla asked.

"Actually, I was going to bring it up tonight but I didn't get the chance," Marla said. She was searching Sharla's face. "You're not upset about it, are you? I mean, given the fact that you wrote a book based on the man, I didn't think you'd mind."

Sharla shook her head. "No, it's not that, it's just....I wish you'd told me so I could have..." She trailed off.

"Could have what?" Marla pressed.

"I don't know," Sharla stammered. "Prepared myself, I guess."

"Prepare?" Marla frowned. "Prepare for what? What's there to prepare for to simply have a chat with someone? You just pick up the phone, say 'hello' and start talking. There's nothing to it."

"Maybe for you," Sharla countered. "You're used to being around big names."

Marla put down her drink and looked at Sharla. "Darling, the only difference between a celebrity and everybody else is having your name in the paper more often than the average Joe. There isn't one person I've met, be it Elton John or Prince Albert who doesn't put their pants on one leg at a time just like every other human being on the planet. Celebrities are still insecure, they still have problems, they can still have a bad day. In short, they're still people and no amount of money ever changes that inner need we all have to feel love and be accepted. Surely, you know that. In a lot of people's eyes, you're a celebrity now. But that doesn't make you immune to being human. Just talk to Tyler like he's human."

"Have you met him?" Sharla asked.

"Once," Marla nodded. "Briefly, at a party a few months ago. Some music fundraiser Larry Dupree threw to raise money for underprivileged kids. I only got to say hello to him. He was in and out, like he was in a real hurry. Seemed like a sweet boy, though. Much taller than I expected."

"How did you get him my number?"

Marla smiled. She became very animated and leaned in to Sharla. "I thought you'd never ask. It just so happens an old college friend of mine, we were in the same sorority together, hails from Georgia. After she graduated, she went back and married her high school sweetheart, a real Southern gentleman. Anyway, her husband is good friends with Thomas Nicks, Tyler Nicks' father. Turns out they did a stint in the Army together and remained friends. When my girlfriend injured her back in a car accident a few years ago, Tommy Nicks was her chiropractor. Well, when I found this out, I asked her if she wouldn't mind seeing if Tom would pass along a phone number to his son from a dear, sweet girl named Sharla Davis."

Marla shrugged and took a sip of her drink.

"Wow," was all Sharla could manage.

"Small world, huh?" Marla chuckled. "Who would have thought that a genteel Southern belle and a little Jewish girl from Queens would end up best friends? Life's full of twists."

Sharla was studying her friend in amazement. "Why'd you do, it Marla? I didn't ask you to."

"You asked me to make sure he got a letter from you."

"Yes, but that was a letter," Sharla reasoned. "Not a phone call."

Marla sighed. "I did it….because you wouldn't have. I don't know. I like you, kid, what can I say? I guess there's something about you that reminds me of myself when I was young. Besides, I think you two need to talk."

Sharla sat up straighter. "About what?"

"About whatever it was that propelled you to write about him in the first place, maybe." Marla said. "I don't know, dear. Just talk. Just…be human."

Marla's cell phone went off.

"I have to take this," she said and opened her phone.

While Marla talked, Sharla went back into the living room and started straightening up, her mind racing. She was picking up stray trash and putting it into a plastic bag when Marla came into the living room several minutes later.

"That was Danté, my new assistant," Marla said. "I've got good news. The *Today Show* wants to interview you."

"Oh?" Sharla raised an eyebrow.

"Yes, and it's perfect timing because you'll be in New York anyway for your book signing."

"And when is that?" Sharla asked.

Marla looked at her watch then back at Sharla. She smiled.

"How soon can you pack?"

Chapter 25: Being Human

No matter how many times she visited, coming to New York always felt to Sharla as if she were about to embark on some new beginning.

In New York, there seemed to be no such thing as celebrities. People were simply people. A film star could walk down the street with not much more acknowledgment than a nod and a smile.

There was a peaceful sense of anonymity that Sharla loved about the place, the kind of anonymity she'd often heard John Lennon speak of before someone infringed on that peace and shattered it and him on the stoop outside his apartment building. But the ability to blend seamlessly into a crowd was still there.

New York—as John had also said—was like Rome in its heyday: the center of Western civilization. A great place to learn about being human.

Sharla savored it. She breathed it in just as she breathed in the wintry air of New York at Christmas, with all of its bright, glittery lights and festive decorations.

Her first day back in the city, Sharla was in Bloomingdales doing some gift shopping when she felt a light tap on her shoulder. She turned around to find herself staring into the chest of a thin, tall woman with striking green eyes and a round face who looked vaguely familiar.

The woman was wearing a light blue button-down dress with a black belt and matching boots. Her shoulder-length brown hair was pulled back in a ponytail. A pair of sunglasses sat perched atop her head, looking as if they might fall down over eyes at any second.

Sharla turned her gaze upwards at the woman, whose 5-foot-10 inch frame easily towered over her. The woman, who was pushing a little girl in a stroller, smiled warmly.

"Sharla, I am so sorry to bother you," the woman said sweetly. "I know you're probably trying to shop in peace, but I just had to come over and tell you how much I enjoyed your book."

The woman began fishing in a large handbag hanging from her shoulder and took out *Beauty in the Ashes.*

"Oh, you're welcome," Sharla said. She began digging around in her own purse for a pen. "Would you like me to sign it?"

"Um, well, that would be nice," the woman answered hesitantly, putting the book back into her handbag, "But I was really wondering if maybe you and I could go somewhere and talk for a little while, maybe grab a bite. If you have time."

Sharla looked at the woman, puzzled and feeling slightly nervous. Her trepidation must have registered on her face. She was about to answer that she didn't have time but the woman interrupted.

"Oh, listen, I'm not crazy or anything," the woman quickly said, holding out her hands. "It's just, I haven't seen you since we both worked at the paper and I thought it might be nice to catch up."

Now Sharla was really confused. Was she supposed to know this lady?

The woman's eyes stayed fixed on Sharla, searching her face. Finally she said, "You don't recognize me, do you?"

"No, I'm afraid not," Sharla admitted. "You look familiar but...you say you worked at the paper with me. At the *Agape Gazette*?"

"Yes," the woman nodded, then quickly added, "We weren't in the same department, though. I worked in advertising."

"Advertising..." Sharla repeated, mainly to herself. She didn't know anyone in advertising. In fact, the only person she really knew of in that department was that slut who'd stolen Paul away from her.

"It's me, Sarah Cummings!" the woman blurted, as if on cue. "Well, it was Cummings. It's Grant now."

Sharla dropped her shopping bag, it's contents spilling out onto the aisle next to the perfume counter. Of course. Sharla recognized her now. Thin, tall…elegant bone structure. Only Sarah's hair was shorter and slightly lighter when she worked in Agape. Sharla had never really gotten a good look at her up close.

"Whoops!" Sarah laughed, bending down to pick up the scattered purchases. Sharla slowly eased down to help her, feeling as if she were in a dream. A bad one.

Sarah looked at Sharla with concerned. "Are you okay?" she asked as she stuffed items back into the Bloomingdales shopping bag. Sharla didn't answer.

"Guess you're really shocked to see me, huh?" Sarah chuckled. "In New York of all places. I bet I'm the last person you thought you'd run into here."

"You got that right," Sharla managed. She hadn't thought about Sarah Cummings, about Paul in a long time. She'd stuffed her feelings about both of them down into a place where she thought she no longer felt any pain. But seeing Sarah standing in front of her face to face, Sharla realized she was still very angry.

That grainy, black and white engagement photo of the two of them taken on the patio of Paul's apartment came to Sharla's mind and she cringed. She began thinking of the many times she'd tried to throw that stupid picture away and couldn't. Of how small and unworthy she felt every time she glanced at it. She'd ended up keeping it until it finally disintegrated after she forgot she'd left it in the pocket of her jeans and washed them. Too bad her wounded heart hadn't been washed away with it.

Now, one of the people who'd helped to make her feel about as big as a cockroach was standing before her asking to go to lunch. How could this woman who had so blatantly disrespected her have the nerve to stand before her now acting so cordial and looking her in the eye as if nothing had ever happened?

Sharla felt like telling the hussy exactly what she thought of her and probably would have had the little girl Sarah had with her not begun to cry.

"It's okay, honey," Sarah cooed to the child. "Mommy's gonna take you to eat in just a minute."

To calm her, she handed the little girl a small baby doll stuffed down inside her stroller and straightened up again.

"She gets so fussy when she's hungry," Sarah explained.

For the first time since Sarah had walked up to her, Sharla really looked at the little girl, whom she guessed was about two, maybe two-and-half-years-old. The child had a round face like her mother but her eyes were large and brown like Paul's. A flurry of loose blondish curls covered her head as she sucked her thumb and hugged her doll, content for the moment.

Sharla thought she was precious. Watching the child melted some of her indignation. Calmness came over her and she knew it was the Holy Spirit cautioning her not to say something she might later regret. Instead, she felt led to keep quiet and hear Sarah out.

"Listen, there's a little Italian place around the corner. Would you mind if we sat down and talked for a minute?"

There was a slight pleading in Sarah's voice—nothing overt, it was just under the surface—that piqued Sharla's curiosity.

"Alright," she curtly agreed. "But I can't stay long."

"No, I understand," Sarah replied, smiling bigger than ever. "Just a few minutes."

With that, she took control of the stroller and she and Sharla walked out of the department store to a quiet outside table under the awning of a nearby small, Italian bistro. After ordering spaghetti for Samantha (Sharla learned that was the name of Sarah's little girl), and watching the child play with her noodles and sauce before finally getting most of the food on her bib and some in her mouth, the two women settled in to talk.

Sarah had a light salad while Sharla only ordered bottled water. At that particular moment, she didn't have much of an appetite.

During the initial course of the conversation, Sharla didn't say much. She just sipped her water and let Sarah talk, which Sarah seemed more than happy to do. Sharla listened politely, all the while wondering what this woman really wanted and what was she up to?

A few minutes into the banter, Sharla learned that after Sarah and Paul married and moved to Florida, the marriage slowly began to disintegrate. The first two years were pretty good, Sarah admitted, but about the third year, Sarah said Paul seemed to lose interest in her and became difficult and argumentative. Sharla nodded. She was familiar with Paul's erratic moods. Sarah remarked that she was confused by the sudden change in her husband, who'd always been so caring and thoughtful before.

"I thought if I could get pregnant, that would help the marriage," she confessed. "I guess I figured having a baby would change things."

"And they did change…for a while," Sarah smiled, looking at her daughter. "After Samantha was born, Paul got this great job offer with a huge financial firm in upstate New York, so we moved here and a little of the old Paul came back. But it didn't last."

Her smile slowly faded as she continued.

"Around the time Samantha turned one, he just seemed to get worse. He was always in a bad mood, I could never do anything right. He wouldn't touch me, started staying away for days. One day I came home and found he'd cleaned out his closet. All his clothes were gone from the dresser…"

She chuckled bitterly. "…He left a note on the bed. It said something like, 'I can't live like this anymore, I'm tired of living a lie,' or something really melodramatic like that. I wish I'd kept it so I could show it to you."

Sharla smiled empathetically. She didn't need to see the note. She'd gotten one of her own.

"Anyway," Sarah went on. "Paul called me later that night to tell me that he'd met some guy out in Soho and had moved in with him and he wanted a divorce."

Sharla never would have admitted it aloud, but hearing about Sarah's marriage woes filled her with a sense of merited vindication. She chuckled to herself. So, there was trouble in paradise…go figure. She did her best to mask her inward satisfaction, trying to keep her expression neutral throughout the conversation, but Sarah's last comment made her gasp and drop her jaw in astonishment.

"What?!" she exclaimed. "A guy? Did you say he met a *guy* and moved in with him?!"

"That's exactly what I said," Sarah answered, folding her arms. "A *man*. Supposedly, some art teacher. His name's Antoíne and Paul says he's the love of his life."

"Oh my God!" Sharla gasped. "Paul's gay?!"

"Apparently," Sarah sighed.

"I can't believe it," Sharla muttered. Never in her wildest dreams would she have figured Paul to be gay.

"Well, believe it because it's trooo, yes it is, it's trooo!" Sarah cooed, spooning some spaghetti into Samantha's mouth. Samantha smiled back and echoed "*Trooo!*" clapping her hands gleefully.

"So," Sarah went on, using a napkin to wipe spaghetti sauce off her fingers, "As you can guess, Paul and I are now in the middle of finalizing a divorce. I'm switching back to my maiden name."

"What about Samantha?" Sharla asked, turning to the little girl with concern.

"Oh, she's with me," Sarah said firmly. "That was one thing Paul and I were able to agree on. He has visitation but I have full custody, which was just fine with him."

"Good Lord," Sharla breathed, shaking her head.

"But listen," Sarah said, briefly touching Sharla's hand. "I didn't ask you to meet me just so I could tell you my problems. There's another reason."

"What?" Sharla swallowed, listening.

"When Paul and I were together, after things really started to go bad, around that time, your first book came out and for weeks all Paul could talk about was how if it hadn't been for him, you never would have written a book…"

Sharla stiffened.

"…He said you should be thanking him because without him, you'd have been nothing…"

Sarah paused, trying to gauge Sharla's reaction.

"Go on," was all Sharla managed through clinched teeth.

"I couldn't understand why he kept going on about you. The more we heard about you and your book, the angrier he became and I just couldn't figure it out. I bought your book to see if maybe there was some clue in it as to what Paul was going on about, and when he found it in the house, he went ballastic. He started yelling and ripping out the pages, ranting that he didn't want anything you'd written in his house…"

"Good grief!" Sharla frowned. Paul really had lost it.

"…So when he'd calmed down," Sarah continued, "I asked him if there'd ever been anything between you two and he wouldn't answer me. Well, a few days later, I happened to be doing some cleaning and I came across a pair of Paul's old blue jeans I was going to give away. When I unfolded the jeans, a picture of you and him fell out, and when I confronted him about it, he finally admitted that you and he had been in a relationship—"

"Wait a minute," Sharla said, leaning forward. "You mean you didn't know he and I were in a relationship?"

Sarah shook her head. "No. He never mentioned you."

Sharla stared at Sarah in disbelief. "But he and I had been together for three years," she argued. "How could you not have known? I was still with him when you…"

Sharla trailed off. She was about to say "When you stole him," but closed her mouth instead, afraid she might completely lose it and more suspicious of Sarah than ever.

Sarah looked away for a moment. Sadness came over her face; it looked genuine.

"I know," she finally said. "I got enough out of Paul to put the pieces together. That's why when I saw you in Bloomingdales, I knew I had to talk to you."

Again, she took Sharla's hand. Sharla didn't jerk away but she felt a little sick inside.

"Sharla, I swear to you I had no idea you were with Paul," Sarah said quietly, looking Sharla directly in the eyes. "When I met him, he told me he wasn't seeing anyone and I didn't have any reason not to believe him."

"What about all my things in his apartment?" Sharla asked, trying to muster as much civility in her voice as possible. "You didn't see any of my clothes, my pictures?"

Sarah shook her head. "I never saw a trace of you in his apartment."

Sarah looked so earnest, Sharla briefly thought she might be telling the truth. Then she thought about the night she'd come home from work and found all of her belongings on her front stoop. And the note Paul had written saying it was over. Three weeks later, he and Sarah got engaged. Sharla was beginning to see that it made sense. He'd removed her and her things out of his life to make room for someone else's. Paul always was a control freak who hated leaving any loose ends. So once he'd done with Sharla, he'd cleaned out every trace of her, making sure he'd completely erased her from his life. As far as Paul was concerned, Sharla Davis had probably ceased to exist. What an affront it must have been to his monumental ego to later have the bestselling book of the woman he'd once dismissed as nothing staring him in the face.

Sharla quit thinking and looked at Sarah. She had stopped talking and was waiting for Sharla to react. Slowly, she removed her hand from over Sharla's.

"I can only imagine what you must think of me," Sarah sighed regretfully, removing Samantha's bib. She took a napkin, dipped it in her water glass and began to clean off her daughter's sauce-stained face.

"I just want you to know," she continued, picking up Samantha and holding her in the crook of one arm. "I never would have continued seeing Paul if I'd known he was with you. I'm not like that. I know you're still upset. I could see it when you recognized me. Frankly, I was surprised you agreed to sit down with me at all but I'm glad you did."

Sharla was about to say something but Sarah stopped her.

"I don't blame you," she continued, briefly hoisting Samantha up on her hip so she could get a better grip on the child. "I guess I might still be mad too if I were in your place. But I really didn't know. And I'm really sorry about what he did, to both of us."

Sarah smiled. Sharla could see she was sincere. She sat back in her chair, touched, not sure what she should say. A sheet of guilt fell over her for having felt so smug about all of Sarah's troubles just a few minutes earlier. Sharla felt the peace of God come over her and the anger she'd been harboring for more than three years suddenly vanished. All of the bitterness and hatred for both Paul and Sarah left her and was replaced by only compassion and most importantly, forgiveness.

"Well," she said, clearing her throat. "It's not like we were married."

"But three years is a long time to be with someone," Sarah countered. "And if I know Paul, he didn't break up with you well, did he?"

Sharla smiled ruefully. "No, he didn't."

Sarah nodded. "Figures." She gingerly placed Samantha back into her stroller and strapped her into place.

"Well, hey," she said, raising up with a newfound spring. "He did you a favor. Heck, he did both of us a favor."

"What favor did he do for you?" Sharla asked, puzzled.

"He gave me her." Sarah looked down at Samantha, who, no sooner than she was strapped in, began dozing peacefully with her doll in her arms, her small round mouth slightly ajar.

"What I went through with him was worth it just to have my daughter. She's the one good thing that's come out of this mess."

Sarah looked directly at Sharla, her eyes warm and smiling. She really did seem to be at peace with it all.

Sharla smiled back. "Well, with your looks, I'm sure you'll have no trouble finding someone to help you raise Samantha."

Sarah frowned and wrinkled her nose as if she'd just smelled something highly unpleasant.

"Oh, God!" she moaned. "I'm not even thinking about being with a man right now. I've been on a few dates but I'm not rushing it. To be honest…" she said, looking down lovingly at Samantha, "I really enjoy being a single mom. And it's not easy finding a man who'll accept Samantha. You'd be surprised at the number of men who, when they find out you have a two-year-old daughter, don't tend to return phone calls."

"You just haven't found the right one," Sharla answered.

"What about you?" Sarah asked. "Are you seeing anyone special?"

"No, I'm still single," Sharla sighed and smiled.

"Well, ditto to you, then," Sarah teased.

Sharla frowned. "Huh?"

"*You* haven't found the right one."

Sharla nodded. For some reason, she thought fleetingly of Tyler.

The two women exchanged phone numbers and promised to keep in touch.

"Oh, hey!" Sarah called, jogging to catch up with Sharla, who was headed out of the restaurant. "You forgot to sign my book."

Sarah again produced *Beauty in the Ashes* and opened it. Sharla signed it:

> To Sarah:
> God bless you and your beautiful daughter!
> Love,
> Sharla Davis

———————————————————

Some time later, as Sharla replayed the recent events on her way back to her hotel, she realized the seed of anger she'd been holding onto for so long had been concocted on the basis of a lie.

All these years, she had villianized Sarah yet Sarah had been just as much in the dark as she was, both of them victims of the deceit of a man who was obviously confused and full of his own self-hatred and bitterness. Yet this man, Sharla marveled with great amusement, was the same man upon whom she'd once thought the sun rose and set.

She sighed and laughed to herself. *What was I thinking?!*

But Sharla knew exactly what she'd been thinking. She had no illusions about her looks. She felt she would never be what any man would have considered as beautiful. And she'd never thought she could do better than Paul, who seemed so intelligent and acted so confident. She remembered thinking that if someone like him could be interested in someone like her, maybe she wasn't so bad after all. She'd based her entire self-image on one man's opinion of her. And when that man rejected her, Sharla had taken it to mean she was worthless. Her feelings of worthlessness had further been justified by the fact that Paul replaced her with what Sharla felt was the antithesis of herself. But Sarah, whom most people would consider very attractive and "worthy," had also been used up and dumped on by the very same man. Her physical beauty hadn't kept her from being hurt.

Sharla could see now that she had used blaming Sarah for the end of her relationship with Paul as a diversion, an excuse for her not to take responsibility for her own lack of forthrightness. She'd wasted so much time being bitter, distracted by anger that had kept her from being free to live.

Thank Jesus He had gotten her out of that unhealthy situation. Sharla truly believed God had put Sarah in her path at a time when He knew Sharla was ready to forgive. And Sarah was right. Paul had done Sharla a tremendous favor—he'd dumped her. What a blessing that turned out to be! If she ever saw Paul again, Sharla thought she'd probably thank him. She'd certainly be praying for him.

To think she had wanted to marry him! That could so easily have been her standing in Sarah's place had God not allowed Paul to break Sharla's heart. But Paul hadn't really broken it. He'd simply wounded it so that God could show her what a magnificent healer He was.

Sharla slid her electronic room card into the door of her hotel suite and walked inside, absently sitting her purse and shopping bag down on the sofa. She stretched. Her neck and shoulders felt tense. Maybe she'd ring downstairs for a masseuse, then take a long, hot bath. Sitting on the edge of her hotel bed, Sharla took out her cell phone and checked her voice messages.

Tyler hadn't called back; it was probably for the best. Things were going to be very busy for Sharla the next few months. The last thing she felt she needed now was to become emotionally preoccupied with Tyler now that she'd finally gotten herself free of her feelings. The vision she'd had a little more than two years ago, once so powerful and clear, had lately grown fuzzy and dull in her memory, the way a dream will often fade upon waking.

Now, gazing out her hotel window, which overlooked a magnificent view of Central Park, Sharla could only think of how grateful to God she was to have come out from under all of her pain and grief, and to be standing on the other side. She knew there would no doubt still be storms in the future—after all, Jesus did say that in this world, there would be trouble—but Sharla felt confident that with God, she could face her troubles head-on, not simply tuck herself away inside her house and pretend nothing was wrong as she'd done before.

Jesus said He had overcome the world.

Philippians 4:13 came to her mind: *"I can do all things through Christ who strengthens me…"*

Sharla sighed and thought briefly about the phone call the other night and her calm, almost blasé reaction. A year—no, even seven short months ago—she would have been in tears she'd missed that call, not to mention traumatized that Tyler hadn't called back. Now, all she felt was peace.

Qué sera sera, whatever will be will be…the future's not ours to see…

Doris Day sang blithely in her head. Sharla chuckled. Ah, well. Perhaps she really had been in love with Tyler's image after all.

Whatever the case, Sharla thought her father was right. The Lord had used Tyler to show her she was worth something in God's eyes, and that was all that mattered. She understood now that no matter how much she may have thought she loved Tyler, she would have made herself and him miserable had she met him when she'd wanted because she didn't have any self-respect or love for *herself.* That was what God had birthed into her these last two years. And the truly amazing part was, He'd used a prematurely gray-haired Soul singer from Georgia who had no idea who she was to do it.

That is what Sharla told Tyler in her letter. Not the part about not being ready for him, but the latter part, about God using him to show her she was valuable. That letter was the hardest she'd ever had to write, yet it was also the most liberating. In it, she'd put aside any pretense. There'd been no hiding behind cute phrases. Just 'thank you.'

After she'd done it, she'd felt she could move on, that it was *okay* to move on. She could get on with her life and let Tyler get on with his. And just when she'd come to a place in her heart where she'd made peace with the possibility that she'd never meet Tyler, he'd called. Sharla laughed to herself. The man had impeccable timing.

No matter. Sharla hadn't tried to figure it all out, there hadn't been time. She'd been back in New York less than a day and already, the city had presented her with something of a surprise. As she continued to sit and look out her hotel window, Sharla wondered what else the city might reveal.

●————————————————————————————————————●

The *Today Show* appearance the next morning was nothing out of the ordinary. The interview, which consisted of a few questions regarding Sharla's new book, lasted about seven minutes. Matt Lauer, who interviewed Sharla, mercifully skirted over the subject of Tyler and her first novel, choosing instead to focus on the new book, for which Sharla was grateful.

After posing for a few pictures with fans outside the *Today Show* studios, Sharla went back to her hotel and snoozed for a bit before arriving at a popular local bookstore near Central Park for her book signing.

Sharla was pleasantly surprised to find that early buzz for *Beauty in the Ashes* had generated quite a crowd outside the store. There was already a line of women (and even a few men) waiting for the signing to start. Sharla stared in amazement at a huge display of the book in the front store window. She still couldn't get over the shock of seeing her name on the front cover of anything, let alone something she wrote.

As she settled in for the signing, Sharla enjoyed hearing the compliments from women who'd obtained advanced copies of the book and said it changed their lives. Many of them told her they identified with Sharla's female protagonist, several commenting that they too had overcome abusive relationships. Although Sharla was appreciative of their praise, she was very clear to point out that if anyone had experienced a change, it was not so much because of her book but because of the power of the Lord Jesus Christ within it.

After about an hour of signing, Sharla fell into a groove of smiling politely at whoever happened to be standing in front of her. Aside from posing for the occasional photo with someone, she took each customer's copy of *Beauty in the Ashes*, signed it and handed it back. She was prepared to do the same for the next individual who walked up.

"Hi, Sharla, nice to finally meet you in person," a voice said to her from across the signing table. It was a man's voice, though Sharla hardly noticed. She was thinking about how many more books she'd be able to sign before her hand gave out. It was starting to cramp.

"Hello," Shara smiled perfunctorily, barely looking up. She automatically picked up her pen with her right hand, while holding out her left for the man's book.

The man placed the book in her hand and Sharla turned to the title page.

She began to write: *Best Wishes & God Bless You...*

"What's your name?" Sharla asked politely but noncommittally, her pen pursed over the page.

"Uh, it's not for me," the male voice said. "It's for my sister. Her name's Janis."

He spelled it for her. Sharla could tell when the man spoke that he was an out-of-towner like her. She nodded and scrawled the name across the bottom of the page. She smiled at the spelling.

"Janis...like Janis Joplin, huh?"

The male voice chuckled. "Yeah. You like her?"

"Love her," Sharla commented enthusiastically. "Love her voice."

Judging from the guy's enthusiastic tone, he was a music fan. Sharla raised her head and looked at the man for the first time.

"Well, tell your sister I said 'thank you.'" She lifted the book to hand it back to the man, whom she noticed was wearing a baseball cap, the brim hung low over his eyes.

"I will," he smiled back. Then, leaning into her a bit, the man said in a very low tone, "I enjoyed your first book myself."

Sharla's eyes locked with the man's. He smiled and very briefly lifted the bill of his cap off his forehead before quickly replacing it back over his eyes. The gesture was quick but no so quick that Sharla wasn't able to get a look at the man's eyes. There was something very familiar about them. They were a lovely dark brown. And very sweet, much like the eyes that had once stared out at her from her computer desktop.

Sharla blinked. She could see a few strands of silver hair poking out rebelliously from underneath the man's cap. Her eyes went back to his face, the cap's brim hung low again so she could no longer really see his eyes. But she didn't need to see them again. The gray hair, the slight Southern drawl to his voice that she hadn't really been able to place until just then, even the way he stood. Sharla knew.

It was Tyler.

Sharla lowered her head a little and leaned in, trying to peak under the brim of Tyler's cap. Tyler raised the cap and looked directly at her for about three seconds, before he shyly lowered his head again and looked away.

The entire exchange couldn't have lasted more than 30 seconds, but Sharla suddenly felt as if she were in an Isaac Asimov novel. One where all time as man knew it had been suspended.

"Well, hello," she half-whispered, more to herself than to Tyler. Her voice sounded surprisingly calm.

"Hi," Tyler smiled. The two of them simply looked at each other for another few seconds before Tyler finally spoke again, his voice low.

"How much longer you got here?" he asked.

Sharla raised her head to survey the line of people still standing before her. She wanted, if at all possible, to make sure everyone that came got to have their book signed.

"Probably about another hour, maybe a little longer," she surmised.

Tyler briefly turned his head back to survey the line, then turned his attention back to Sharla. "You hungry?" he asked.

Sharla smiled and thought for a moment. "I could eat."

Just then, a security guard walked up and politely tapped Tyler on the shoulder.

"Excuse me, sir, but you're holding up the line. Ms. Davis has a time limit."

There were a few murmurs of agreement from within the line. Sharla opened her mouth to admonish the security guard, who obviously hadn't recognized Tyler, but Tyler shook his head and put a finger to his lips. He quickly stepped aside to make room for the lady behind him, who voiced her disapproval with his lingering by giving him a sideways, annoyed once-over. Tyler simply smiled at her, tipped the brim of his cap and whispered "sorry." He then shot a mischievous wink to Sharla. She responded with a little smile that Tyler didn't get to see because the lady behind him was now standing directly in front of her, holding out two books and blocking Sharla's view. The lady wanted a photo with her, as did the next three people that came after her. Sharla became so engrossed in taking pictures, that when she finally had a chance to look up at where Tyler had been standing, she saw he was no longer there. Her eyes scanned the entire bookstore for him, but he was gone.

When the line had trickled down to only five or six more people almost an hour later, a bookstore employee tapped Sharla on the shoulder and handed her a note. She briefly paused her conversation with the latest book holder—a nice Indian lady from Pakistan—unfolded the note and read it:

meet me out front

Sharla glanced around the store but saw no one. The note wasn't signed but she knew instinctively who it was from. After surveying what was left of the line, Sharla motioned to the security guard, who walked over to her followed by one of the bookstore's managers.

"I'll see these last few people," she told them, "but then I have to leave, so please don't let anyone else in line."

The security guard nodded, as did the manager who made the announcement just as an elderly lady stepped up behind the last person in line, tightly clutching a copy of Sharla's book in her wrinkled hands.

"I'm sorry, ma'am," the manager told the woman. "Ms. Davis isn't signing anymore books."

The old woman looked disappointed but smiled. "Oh." she sighed. "I tried to get here earlier but the bus was late."

Sharla heard the conversation and looked at the woman. Something about the lady touched Sharla, though she couldn't put her finger on what it was. She could see the woman was tired and a bit frail. Her clothes were old and very simple, her head covered by a knitted cap. Her face looked stung by the wind, as if she'd traveled a good distance to get there. The woman was turning to leave when Sharla called out, "Ma'am, wait!"

The elderly lady turned around.

Sharla motioned for her to get back in line. "I'll sign your book."

The woman looked reluctantly at the manager then back at Sharla.

"It's okay," Sharla said. She looked at the manager who nodded to the woman to return to the line.

"That's it, though, no more." The comment was directed at bookstore staff, though Sharla was smiling at the elderly woman when she said it.

"Thank you for waiting for me," the old woman said when it was her turn. "You must be tired."

Sharla smiled and handed the elderly lady her book.

"Not really," she replied. "Thank you for coming." She gingerly patted the old woman's hand and rose to leave.

Much to the chagrin of the personal assistant assigned to pick her up, Sharla said she'd decided not to go straight back to her hotel, but preferred to walk around for a while. The assistant felt responsible for Sharla and warned her it might be dangerous for a woman walking around New York alone.

"Who said I'd be alone?" Sharla slyly asked. The assistant, who didn't know Sharla very well but knew she was a Christian, looked slightly shocked.

"Don't worry," Sharla laughed, patting the poor nervous creature on the shoulder. "I won't be doing anything immoral or illegal."

"Really, I'll be fine," she continued. "I have my cell phone, the hotel's only a few blocks from here and if I need to I can take a cab somewhere. I absolve you of any responsibility for my well-being. Go. Do something for yourself. I won't tell."

The assistant finally left, reluctantly.

As Sharla exited the front of the store, she realized she wasn't sure what to expect. She presumed Tyler would be waiting for her in a car, probably a limo. But when she stepped outside, she saw nothing. No car with dark-tinted windows parked along the curb with its engine running, certainly no limousines.

Sharla looked around but didn't see anyone. A taxi pulled up to the curb and a party of four exited and made their way inside the bookstore, passing Sharla absently.

Sharla rubbed her right hand. There was a dull ache in it from signing for two hours. Sharla poked her head out onto the street at the cars rounding the corner. She stood there for a moment, the cold New York air on her face. It was uncharacteristically warm for Christmastime. Sharla guessed it was around 50 degrees right now, though the temperature would no doubt plummet later that evening. Snow was in the night's forecast.

This was ridiculous, Sharla thought, standing on the sidewalk waiting for she-wasn't-sure-what. She didn't even know what kind of car Tyler was in. Maybe they should have planned this out a little beforehand. She should have at least thought to ask him for his cell phone number.

Sharla took a step backwards and felt a tug at her elbow. She smiled and turned around expectantly. It was the frail, elderly woman.

"I didn't get to say this inside," the woman smiled, "But I just wanted to tell you how much your book has blessed me."

"Thank you," Sharla said, though her mind was a million miles from the woman's comments.

"I have a daughter who was in an abusive relationship," the woman continued. "I gave her your book, she read it and she recently moved into a shelter and has joined a local church. I really believe it was all because of what she read in your book."

Sharla was looking through the bookstore's front glass window to the back of the store for gray-haired men in baseball caps. "That's very sweet of you to say, but I didn't do anything for your daughter. It's God that helped her. He just used my book as a means, that's all."

"Well, you're very modest," the woman said. She paused for a second then said: "Are you married?"

Sharla frowned slightly, wondering why the woman was asking.

"No, ma'am."

The woman looked at Sharla thoughtfully and resumed her friendly smile. "You will be soon. I can sense it."

Sharla took an involuntary step back. "Really? What makes you sense that?"

"I don't know," the woman shrugged. "You just have a look about you, I guess. Anyway, I'm sure you've got somewhere to be. I just wanted to thank you for your book."

She then walked away but paused as if she'd just remembered something else. Turning back to Sharla, she said, "I hope you don't mind me saying this, but I think your second book is much better than your first. Not that your first wasn't good, but this one really says something. That Tyler Nicks is alright but…" She held up *Beauty in the Ashes…*

"…this book is a real blessing."

The woman looked at Sharla, worried she'd been too forward. "I hope you're not offended."

Sharla smiled and shook her head. "No, I'm not offended. In fact, I agree. I didn't write my first book for anyone but me, really. This one," she gestured to the book the woman held, "was for others."

"Well, I suppose you had to write that first one in order to write the second one. One fueled the other?"

Sharla thought for a moment. The old lady had a point. "I hadn't thought about it like that," she confessed. "But you're probably right."

"Well, God bless you, dear." the old lady said. "Merry Christmas."

"Merry Christmas," Sharla echoed. She watched the old lady as she ambled down the sidewalk towards a nearby bus stop. Instinctively, Sharla followed her, though she wasn't sure why.

"Excuse me," she said, stopping the lady. "This is none of my business but do you mind if I ask where you're going?"

"I'm going to catch the bus home," the old woman answered.

"How far away do you live?" Sharla asked.

"Oh, a good ways. You probably couldn't tell," the woman joked, tugging at her clothes. "But this is not my part of town."

Sharla chuckled.

"No, I just came to have my book signed," she said.

"Will you have to change buses?" Sharla asked.

"Yes."

Sharla thought for a moment, then reached inside her handbag. She pulled out three $100 bills and handed them to the woman. "Here," she said. "Take a cab."

The woman looked at the money, her eyes growing huge. "Oh, goodness no, I couldn't take this!" She tried to hand the money back to Sharla but Sharla refused it.

"No, I insist. I want you to have it."

"But..." the woman looked around, then whispered. "...but this is too much! I don't live that far!"

"So take the rest and use it for something else," Sharla suggested. "By your daughter a Christmas present."

The woman's eyes widened but she didn't speak. She merely stood before Sharla, dumbfounded. Sharla used the woman's silence as an opportunity to hail a cab that was just rounding the corner. It stopped in front of her and the old woman. Sharla opened the back door, gingerly helped the woman inside, then addressed the driver: "She'll tell you where she wants to go."

"I...I don't know what to say..." the woman finally spoke, her words trailing off. Tears were forming in her eyes. "This morning, I prayed to God that He would make a way for me to help my daughter and her kids when they get out of the shelter. My daughter doesn't have a job and I'm a widow on a fixed income. I didn't know what we were going to do this Christmas, how I'd afford anything for my grand babies."

She reached out and hugged Sharla tightly around the neck. "Thank you."

"You're welcome," Sharla said. "I'll be praying for you."

"God bless you!" the woman said as Sharla closed the cab's door and the vehicle pulled out into the street. The woman waved and Sharla waved back as she watched the car disappear into traffic.

As the taxi grew smaller, it suddenly occurred to Sharla that she hadn't gotten the woman's name. But that was all right. God knew who she was.

When the cab was out of sight, Sharla broke her gaze and turned around to head back to the store. As she approached, she saw Tyler standing in front of the bookstore admiring her book display in the front store window. Sharla took in an involuntary quick breath, startled to see him standing in front of her, as if he'd appeared out of nowhere.

She walked towards him slowly, wondering how long he'd been standing there.

"Hey," she said, sidling up next to him.

Tyler turned in Sharla's direction, his expression momentarily that of someone deep in thought. He smiled when he recognized Sharla.

"Hey," he answered back.

"Where did you come from?" Sharla asked, looking around. "I didn't see you when I came out."

"From around the corner," he said, pointing to the corner closest to the front of the bookstore and opposite where Sharla and the elderly woman had stood moments before.

"This is a nice display," he commented, pointing at the rows of Sharla's books laid out in the window next to a poster with her photo on it that read: **Book Signing with the Author, Today Only**.

"Yeah," Sharla agreed. "It's kind of surreal for me to look at it and think 'that's my book in there.'"

Tyler nodded soberly and looked back at Sharla. "I know the feeling."

"Did you…hear any of the conversation I was having with that old lady just now?" Sharla asked cautiously. She was hoping Tyler hadn't seen her give the woman any money. She didn't want Tyler to think she'd done it to impress him.

"Not really," Tyler said. "Just that she thought your second book was better than your first." He said the last part in a slightly offended tone but his little smile gave it away at the end.

Sharla chuckled. "It's just one person's opinion."

"Yeah, I'm not mad," Tyler said. Then: "Hey, you wanna grab something to eat?"

"Sure, I'm starving."

"Where would you like to go?"

"I don't care," Sharla shrugged, looking around. "Where's your car?"

"I'm not in one."

Sharla frowned. "How did you get here?"

"I walked," Tyler said matter-of-factly.

"You walked?" Sharla was surprised. "From where?"

"From my hotel."

"Where's your hotel?"

Tyler thought for a moment. "About nine or ten blocks away."

Sharla's eyebrows went up but Tyler seemed nonplussed. "I like to walk," he explained. "It's good exercise."

Sharla smiled. Tyler looked at her, searching her face. "What?"

Sharla chuckled and shrugged sheepishly. "It's just...I don't know. I figured you'd probably have a car. Like a limo or something."

Now it was Tyler's turn to chuckle.

Sharla rolled her eyes in embarrassment. "I know, I know, it sounds stupid, but I figured you being a celebrity and all, you'd send for your driver... you know..."

She trailed off, feeling too silly to continue.

"Well, you're a celebrity too, aren't you?" Tyler challenged playfully. "Where's your limo?"

"Ugh, please!" Sharla grimaced. "I don't consider myself a celebrity. And my hotel's just two blocks from here."

"Well, I'm not big on taking limousines," Tyler countered. He fished his cell phone out of his coat pocket. "I can get us a car, if you want."

He was about to dial but Sharla stopped him.

"No, that's okay. It's nice out. Let's walk."

They walked a little ways, trying to figure out where to grab a bite when Sharla spied a pizza vendor at a corner. After getting a couple of huge slices each and drinks, they set down on a bench near Strawberry Fields in Central Park. The gothic architecture of the Dakota towered over the park as they sat and people watched.

The rumors about Tyler's demeanor were true. Sharla found him easy to talk to, very well-mannered and very engaging. The fact that he was considerably more striking in person didn't escape Sharla's notice either. The old saying she'd heard about the camera adding 15 pounds was true. Tyler was thinner in person, but every bit as tall as she'd expected. Donning a dark baseball cap that hid his gray pate and wearing jeans, sneakers and a black leather jacket over a dark blue sweater, he looked extremely ordinary. Anyone—any woman—would probably not stop for a second glance. Not until he took his hat off to expose that headlight of silver hair and those gorgeous dark brown eyes, which, in Sharla's opinion, were his best feature.

As they talked, Sharla hoped Tyler couldn't see just how smitten she was with his beauty. She tried not to stare. Tyler, for his part, appeared oblivious of his effect on women, something at which Sharla quietly marveled. He seemed to have no idea of how good-looking he really was, and didn't carry himself with the air of conceited entitlement some handsome men possessed. In fact, he acted just the opposite. He was shy and quiet, almost self-deprecating. Yet Sharla saw he had a quiet charm and a quick-witted intelligence about him that made him very charming.

They talked a little about their careers and some of the pitfalls of success. Figuring it too sensitive a subject, Sharla shied away from any talk about Venice Dupree, but just for fun, she did ask Tyler what he thought about

Dustin Limbergate, a young Pop star who recently attacked Tyler in a music magazine by calling him 'a no-talent hack.'

Tyler answered in fun. He simply looked at Sharla with a huge grin and said, "Dustin, who?"

This made Sharla laugh so hard, she almost choked on a slice of her pizza.

Tyler did confide to Sharla that he was readying himself for his first big solo tour. Plans were in the works, he said, for him to get back on the road with his old band, renamed the New Atlanta Soul Review, who had amassed their own following while Tyler was furloughed on ANBS. Sharla immediately saw how Tyler's eyes lit with excitement as he talked about finally being able to head back out on the road and promoting his new album.

"That's why I'm in New York right now," he explained, taking another bite of his pizza and dabbing at the corner of his mouth with a napkin.

"How long are you here for?" Sharla asked.

Tyler shrugged. "Not long. Couple of days. You?"

"I fly out tomorrow," Sharla said.

"Goin' home?"

Sharla took a sip of her drink. "Nope. Cincinnati, I think. I'm doing a book signing tour. 10 cities."

"Oh, that's right," Tyler nodded. "Forgot."

"So," Sharla continued. "If you're here on business…" she frowned. "What are you doing *here*?" She pointed a finger at the park bench they sat on.

Tyler finished the last of his pizza and leaned back on the bench, absently rubbing his hands on his jeans. He looked straight ahead as he spoke, but Sharla could see that familiar, boyish grin spreading at the corners of his lips.

"I'm getting some fresh air," he said finally. "And talking to you."

"Shouldn't you be in some meeting?" Sharla teased.

"I just got outta one," Tyler said soberly. There was no smile this time. Sharla wanted to ask how the meeting went but she was afraid to intrude. She figured if Tyler wanted to talk about it, he would have. She decided to change the subject instead.

"How'd you know I was here?"

"Saw you on TV this morning." Tyler kept looking straight ahead, his eyes planted on a man playing Frisbee with his dog. He took a sip of his drink and looked back at Sharla. "I had some time off today so I figured I'd go down to the bookstore and see you."

Sharla leaned forward. "You mean you really stood in line?"

"Yeah," Tyler shrugged.

"For almost an hour?"

Tyler looked at Sharla and thought for a moment. "It went pretty fast," he reasoned. "I didn't wait long."

"What if it had been a long wait?" Sharla asked.

"Then, I guess I would have had to meet you another time."

Sharla was stunned. "Why didn't you just call me again? I told Ines to give you my cell number."

"Who's Ines?"

"My housekeeper."

"Oh," Tyler nodded. "She did."

Sharla's eyebrows went up. "What?"

"I called you last night but your housekeeper said you'd left for New York. She gave me your cell but when I saw you on the *Today Show* this morning, I thought I'd just see you in person."

Sharla couldn't believe what she was hearing. "Why did you do that? You didn't have to stand in line to see me."

"I know," Tyler admitted. "But I like the element of surprise." That mischievous grin returned. "Were you surprised?"

"Yes, I was!" Sharla smiled.

The two of them sat in silence for a while, watching passersby. Finally, Tyler turned to Sharla. He cleared his throat nervously, then said, "Hey, um, can I ask you somethin'?"

"Sure," Sharla said, wondering.

"Did you ever get those flowers I sent you?"

Sharla eyes widened. "Yes!" she exclaimed. "They were beautiful. I would have let you know I got them but the card that came with them didn't have a return address or a number or anything...."

"There was nothing on the card?" Tyler asked, a little perturbed.

"Well, there was a nice note but nothing else, no contact number," Sharla sounded almost apologetic, as if the matter was her fault. She nervously began fiddling with the leftover crust of her pizza.

Tyler frowned. "Man, I thought for sure I told the florist to put my number on the card."

Sharla stopped playing with the pizza crust and sat deathly still, her mind racing.

"You meant to leave a number?" she asked incredulously.

"Yeah," Tyler nodded. "I specifically told the florist to put my cell phone number on the card."

Sharla's smile was huge. On the inside. Outwardly, she made sure her face maintained a neutral expression.

"Well, I guess they forgot or misunderstood. It was a beautiful arrangement, though. Thank you." She spoke slowly, with deliberate calmness. Then: "How did you know I liked roses?"

"Doesn't every woman like roses?" His tone was playful and warm, his smile captivating.

"I guess," Sharla chuckled. "I'd never really thought about it. I just know what I like."

The two didn't speak again for about a full minute. They simply sat quietly, taking in the scenery for a while before Tyler spoke.

"Thank you for the letter," he interjected. The subject came from out of left field, catching Sharla off guard. She looked at Tyler, searching for some hint of what he'd really thought about her letter on his face, but he was only smiling at her, nothing more.

"You're welcome," she said, her voice slightly shaky. "I'm glad you got it."

"Yeah, I got it," Tyler said. "It was very sweet."

"Good." Sharla smiled and looked down at the ground.

The two of them sat quietly for another minute. Then Tyler scratched the tip of his nose and rested a hand on his knee. "You know, I never really got a chance to talk to you about *Chasing Trevor.*"

Sharla sighed, afraid of what might be coming next. "No, you didn't."

"I really did enjoy it," Tyler said. "I meant that."

"Good, I'm glad," Sharla exhaled, a huge smile surfacing on her face. "I was worried you didn't like it."

"No, no, I did," Tyler said. "It was real nice. I was flattered."

Tyler looked away from Sharla and down at the ground. "I, um, I'd like to know how you came up with the idea," he said slowly. "If you'd be willing to talk about it."

He grazed Sharla briefly with his eyes. "Not now," he added. "But… sometime…" he trailed off, picking at a loose splinter on the bench.

"Sure," Sharla beamed. "I'd like that."

"Maybe," he continued, clearing his throat. "Maybe you could sign my copy."

Sharla froze. Something her mother had said at the party before Sharla left for New York came to her:

Who knows? Maybe Mr. Right is out there waiting for you to sign a copy of your book for him.

Sharla involuntarily put a hand to her mouth and smiled. Never in her wildest imagination had she thought this was the way she would meet the man God had shown her on her television set more than two years ago.

Tears were trying to well in her eyes but she willed them back. She wasn't going to cry, not now. Instead, she merely swallowed and said, "I would love that."

"Good," Tyler said. "Why don't we talk about it over dinner tonight?"

"Alright," Sharla replied, seeing the prophecy God had spoken over her more vividly than ever before. "Let's have dinner." Then: "Do you think it was coincidence you and I both happened to be in New York at the same time?"

Tyler frowned momentarily. "Well, I don't know about that. Could be coincidence, could be….something else."

Sharla sat up straighter. "Like….God?"

Tyler nodded. "Sure, why not? I'm not big on coincidence. I like to think things happen for a reason."

"Like you winning *America's Next Big Star?*"

"Yeah," Tyler agreed, pointing at Sharla. "Or you writing a spoof about it."

The pair laughed then sat quietly for a moment, smiling at one another.

"You have to wear a hat everywhere you go now?" Sharla asked, glancing at Tyler's cap.

"Just about." Tyler repositioned the cap on his head.

"Doesn't that get kind of bothersome?" Sharla asked earnestly. "I mean, doesn't your head ever get hot?"

Tyler laughed a sweet belly laugh that was music to Sharla's ears. "Uh, yeah, sometimes. But I really don't mind. Saves me from havin' to comb my hair. Such is the price of fame. Or whatever." He shrugged.

Sharla looked around. "But this is New York, you know," she said. "People don't bother with celebrities here. In fact, they go out of their way not to notice people." Sharla stared at Tyler intently. "I bet you could take your cap off here."

Tyler looked around the park. There weren't many people in their area.

"I dare you to take your cap off."

No sooner than the words came out, Sharla wondered who'd spoken them. She'd never dared anybody to do anything before. It wasn't like her to be so impetuous.

Tyler turned to her. "You serious?"

Sharla shrugged. "Sure, why not?"

Tyler continued to study Sharla intently for a moment. Then: "Alright. Here goes." With that, Tyler lifted his arm to the bill of his cap and began to raise it off his forehead. As he did so, Sharla suddenly realized what she'd asked him to do and grabbed his arm.

"No, don't!" she said. She realized she was touching him and loosened her grip. Slowly.

"Why?" Tyler chuckled.

Sharla wasn't sure what to say that wouldn't sound extremely silly, so she simply stated the obvious. "Someone might recognize you."

"Right," Tyler agreed. "That was the whole point of the dare, wasn't it?"

"Well, yes, but...I changed my mind," Sharla said weakly.

Tyler frowned. "Why?"

Sharla didn't know what to say. How could she explain to a man she'd only just met that the reason she didn't want him to reveal himself was because she didn't want to lose him to a crowd? Why she'd dared him to do something like take off his cap in the first place was beyond her. The only explanation she could come up with was that being around Tyler was freeing. She could have told Tyler that but she didn't.

Instead, she said, "Do you really want to attract a crowd?"

Tyler looked around. "There aren't that many people here. And you did dare me," he reminded.

"I know," Sharla sighed, wishing she hadn't.

Just then, a small rubber football landed at Tyler's feet. Tyler stooped down to pick it up as a little boy who looked to be around seven or eight walked up to the two of them and stood directly in front of Tyler.

"This yours?" Tyler asked the boy.

"Yes," the boy said, holding out his hands for the ball.

"Tell ya what," he said, smiling at the child. "You go over there to that tree and I'll throw it to you."

The little boy's eyes lit up and he anxiously ran about two feet back to a tree in the park across from the benches. Tyler softly threw the ball to the boy who caught it and threw it back to him. Their impromptu game of catch went on for a few more minutes with Sharla looking on before a woman who was turned out to be the boy's mother walked up to her son.

"Evan!" she called. "I told you not to wander around the park. What are you doing?"

"Playing catch," the boy said.

"With who?"

"Him." Evan pointed to the benches where Tyler stood and Sharla sat.

Evan's mother walked him over to the bench and Tyler handed him the ball. "Here you go, bro," Tyler said to the child. "You've got a good arm."

"What do you say, Evan?" his mother prompted.

"Thank you," Evan managed.

"You're welcome," Tyler smiled and put out his hand to the boy. Evan shook it, then gave Tyler five.

"I'm sorry he bothered you," Evan's mother said to Tyler. "He's so hyper I can hardly keep track of him."

"It's okay," Tyler assured her. "I didn't mind, it was my idea."

"I guess he misses his dad," Evan's mom said, smoothing down her son's hair affectionately. "He's in Iraq."

"I like your hat," Evan said, pointing at Tyler's cap.

"You do?" Tyler said, glancing in Sharla's direction. "Well, I tell you what then, you can have it." He removed the cap and gave it to the little boy.

"Thanks!" Evan said ecstatically. He put the cap on and it fell over his eyes. Tyler straightened it for him.

When Evan's mother saw Tyler's shock of gray, she looked at him more closely, and the look on her face told Sharla she recognized Tyler.

"Um…excuse me, but you look familiar," the woman said slowly. "Are you…are you…?" The woman hesitated then said. "Has anyone ever told you you look like Tyler Nicks, that gray-haired guy from America's Next Big Star?"

Tyler smiled, looking at Sharla. Looks like the dare was back on. "Yeah, I get that sometimes."

Inching closer to him, the woman studied Tyler's face intently before announcing more to herself than anything else, "You *are* Tyler Nicks!"

Tyler lowered his head shyly. "Yes, ma'am," he admitted.

The woman put her hands on her hips. "I knew it! I'm a big fan of yours. I voted for you."

"Thank you, I appreciate that," Tyler said.

"Would you mind signing an autograph?" the woman asked. "Not for me, but for Evan."

Sharla sighed. She'd heard that line before.

"Sure," Tyler nodded. "Do you have a pen?"

"I do," Sharla offered, searching in her purse.

"Hey, Evan," Tyler called, "Can I see your ball for a sec?"

Reluctantly, Evan handed over the football and Tyler signed it.

"What do you say, Evan?" his mother prompted again.

"Thanks, Tyler," the boy chimed and everyone laughed.

Tyler's 'headlight' began to attract a small crowd. He ended up doing a mini signing of his own with some of the families—most of them single mothers—in the park who'd noticed him.

Just as he'd done for her earlier, Sharla waited patiently for Tyler to finish chatting with the fans. But instead of feeling less of him, Sharla felt more of Tyler as she watched him sign autographs and pose for a few photos with people. She found herself feeling quite proud to be witnessing him interact with people in person. He was very warm and children seemed to gravitate to him. Occasionally, in between fans, Tyler would look back at Sharla and wink. Sharla smiled. She wondered if what she and Tyler had done this afternoon would be considered a date and decided that it probably was not. Today had simply been about being human.

Sharla's cell phone rang. It was Ida. Sharla quickly explained to her mother that there wasn't time to talk. The autograph seekers were gone; Tyler was walking towards the bench. Sharla smiled and told her mother she would call her later.

Right now, she was anxious to get back to the business of being human.

Epilogue

My story—Sharla's story—has a happy ending. But if you've been following my journey from the beginning, you already knew that.

Eight months into our courtship, Tyler proposed to me on his tour bus, under a giant harvest moon, with the ocean rippling past as we drove down a beautiful stretch of Texas road in a city near the Mexican border called Corpus Christi. The stretch of road was aptly named Ocean Drive.

I suppose there are many women who wouldn't find this scenario very romantic as proposals go, but I cried when he gave me the ring because I know how important that setting was for Tyler, a man who has essentially been married to the road. Now I'm going to be a part of that and I couldn't be happier.

We're planning the proverbial June wedding. Everyone, especially, my mother, is thrilled. Now she's gone from nagging me about finding a man to asking when she can expect a grandchild.

As usual, it seems I'm working under a deadline.

In the meantime, Hollywood's calling. Three studios are currently bidding for the rights to *Chasing Trevor*. I really don't care which studio gets it. No matter who it is, I already have final script approval and will be helping to write the screenplay, so that's basically all I'm concerned about. I have to admit, though, I'm really excited about the entire process. Rumor has it both George Clooney and Richard Gere have been approached to play Trevor. I don't know who they've got in mind for Dora but personally, I hope they cast an unknown. God specializes in them.

For now, it might please you to know that I have another book in the works. This one is completely autobiographical; all about the road of faith

God placed me on. In fact, you might recognize some of the story when you read it. I hope so, anyway.

I have to say that because I started my story with the ending, I would think it should come as no surprise that Tyler and I are engaged. But oddly enough, for me, it has come as a total shock. Having a vision is one thing, but watching God bring it to pass before your eyes is quite another, especially when what's currently in front of you in no way resembles what God says He's going to give you.

That God would take me, a timid, overweight, sad young woman and use her to tell someone about what it means to have faith was ridiculous just a few short years ago. Even more ridiculous was God's revelation that He had already chosen someone to love me just as He loved me. That is why I started my testimony at the end. Because I've discovered that it's not so much about what happens when we get to the realization of a dream, but about what went on while we were striving to get there.

I wanted to tell you not about what God said He would do—for just as His Word states, God is faithful to keep His promises—but about what it took for me to get to the place in my life where I could receive what God had.

To say that Tyler was the man of my dreams would be inaccurate. My future husband was the man of *God's* dream, the dream that God always had for me. Who I thought Tyler was, his so-called status, made no difference to God. Tyler's fame was never an obstacle for Him, but it was to me, and that is what God showed me I had to lay down at His feet before I could receive anything.

If I learned nothing from this journey, I learned that God may not always grant you everything you want. But if you trust Him, he will always give you precisely what you need.

In His way and in His time.

The End

Printed in the United States
123994LV00005B/49-57/A

9 781434 325006